Culture and
Customs of
Venezuela

Recent Titles in
Culture and Customs of Latin America and the Caribbean

Culture and Customs of Argentina
David William Foster, Melissa Fitch Lockhart, and Darrell B. Lockhart

Culture and Customs of Colombia
Raymond Leslie Williams and Kevin G. Guerrieri

Culture and Customs of the Dominican Republic
Isabel Z. Brown

Culture and Customs of Ecuador
Michael Handelsman

Culture and Customs of Costa Rica
Chalene Helmuth

Culture and Customs of Chile
Guillermo I. Castillo-Feliú

Culture and Customs of Guatemala
Maureen E. Shea

Culture and Customs of Cuba
William Luis

Culture and Customs of Haiti
J. Michael Dash

Culture and Customs of Jamaica
Martin Mordecai and Pamela Mordecai

Culture and Customs of El Salvador
Roy C. Boland

Culture and Customs of Venezuela

∾

Mark Dinneen

Culture and Customs of Latin America
and the Caribbean
Peter Standish, Series Editor

GREENWOOD PRESS
Westport, Connecticut • London

Library of Congress Cataloging-in-Publication Data

Dinneen, Mark.
    Culture and customs of Venezuela / Mark Dinneen.
       p.   cm.—(Culture and customs of Latin America and the Caribbean, ISSN 1521–8856)
    Includes bibliographical references and index.
    ISBN 0–313–30639–7 (alk. paper)
    1. Venezuela—Civilization—20th century.   2. Venezuela—Social life and customs—20th
century. I. Title. II. Series.
    F2326.D55   2001
    987.06'3—dc21   00–057649

British Library Cataloguing in Publication Data is available.

Library of Congress Catalog Card Number: 00–057649
ISBN: 0–313–30639–7
ISSN: 1521–8856

First published in 2001

Greenwood Press, 88 Post Road West, Westport, CT 06881
An imprint of Greenwood Publishing Group, Inc.
www.greenwood.com

Printed in the United States of America

The paper used in this book complies with the
Permanent Paper Standard issued by the National
Information Standards Organization (Z39.48–1984).

10 9 8 7 6 5 4 3 2 1

For Gladys

Contents

Illustrations

Series Foreword

"CULTURE" is a problematic word. In everyday language we tend to use it in at least two senses. On the one hand we speak of cultured people and places full of culture, uses that imply a knowledge or presence of certain forms of behavior or of artistic expression that are socially prestigious. In this sense large cities and prosperous people tend to be seen as the most cultured. On the other hand, there is an interpretation of "culture" that is broader and more anthropological; culture in this broader sense refers to whatever traditions, beliefs, customs, and creative activities characterize a given community—in short, it refers to what makes that community different from others. In this second sense, everyone has culture; indeed, it is impossible to be without culture.

The problems associated with the idea of culture have been exacerbated in recent years by two trends: less respectful use of language and a greater blurring of cultural differences. Nowadays, "culture" often means little more than behavior, attitude, or atmosphere. We hear about the culture of the boardroom, of the football team, of the marketplace; there are books with titles like *The Culture of War* by Richard Gabriel (Greenwood, 1990) or *The Culture of Narcissism* by Christopher Lasch (1979). In fact, as Christopher Clausen points out in an article published in the *American Scholar* (Summer 1996), we have gotten ourselves into trouble by using the term so sloppily.

People who study culture generally assume that culture (in the anthropological sense) is learned, not genetically determined. Another general assumption made in these days of multiculturalism has been that cultural differences should be respected rather than put under pressure to change.

But these assumptions, too, have sometimes proved to be problematic. For instance, multiculturalism is a fine ideal, but in practice it is not always easy to reconcile with the beliefs of the very people who advocate it: for example, is female circumcision an issue of human rights or just a different cultural practice?

The blurring of cultural differences is a process that began with the steamship, increased with radio, and is now racing ahead with the Internet. We are becoming globally homogenized. Since the English-speaking world (and the United States in particular) is the dominant force behind this process of homogenization, it behooves us to make efforts to understand the sensibilities of members of other cultures.

This series of books, a contribution toward that greater understanding, deals with the neighbors of the United States, with people who have just as much right to call themselves Americans. What are the historical, institutional, religious, and artistic features that make up the modern culture of such peoples as the Haitians, the Chileans, the Jamaicans, and the Guatemalans? How are their habits and assumptions different from our own? What can we learn from them? As we familiarize ourselves with the ways of other countries, we come to see our own from a new perspective.

Each volume in the series focuses on a single country. With slight variations to accommodate national differences, each begins by outlining the historical, political, ethnic, geographical, and linguistic context, as well as the religious and social customs, and then proceeds to a discussion of a variety of artistic activities, including the media, the cinema, music, literature, and the visual and performing arts. The authors are all intimately acquainted with the countries concerned: some were born or brought up in them, and each has a professional commitment to enhancing the understanding of the culture in question.

We are inclined to suppose that our ways of thinking and behaving are normal. And so they are . . . for us. We all need to realize that ours is only one culture among many, and that it is hard to establish by any rational criteria that ours as a whole is any better (or worse) than any other. As individual members of our immediate community, we know that we must learn to respect our differences from one another. Respect for differences between cultures is no less vital. This is particularly true of the United States, a nation of immigrants, but one that sometimes seems to be bent on destroying variety at home, and, worse still, on having others follow suit. By learning about other people's cultures, we come to understand and respect them; we earn their respect for us; and, not least, we see ourselves in a new light.

Peter Standish
East Carolina University

Introduction

VENEZUELA IS UNDOUBTEDLY one of the least known countries of Latin America. Even within the field of Latin American studies in the United States, it has tended to occupy a marginal position, with much more attention directed toward other nations of the region, such as Mexico, Brazil, Colombia, Argentina, and Cuba. Yet Venezuela is a country of over 22 million people (1996 figures), whose central location on the continent makes it an important point of intersection between North America, South America, and the Caribbean. It is a major trading partner of the United States. The United States accounts for over 50% of its foreign investment and over 50% of its trade (*Venezuela Today*, DTI/LATAG, London, 1995, p. 5). In 1996, Venezuela became the largest supplier of petroleum to the United States, and the oil trade has served to forge particularly close links between the two countries (Box, 1997, 1464). Indeed, the strength of U.S. influence in virtually all areas of Venezuelan life became one of the most controversial topics of debate in Venezuela in the latter decades of the twentieth century.

Culturally and socially, Venezuela has much in common with the other nations of Latin America, but, as in the case of all the others, the peculiarities of its history and geography have given it distinctive features of its own. Without doubt, the most significant has been the development of the oil industry in the course of the twentieth century, which, since the 1960s, has enabled the country to sustain a stable democratic system of government and a strong and prosperous state. Indeed, that to a large extent explains the relative neglect of Venezuela for so many decades by commentators and scholars overseas, for their attention has been drawn toward the economic and political turbulence in other parts of the continent, where power has

Map of Venezuela

often been held either by revolutionary or radical regimes, or by military dictatorships. In the 1980s and 1990s, however, Venezuela's apparent stability experienced severe strain, shaken by economic crisis and political unrest including two attempted coups. As a result, a process of significant social and political change began. That process, and the many uncertainties the country faces as it enters the new millennium, may well attract more international attention over the years to come.

First appearances are deceptive in Venezuela. The visitor who arrives in Caracas sees a modern and apparently prosperous city, full of skyscrapers, broad freeways, and seemingly endless billboards and neon lights—strongly reminiscent of cities in the United States. Yet acute poverty exists alongside the prosperity, and a large percentage of the Caracas population lives in the very different world of the ramshackle shantytowns that have expanded rapidly. Imported American culture is evident everywhere, but it intermingles with local cultural expressions and customs. Despite the influx of outside influences, many distinctive traditions continue throughout the country, varying according to the region and the community. Sharp contrasts and immense variety are what most characterize modern Venezuela. The richness and diversity of its culture, however, are not given due recognition by observers from outside. Nor are the country's artistic achievements. It has been noted that Venezuela "has produced neither a Neruda, an Orozco nor a Villalobos" (Waddell, 1990, xv). Yet it has produced artists of the caliber of the novelist Rómulo Gallegos, the painter Armando Reverón, the playwright and filmmaker Román Chalbaud, and the architect Carlos Villanueva, among others. These men have made an outstanding and original contribution to their respective arts, and their work is of a quality equal to anything produced elsewhere in Latin America, even if international acclaim has been limited. In addition to these achievements in so-called high art, Venezuela has many vibrant expressions of popular culture, seen, for example, in music, religious ritual, and the numerous festivals that take place in towns and villages across the country. A major part of the nation's social and cultural life, they too will be discussed in the chapters that follow. The vitality and variety of Venezuelan culture merits greater recognition. It is hoped that this book will make a small contribution to that process.

REFERENCES

Box, Ben, ed. *The 1997 South American Handbook.* Bath, England: Footprint Handbooks, 1997.
Waddell, D.A.G. *Venezuela.* Oxford: Clio Press, 1990.

Chronology

1498	Christopher Columbus explores the island of Trinidad and the coast of Venezuela.
1503	The Spanish Crown grants permission for settlers to exploit the slave labor of the Caribbean Indians.
1525	African slaves are introduced into Venezuela.
1528	The Spanish government cedes Venezuela to the German banking house Welser, with which it has run up large debts. The company spends almost twenty years trying in vain to develop profitable enterprises before returning the territory to Spanish control.
1567	Caracas is founded, one of a number of cities established in Venezuela since the 1520s.
1600–1700	The cultivation of cacao is developed as a major part of the colony's economy; more towns and cities are founded.
1728	The Basque firm Compañía Guipuzcoana (Caracas Company) is given a trading monopoly over Venezuela, which lasts until the 1780s.
1777	The Spanish Crown creates the Captaincy-General of Venezuela, the culmination of a slow process of political and administrative integration.

1811   The first independence movement against Spain, led by Francisco de Miranda, culminates in a declaration of independence on July 5 and the foundation of the First Republic of Venezuela. Spanish forces regained control ten months later.

1813   Simón Bolívar leads a new independence movement and, taking Caracas in August, declares the Second Republic. That, too, is short-lived, collapsing after a few months.

1817   Bolívar returns to Venezuela, after a sojourn overseas, to begin the final campaign for independence.

1819   Bolívar achieves a military victory over Spanish forces in Colombia, and in December the revolutionaries proclaim the Republic of Gran Colombia, a single centralized state incorporating the present-day republics of Colombia, Panama, Venezuela, and Ecuador.

1821   Bolívar decisively defeats the Spanish at the battle of Carabobo, securing the independence of Venezuela. He is subsequently declared president of Gran Colombia, with its capital in Bogotá.

1830   A separatist movement in Venezuela is finally successful. Gran Colombia breaks up, and the Republic of Venezuela is declared, with José Antonio Páez its first president. Defeated in his plans for a unified Gran Colombia, Bolívar sets off for exile, but dies in Colombia on December 17.

1854   Slavery is abolished in Venezuela.

1859–1863   After many years of violence and unrest, Venezuela is plunged into a rebellion and civil war, the Federal Wars, between Conservative and Liberal forces.

1870   Antonio Guzmán Blanco seizes the presidency. The dominant force in Venezuelan politics for the next eighteen years, he carries out a program of liberal reforms.

1902   European military forces blockade the Venezuelan coast and threaten to invade unless the Venezuelan government pays its debts to them.

1903	Another period of civil war is ended by General Juan Vincente Gómez's victory at the battle of Ciudad Bolívar.
1908	Gómez seizes the presidency. He dominates the country until 1935 with ruthless authoritarian governments.
1917	The first discovery of oil is made.
1922	Vast quantities of oil are discovered in Lake Maracaibo, dramatically transforming the Venezuelan economy.
1926	Oil becomes Venezuela's major export. Agricultural products had dominated until then.
1935	The death of Gómez opens the way for a period of free political activity and free expression, during which Venezuela's modern political parties are formed, notably Acción Democrática in 1941 and COPEI (Committee for the Organization of Independent Electoral Politics) in 1946.
1948	A military coup installs a new dictatorship.
1958	The military regime, led by General Marcos Pérez Jiménez, is overthrown. In December, Rómulo Betancourt is elected President of the new civilian government.
1960	The Organization of Petroleum Exporting Countries (OPEC) is founded, with Venezuela one of the founder members.
1962	The Betancourt government finally represses the armed struggle launched by guerrilla groups seeking a socialist revolution.
1968	Rafael Caldera of COPEI becomes the first opposition candidate to gain the presidency through direct elections.
1973	Carlos Andrés Pérez of Acción Democrática is elected president. The Yom Kippur war between Arabs and Israelis triggers a spectacular rise in world oil prices, generating a period of economic boom in Venezuela.
1975	The Pérez government passes laws to nationalize the iron, steel, and oil industries.
1976	Petroleum industry nationalized by Pérez government.

1983	The debt crisis, fall in oil prices, and devaluation of the national currency signal the end of the oil boom.
1989	Another government under Carlos Andrés Pérez seeks to implement tough austerity measures. In response, violent riots break out in Caracas on February 27.
1992	Two attempted military coups are suppressed by troops loyal to the government.
1993	Facing corruption charges, President Pérez is impeached.
1994	The economic crisis reaches a new level of gravity with the collapse of a large portion of the financial system.
1998	With the country still facing severe economic problems and popular discontent, presidential elections are held in December, and are won, with a massive majority, by one of the coup leaders of 1992, Hugo Chávez, with his Polo Patriótico coalition party. A humiliating defeat for the discredited traditional parties that had dominated since 1958, his victory signified a new phase in the country's political life. Chávez promised a new constitution and wide-ranging reforms.
1999	The new constitution is approved by referendum on December 15. At the same time, the country suffers the worst natural disaster of its history when floods and landslides destroy towns on the coast north of Caracas. Up to fifty thousand are feared killed, and many more are made homeless.
2000	Against the background of record unemployment, rising crime figures and a shrinking economy, the biggest elections in Venezuela's history, required because of the new constitution, are held on July 30. Chávez is comfortably reelected.

1

Context

THIS CHAPTER AIMS to acquaint the reader with the key historical, economic, and social factors that have shaped Venezuela's cultural development up to the end of the twentieth century. A list of major historical events is given in the chronology, so Chapter 1 concentrates on developments, circumstances, and phenomena that have had an indelible and lasting impact, and have helped to make the country's cultural life distinctive. By reviewing the impact of oil, regional cultural differences, and state policy on education and culture, this chapter will provide a broad framework within which to place the various art forms and cultural expressions discussed in the rest of the book.

EARLY HISTORY

Having carried out two expeditions for Spain that explored the Caribbean and the outlying islands of the American continent, Christopher Columbus led a third voyage, in 1498, that took him to the delta of the Orinoco River and along the Venezuelan coast. Venezuela thus became the first part of the New World mainland that the Spanish encountered and explored. The following year, Spanish merchants financed another expedition, this time under the command of Alonso de Ojeda, that further explored the coastline. "A member of that voyage supposedly gave the land its name. Amerigo Vespucci is said to have referred to it as Venezuela, meaning Little Venice, as an ironic comparison with the European city when he saw the wooden huts on stilts that the Indians constructed in shallow waters near Lake Maracaibo."

The country's mestizo culture has its roots in the earliest days of the long and arduous process of colonization carried out by the Spanish. Interbreeding between Europeans and Indians was a natural consequence of the scarcity of women among the first Spanish colonists. In later centuries, African slaves and immigrants from other parts of Europe added to the process of miscegenation, making Venezuela one of the most racially mixed countries of Latin America. At the end of the twentieth century, 69% of the population considered themselves to be of mixed race (Ferguson, 1994, 11). The interaction of different cultural traditions has produced the rich variety of hybrid forms of expression, beliefs, and customs that is undoubtedly one of the most distinctive features of modern Venezuelan culture. Many of them will be discussed in later chapters, such as the music that merges European and African forms, the culinary traditions that combine Spanish and Indian practices, and the religious rituals that fuse indigenous, African, and European elements.

The indigenous peoples the Spanish found in Venezuela were divided into scattered and largely nomadic communities, and there were no sophisticated civilizations equivalent to the Aztecs or Incas. Unlike such countries as Mexico and Peru, therefore, Venezuela does not have a great Indian heritage or highly visible Indian cultures in the present. A census in 1992 numbered the indigenous people at 315,815, divided into twenty-five different ethnic groups, about 1.5% of the Venezuelan population. Some claim the figure to be slightly higher. In order to preserve their cultural traditions and to fight to protect their lands against rapacious speculators, the indigenous communities became increasingly organized in the latter part of the twentieth century. This process culminated in 1989 with the foundation of the National Indigenous Council of Venezuela, CONIVE, composed of twenty regional Indian organizations. Despite the repression indigenous culture has endured through the centuries, significant elements of it are still evident in the interior of Venezuela, particularly in some of the remoter parts. It is estimated that as many as twenty-eight indigenous languages are still spoken, and many of the communities have maintained their traditional forms of housing, their religious rituals, their myths and legends, and a wide variety of arts and crafts.

Concentrating on the greater wealth offered by the populous Indian civilizations elsewhere in America, the Spanish paid relatively little attention to Venezuela during the first two centuries of the colonial period. Cities were founded, and agriculture and cattle raising were established as viable economic activities, but development was slow. This was particularly so in the cultural sphere. The first university in Venezuela dates from 1725, compared with 1553 in Mexico, 1621 in Colombia, and 1622 in Argentina; and the first printing press did not arrive until 1808, whereas a press was established in Mexico in 1535 (Vilda, 1983, 19). Not surprisingly, notable examples of colonial art and architecture are relatively few in Venezuela. Finally, in the eighteenth century, the highly prosperous export of cacao at last made the colony one of the strongest economies in Spanish America.

Various factors merged to give rise to the wars of independence in the early nineteenth century. The trade laws benefited Spain to the detriment of Venezuelan producers; the wealthiest classes of the colony resented the fact that their economic position did not give them a corresponding degree of political power; and the revolutionary ideas emanating from Europe at the end of the eighteenth century had a significant influence. The final break with Spanish power was triggered by Napoleon's invasion of Spain in 1808, which created a constitutional crisis in the Spanish colonies. The Venezuelan revolutionaries declared independence in 1811, but it would take a decade of bitter military conflict to fully secure it. From 1821 to 1830, Venezuela existed as part of the Republic of Gran Colombia, a union also comprising what at present are Colombia, Panama, and Ecuador. However, a separatist movement led by José Antonio Páez steadily gathered momentum in Venezuela, and it was declared a republic in its own right in 1830.

SIMÓN BOLÍVAR

Venezuela provided several of the most outstanding figures of Latin America independence, notably Francisco de Miranda (1750–1816), Antonio José de Sucre (1795–1830), and, the most prominent of them all, Simón Bolívar (1783–1830). Some of the Venezuelan revolutionaries were instrumental in the liberation of neighboring territories as well, and Bolívar in particular is still revered in Colombia, Ecuador, Peru, and Bolivia for his part in the gaining of their independence. Venezuela's vanguard role in the overthrow of Spanish colonialism is proudly recorded in monuments and iconography across the country. Dominant among them are those dedicated to Bolívar, who is frequently referred to as "The Liberator," the title bestowed upon him in 1813, during a period of ascendancy of the revolutionary forces. Bolívar is undoubtedly Latin America's most famous and alluring historical figure. That was clearly demonstrated in 1983, when numerous acts of homage took place throughout the continent to mark the bicentennial of his birth. He successfully led a remarkable political and military campaign against the Spanish, but unlike most other independence leaders he believed that freedom from colonialism should open the way for progressive reform and social change. He had a clear vision of the future of the region, and argued fervently for a united Latin America. That objective was defeated and separatism pre-

Statue of Simón Bolívar, Caracas. Photo courtesy of Mark Dinneen.

vailed, but the ideal, forever associated with Bolívar, persists in Latin America to the present day.

It is difficult to exaggerate the role that the figure of Bolívar plays in modern Venezuelan culture. The principal national icon, he has been converted into a cult. For the country's governments, he has been the most important symbol for developing a sense of national identity and unity. It began with the Guzmán Blanco regime in the 1870s and 1880s, which sought to overcome decades of disorder and violence by constructing a strong, centralized state. It promoted patriotic art glorifying the struggle against colonialism, and built the Pantheon in Caracas to house the remains of Bolívar and other independence heroes. Completed in 1876, the Pantheon is Venezuela's most important shrine. The Gómez government consolidated the process in the early twentieth century, building a museum dedicated to Bolívar's life and reconstructing the house where he was born in the center of Caracas. Today in Venezuela his name is evoked constantly. The country's currency, main airport, and highest mountain peak are named after him, as are numerous buildings, streets, and squares in towns throughout the nation. A city, a state, and a country carry his name, though the country, of course, is Bolivia, named in his honor in 1825, rather than his homeland. There has been an attempt to rectify that, however. The new constitution of 1999, introduced by the government of Hugo Chávez and approved by referendum, changed the official title of the nation to the Bolivarian Republic of Venezuela.

Bolívar's hold over the Venezuelan imagination has remained strong. As will be seen in subsequent chapters, his life and exploits have been featured in numerous books, paintings, television programs, and songs, and his spirit is evoked in popular religious rituals. Many of those expressions have reinforced the myth of Bolívar, presenting him as an idealized national hero, which was cultivated in offical art from the 1870s on and culminated in the paintings of Tito Salas (1888–1974), depicting Bolívar as a Godlike figure. The image has been so strong that attempts to revise it have been relatively few and have always encountered controversy, as was the case with work published by the political scientist Luis Castro Leiva (1943–1999) in the 1980s and 1990s that criticized the thought and influence of Bolívar. Significantly, most works of art seeking to demythify Bolívar have come from outside Venezuela, the best-known example undoubtedly being the 1989 novel *El general en su laberinto* (The General in His Labyrinth), written by Colombia's Gabriel García Márquez. It focuses on Bolívar in the final days of his life, chronically ill, bitterly disillusioned, and isolated. It was generally well received by literary critics, but incurred the displeasure of some politicians and political commentators, who regarded the view presented of The Liberator to be demeaning and insulting.

THE IMPACT OF OIL

Venezuela paid a high cost for independence, with the population reduced by almost a third and immense damage to the economy. The task of consolidating the new republic was enormous, and it was further hampered during most of the nineteenth century by the uprisings and wars that resulted from factional and regional conflicts. The dominant classes were deeply divided over their vision of the future of the country, with conservatives pitched against liberals and centralists against federalists, but in many of the conflicts personal ambition played a more important role than ideas. Such turbulence explains not only the lack of real economic progress for most of the nineteenth century but also the limited results of artistic creativity. Creative energy tended to be absorbed into political, legal, and social projects. Much of the art that was produced was highly imitative, for the dominant elite looked toward French cultural models, deemed to be the most sophisticated in the

Twin monoliths dedicated to the Heroes of Independence, Caracas. Thousands of
monuments across Venezuela recall Bolívar and other independence fighters. Photo
courtesy of Mark Dinneen.

world, for their architecture, literature, and fine art. The Gómez dictatorship
that took power in 1908 imposed political order and stability, but at a huge
social cost; all opposition was crushed and human rights were abused as a
matter of course. Censorship was strict, and intellectual and artistic activity
rigorously controlled. It was during the Gómez years, however, that there
occurred the event that would have by far the greatest impact on Venezuelan
society and culture in the twentieth century: the discovery of oil.

It is probable that no other Latin American economy has changed so
dramatically and so rapidly as did that of Venezuela on account of petroleum.
In 1925, petroleum overtook coffee as the country's main export, and its
dominant role within the national economy increased steadily as the century
progressed. By 1928, Venezuela had become the world's largest exporter of
oil and its second largest producer, after the United States. The sudden
transformation of a poor, agrarian economy with little industry and limited

infrastructure into a modern, prosperous, oil-exporting economy inevitably generated profound changes in most other areas of national life. After the Gómez dictatorship, petroleum revenues provided the stability and sound financial basis for the creation of a new, democratic political system and modern administrative structures. Oil income enabled the state to acquire new industries and undertake numerous projects. By the mid-1940s, the building of roads, hospitals, and schools reached unprecedented levels. Cities, most notably Caracas and Maracaibo, were transformed by a surge in urban construction, the new wealth evident in the housing and leisure facilities provided for the plutocracy. The middle classes expanded, the shift of the population to the cities intensified decade by decade, and immigration increased significantly. It was estimated that foreigners constituted about 1% of the population in 1935; by 1957 that figure was 8%, and rising (Lieuwen, 1965, 13). Italians and Spaniards formed the largest groups. These immigrants, the majority of whom were attracted to the employment opportunities being created in the cities, contributed much to Venezuelan economic, social, and cultural life in the latter part of the century.

Use of the oil wealth varied considerably from one government to another. The military dictatorships of Gómez (1920s and 1930s) and of Pérez Jiménez (1950s) invested little in cultural or artistic activity, tending to regard it with suspicion, but spent lavishly on ostentatious public buildings and monuments. In contrast, the civilian governments that held power in between them spoke of "sowing the oil," using its revenues for social and economic improvement; and education was one of the main areas that benefited. In 1973 there was a quadrupling of crude oil prices, brought about by the petroleum-producing nations in the wake of the Arab–Israeli war. As a result, the period 1973–1983 was one of boom in Venezuela. Oil was responsible for as much as 95% of the country's export earnings (Brooks, 1982, 829), and Venezuelans enjoyed the highest per capita income in Latin America (Galeano, 1997, 165). The state had greater economic power than ever before, and the government of Carlos Andrés Pérez increased public spending to new levels. In fact, it spent more in absolute terms during its five years in office than all the governments during the previous 143 years put together. Funds were poured into education, health and welfare programs, and new cultural projects, with such areas as architecture, the plastic arts, and the cinema receiving a massive infusion of government money. In fact, virtually all forms of cultural expression were affected in one way or another by the influx of petro-dollars. Private funding increased along with that of the state. The consumer boom generated by the more prosperous elements of the population led to increased private-sector sponsorship of cultural events and a rapid expansion of the advertising industry, which provided more revenue for television, the press, and the magazine industry.

However, the oil boom also produced many problems or exacerbated existing ones, and observers soon drew attention to the severe contradictions at the heart of the country's development. The concentration on petroleum, though producing great wealth, also made the economy highly dependent on foreign markets and vulnerable to events elsewhere in the world. In addition, it led to the neglect of other areas of economic production, with serious social consequences. Social inequality was aggravated, and the stark contrasts between the rich and the poor, the modern and the traditional, and the city and the countryside became major themes in works of literature and songs of protest. The way successive governments spent the oil earnings was soon criticized, and evidence of mismanagement and corruption was produced.

Inevitably, petroleum provoked a debate about the changes it effected on national culture. Critics expressed concern that the influx of petrodollars intensified cultural dependency on the United States, pointing to the increasing number of American films, television programs, magazines, and consumer products entering the country. Many lamented the erosion of national customs and traditions likely to result from the high consumerism and the adoption of American lifestyles that were more and more apparent in the cities. In response, there emerged new efforts to emphasize the *criollo*—the national. They were evident in both artistic expression and commercial ventures, such as shops selling traditional handicrafts and restaurants advertising *comida criolla*, popular national cuisine. In fact, the debate over foreign influences and national culture continued in one form or another throughout the rest of the twentieth century. It played a significant role in shaping much of the artistic expression that will be discussed in later chapters. Some have understood it in terms of a conflict between two opposed sets of values, but, as will be seen, many of Venezuela's most successful artists have sought a middle course, assimilating cosmopolitan cultural forms in order to reexamine national concerns and realities in their work.

VENEZUELA AT THE END OF THE TWENTIETH CENTURY

Venezuela confronted grave problems in the early 1980s. An acute financial crisis was provoked by a fall in oil prices and mounting national debt, for governments had borrowed heavily on the expectation of high petroleum revenues. A steep rise in inflation and unemployment seriously eroded the

Hugo Chávez during his presidential campaign in 1998. He won the election in December of that year. Photo courtesy of Archivo El Nacional.

living standards of most social classes, particularly the poorest sectors, whose hardship was intensified by cuts in social spending. Tension mounted. The attempt by President Pérez to implement a severe austerity program led to major riots in Caracas in February 1989, resulting in hundreds of deaths. Amid continuing popular discontent, and accusations of government incompetence and corruption, two military coups were attempted in 1992. Both were repressed, but it was clear that the economic stability and solid democratic political system which had steadily been consolidated over the decades could no longer be taken for granted.

The widespread disillusion and the desire for real change were clearly expressed in the 1998 presidential election. It was won by Hugo Chávez, leader of one of the attempted coups six years earlier, and his Polo Patriótico, a new coalition. Promising radical reform, including a new constitution and an end to corruption, Chávez gained massive support from the poorest sectors of Venezuelan society, which had frequently been ignored by the traditional parties. Constantly invoking the legacy of Bolívar, which he claimed to be the main inspiration of his politics, he developed a mixture of populism and nationalism that restored hope and self-esteem to many voters. However, the breaking of the two-party system that had dominated the country since 1958, the debate over the constitution, and the changes promised all created an air of uncertainty. A new phase of the nation's political life was under way. Inevitably, the circumstances of the 1990s adversely affected cultural activity as well. The drastic reduction in government support, the contraction of the economy, and the lack of clear cultural policy because of the political uncertainty led to a decline in artistic production and educational initiatives.

URBANIZATION

Rapid urbanization has been one of the most striking social features of twentieth-century Latin America, and no country has been more profoundly affected than Venezuela. According to some statistics from 1990, as much as 90.5% of the population was living in urban areas, which would make Venezuela the most urbanized country of the region (Cubitt, 1995, 151). In the 1950s, the majority of Venezuelans still lived in the countryside, so the transformation was rapid. As in other Latin American countries, migration from the rural areas is the main explanation, and in the case of Venezuela the process was accelerated by the petroleum boom, which sharply exacerbated the disparity between facilities, opportunities, and living standards in the countryside and those in the city. Cities such as Barquisimeto, Maracaibo, and Valencia experienced notable growth, but it was Caracas that received most government funding, and where expansion and social and cultural change were most dramatic.

That funding for the capital produced many impressive buildings, cultural facilities, and shopping centers, as well as some significant improvements in city services, most notably the highly efficient subway system, opened in 1983. It is in the crowded city, however, where social inequality in Venezuela is most apparent. On steep slopes unsuitable for standard housing, squatter settlements, or shantytowns, have been erected, often overlooking blocks of expensive apartments. As one observer notes, the inhabitants of Caracas have devised special terminology to denote such contrasts. *Urbanización* signifies a relatively prosperous area of planned housing, whereas *barrio* refers to poor districts. *Rancho* signifies the owner-built shack typical of the shantytown, and is at the opposite end of the social scale to the *quinta*, the large house of the well-to-do (Ferguson, 1994, 46).

Social deprivation, violence, and crime increased appreciably in the last decades of the twentieth century, and they became major issues of popular concern, regularly discussed in the media and recurring topics in literature and film. Notable among such works were a number of testimonial novels based on the experience of marginalized city dwellers living in a world of

High-rise apartment blocks and freeways of modern Caracas. Photo by Nelson Garrido. Courtesy of the Fundación Bigott.

poverty and crime. The most celebrated was *Soy un delincuente* (I'm a Criminal), supposedly the testimony of a young armed robber named Ramón Antonio Brizuela but in fact the work of the writer Gustavo Santander Laya. Published in 1974, it was a phenomenal success, and was made into an equally successful film.

For thousands of Venezuelans, such writing and films opened up a world that existed on their doorstep but was remote from their experience, too hostile and dangerous to enter. However, the impact of modern urban life on the arts extended beyond specific social issues. Novelists, dramatists, artists, and filmmakers began to explore the broader subject of alienation and isolation in the city, presenting an urban environment that promised much but often brought frustration and disillusion. In terms of artistic production, the expanding city presented artists with both new challenges and new opportunities, for it offered increased facilities and institutional support.

It is also in the big cities, above all in Caracas, that the intermingling and merging of different cultural forms is most evident. Many migrants arriving from the interior continued their rural customs, such as magical religious practices and traditional forms of medicine, while adopting new ways in order to accommodate themselves to urban patterns of life. New hybrid cultural expressions frequently resulted. However, Caracas has also long been the principal point of entry for customs, fashions, and cultural models from overseas, many of which were rapidly assimilated by the wealthy sectors of the city's population. This medley of influences has been a powerful creative force in the arts, perhaps above all in popular music, which has constantly blended national and foreign, traditional and modern forms.

As Caracas expanded, it became more cosmopolitan. Nowhere was that process more noticeable than in the city's commercial life and leisure industry. International fast-food chains appeared a few blocks away from traditional cafés, snack bars, and restaurants. Smart shops selling imported consumer products opened not far from family-run general stores. The fare offered by concert halls and clubs became increasingly varied, with Anglo-Saxon popular music alternating with equally popular Venezuelan and Latin American forms. Understandably, many of those in the city have lamented its rapid transformation. They have argued that too much heritage has been discarded in the rush for modernization, exemplified by the destruction of numerous old buildings to make way for towering apartment blocks. In the interior of the country, many others have protested the centralization of decision making and of resources in Caracas. By the end of the twentieth century it had nonetheless become one of Latin America's most dynamic cultural centers, winning international recognition for many of its arts facilities.

REGIONAL CULTURES

Despite the dominance of urban patterns of life, there is still considerable cultural variation across Venezuela. Geographical and historical factors provide the explanation. During the era of colonization, the different landscapes and natural resources of each region determined distinctive forms of settlement, work practices, and social organization, and the type of administration imposed by the Spanish tended to reinforce those separate regional identities.

Modern Caracas. Photograph courtesy of Mark Dinneen.

Until the late eighteenth century the territory that comprises the country today was divided into a number of provinces which had very little contact with one another, and were under the control of different external authorities. In the east, the province of Margarita, created in 1525, was dependent upon the political, legal, and military control of the Spanish administration in Santo Domingo, in what is today the Dominican Republic. In 1528, the province of Venezuela was formed, composed of today's Federal District of Caracas and the central and western states, and also was placed under the jurisdiction of Santo Domingo. Some other provinces, however, to the east and south, including the island of Trinidad, the Amazon region, and that of the Orinoco delta, were subject to the legal control of the authorities in Bogotá, Colombia. Only slowly and belatedly did those provinces become more integrated, politically and economically. In an effort to govern them more effectively, the Spanish Crown embarked on a gradual process of administrative unification in the course of the eighteenth century. This was consolidated in 1777 by uniting them into one territory as the Captaincy-General of Venezuela. That arrangement, giving the territory a more autonomous status, was its first significant step toward political integration.

However, the new administrative unit had little time to solidify. The first uprisings against Spanish rule had already occurred. In the nineteenth century, with independence won, regional interests often rose up to resist the central government of the new republic, on occasions openly declaring their desire for separate status. The western province of Maracaibo is the major example, with five genuine attempts at separation between 1821 and 1935. Regionalist sentiment remained strong in that part of the country, today the state of Zulia, throughout the twentieth century. It is largely explained by its economic strength, as the country's most important oil-producing region, and by the resentment felt by many of its inhabitants toward the strongly centralized state apparatus and the domination of Caracas. By the latter part of the century there was little real support for outright separation, but some of its politicians argued for regional autonomy, similar to that granted by the Spanish government to regions in Spain. The idea was taken up by some in other districts of Venezuela. Regionalism as a political movement, however, has had little real force. Its main significance in recent decades has been at the cultural level. Through their music, festivals, dances, crafts, and customs, regions have sought to assert their distinct identity.

Zulia is one of the states in the northern coastal belt of the country, which was the first part of Venezuela colonized by the Spanish. They established their first settlements on the outlying islands and then along the mainland coast. Coro, between Maracaibo and Caracas, is one of the oldest towns in South America, dating from 1527. Attempts to settle the interior of the country were very limited during the colonial period, first because the climate and environment were so inhospitable, and second because from the coast lucrative trade could be carried out with other areas of the Caribbean. The northern coastal region has remained the most populous of Venezuela ever since. In the twentieth century, agriculture, commerce, oil, and more recently tourism have made it the most developed part of the country. Now a great majority of the Venezuelan population lives there, within a hundred miles or so of the sea. It is where urbanization has been strongest, and where most of the large cities are located, including Caracas, Maracaibo, and Valencia. Its great mixture of peoples means that it is also the part of the country with the greatest cultural variety. In the west of Zulia, near the border with Colombia, the Guajiro Indians retain their language and traditional dress and customs. In other parts of the coastal belt, in such states as Aragua, elements of Afro-Venezuelan culture are evident, particularly in dance and music. Large numbers of African slaves were introduced into those areas in the seventeenth and eighteenth centuries, to work on the thriving cacao plantations. In the latter twentieth century, the cultural influences of different immigrant groups were added, for many settled in the cities close to the coast, attracted by their economic dynamism.

In sharp contrast to the coastal belt are the vast plains or llanos inland and to the south, sparsely populated and largely undeveloped. Cattle raising was established there centuries ago and remains the principal economic activity. Many of the traditions associated with llano life and work have continued to the present, albeit in a modified form, and the region is renowned for its folkloric cultural expressions, most of which have evolved from old Spanish forms. Its music, songs, dances, stories, and legends, which have inspired many professional musicians and writers, still find a receptive audience in Caracas and other big cities. It is not difficult to understand. Llano culture offers an alluring alternative to urban existence, though it has, of course, become idealized. The fragmented and chaotic life of the city is frequently contrasted with the more communal, harmonious life of the plains. Against the concrete jungle of modern Caracas the notion of a more wholesome life in wild, open nature has strong appeal. The plains are associated with freedom, independence, and the preservation of important values from the past. To many living in a society of rapid change and modernization, llano culture represents traditional Venezuelan identity with deep historical roots. The plains have been mythologized, and many works of art, especially works of fiction, have contributed to the process That, however, is not to deny the vitality and creativity of the region's culture, still expressed in a wide range of forms.

In the west of the country are the Venezuelan Andes, a region comprising the states of Mérida, Táchira, and Trujillo, and distinguished from other areas of the country by its mountainous terrain and temperate climate. Because of its fertile valleys it became an important center of agricultural production during the colonial period, especially of wheat, and in the late nineteenth century the cultivation of coffee thrived there, making Venezuela one of the world's major exporters of the crop. The region is renowned for the distinctive architecture styles, customs, crafts, and culinary traditions that have resulted from the peculiarities of its environment. Catholicism has its deepest roots in this region, and it has marked many of the traditions and popular arts, particularly religious paintings, sculptures, and pottery. The most celebrated of the many popular artists of the region is Juan Félix Sánchez (1900–1997), who, having carved many saints, Virgins, and crucifixes, constructed an entire chapel with thousands of stones, earning himself the nickname Architect of the Andes.

Finally, south of the Orinoco River is the largest region of the country, known as Guayana. Formed by the state of Bolívar and the Federal Territory of Amazonas, it comprises nearly half the national territory but contains little more than 5% of the population. Its most distinctive forms of cultural expression derive from its many indigenous groups, such as the Pemón, the Piaroa, and the Yanomami. There is, however, a rapidly growing urban area concentrated around Ciudad Guayana (or Santo Tomé de Guayana), its largest city. It is the result of industrial development based on the region's rich natural resources, especially iron ore. Further expansion of industry and population is planned for this major center of mining and metal processing.

The extraordinary geographical diversity of Venezuela, long proclaimed by the tourist literature that extols its beaches, mountains, plains, and jungles, is echoed at the cultural level. Though centralized government and economic modernization helped to unify the country politically and to forge a sense of national identity, every region proudly asserts its own individuality.

EDUCATION AND CULTURAL POLICY

The foundations of Venezuela's state education system and modern cultural institutions were laid in the years that followed the end of the Gómez dictatorship in 1935. Cultural activity had endured decades of oppression and stagnancy under Gómez. What little there was, was rigorously controlled by the regime, and public art was trite and acquiescent. The only expressions of dissent were made clandestinely. One significant cultural institution was created in the public domain, however. In 1931 a group of society women in Caracas founded an arts center called the Ateneo. It presented concerts, exhibitions, talks, and social events for the elite, but in later decades, freed from restriction, it became one of the country's foremost organizations for the diffusion of diverse currents in all the arts.

There was an explosion of cultural activity and artistic expression after the death of Gómez. Artists established new groups, societies, and journals, and opened their work to new tendencies from overseas. Social and political issues, the discussion of which had long been prohibited, were now vigorously debated in pamphlets, press articles, and essays. The state initiated a process of institutional reform, aiming to create the organizations necessary to promote and support cultural and artistic development. A Directorate of Culture was created within the Ministry of Education to oversee the process. Schools of graphic art, dance, and music, and the Venezuelan Symphony Orchestra were radically restructured, and new museums of fine art and natural science were inaugurated. Supported by oil earnings, these modest efforts by the state were built upon in later decades, albeit in fits and starts, and always accompanied by arguments over priorities and the appropriateness of government spending.

The reform of education was central to the overall program of modernization. In 1936, the illiteracy rate in Venezuela was 71%, and only 20% of children attended school. In the 1990s, illiteracy was 11% and approximately 97% of children received basic education. (Lieuwen, 1965, 18; Cubitt, 1995, 245). Such statistics indicate the steady progress in the development of education in the twentieth century. While in power in the 1940s, politicians such as Rómulo Betancourt and Rómulo Gallegos, anxious to accelerate reform, invested heavily in an aggressive public education policy, which they saw as a major priority of the state. Later, the revenues from oil funded a further expansion of education at all levels, especially in the 1970s, when government spending on the sector was highest. Access to higher education was increased dramatically, and grants, such as those offered by the Gran Mariscal de Ayacucho Foundation, created in 1974, helped students to study at both national and foreign universities. The number of universities in Venezuela rose from four in 1958 to twenty-four in the early 1990s, by which time there were also over one hundred higher education institutes offering a wide range of courses (Ferguson, 1994, 73). For those able to study only at home, the Open University was launched in 1978, offering specially designed materials and classes via the state television channels. The private sector played an increasingly significant part in this general expansion. Thirteen of the twenty-four universities were private, as were many of the new schools and colleges.

Such statistics tell only part of the story, however, for the state education system faced serious problems at the end of the twentieth century. Many educators argued that it had become outdated and inefficient, and that expansion had emphasized quantity but had neglected quality. Alarming evidence was produced to highlight the gravity of the situation. Dropout rates at both the school and the university level were extremely high, rising as the national economic situation worsened. State primary and secondary schools suffered the effects of reductions in the government budget: deterioration of facilities and the value of teachers' pay. Faced with the deficiencies in the state sector, more and more families who could afford it turned to private schools to educate their children. In many of the state universities, production remained low even though costs had risen steadily over the years, and critics pointed out that equivalent universities abroad produced many more graduates. Cumbersome bureaucracy frequently resulted in inefficiency and wasted resources at all levels of the state system, and some observers called for its complete overhaul, arguing that, due to its structural and organizational defects, it was failing badly as an instrument for national development.

The state's policy on, and investment in, other spheres of cultural activity likewise produced uneven results. Some bold initiatives did lead to noteworthy achievements. One of the best examples is Monte Ávila, the state-owned publishing company established in 1968, which soon became the largest publisher in the country. Run without a profit-making objective, the prices of its books were kept low in order to make them as widely accessible as possible. That policy and the quality and range of its books, covering the arts, history, philosophy, and the social sciences, account for the high reputation it enjoys throughout Latin America. For many critics, however, state cultural policy suffered from a lack of clear objectives and long-term planning. It has been argued that too much effort and income were spent on lavish, showpiece projects, often poorly conceived, in which political interests frequently prevailed over the concern for cultural development (Vilda, 1984, 32).

In the 1960s, the government decided to create an institution to coordinate and implement state support for culture and the arts. The National Institute for Culture and Fine Art, INCIBA, was founded in 1964, and its eleven-year history highlights many of the difficulties that undermined state cultural policy for the rest of the century. From the beginning it was beset with organizational and financial problems. It failed to receive adequate government backing, and never obtained more than 10% of total state spending on culture. Nor was it ever able to play the coordinating role that it had been assigned. Groups and organizations around the country worked independently on their own projects, and cultural activity remained fragmented and dispersed, with efforts often duplicated and resources wasted. In the 1970s the Pérez government recognized the deficiencies in state cultural policy, and in 1975 it founded a new organization, the National Council for Culture (CONAC), as the principal state agency for cultural matters. Its wide range of responsibilities included granting subsidies for the arts; organizing cultural events in Venezuela and overseas; creating workshops, exhibitions, and courses; and awarding national prizes. It, too, was the subject of controversy, with the effectiveness of its role periodically questioned.

Cultural policy was steadily given a higher profile by government in the last decades of the twentieth century, but the serious limitations of its implementation were clear. With priority given to supporting the fine arts, large sectors of the population remained excluded. Furthermore, relatively little effort was made to widen active participation in cultural activity, with art treated as the specialist occupation of a few and the majority of Venezuelans regarded as its passive recipients. Accusations of elitism and paternalism were common. One concrete result was the attempts in the 1980s to set up new, community-based groups that, in opposition to government-backed initiatives, sought to popularize the arts by drawing participants from the wider public. Though frequently suffering from a lack of resources and working in isolation, they represented a significant alternative to state-sponsored cultural expression.

THE CHANGING ROLE OF WOMEN

In the line with the general trend throughout Latin America, women's participation in virtually all levels of Venezuelan society increased significantly in the latter part of the twentieth century. In earlier decades, they were almost invariably confined to the traditional role of wife and mother. Gaining a political voice and opening access to educational and work opportunities was a long and difficult process, however. Women played an important part in the clandestine opposition to the Gómez dictatorship in the 1920s and 1930s, and in the 1940s, through organizations such as the Venezuelan Women's Association, they began to campaign for their political and civil rights. Women were finally granted the vote in 1947, and by the 1980s they were challenging the male dominance of the political system, serving as ministers, deputies, and senators. Venezuela's first woman presidential candidate was chosen in 1988. These were significant advances, although, given that women formed over half the country's electorate, the actual number in positions of political influence was still low at the close of the century. And for those from poor backgrounds, without educational qualifications, opportunities rarely extended beyond low-paid work in factories, shops, or domestic service.

Greater access to education has obviously been crucial to women's wider involvement in the middle-class professions. Many took advantage of the major expansion of higher education that occurred in the 1970s and 1980s, and by the 1990s the majority of students at that level were women. Some of those women graduates moved into the traditionally male-dominated professions, such as architecture and engineering, but most found careers in education, administration, and commerce. On the other hand, relatively few obtained executive and managerial posts, which suggests that discrimination still limited their professional advancement. Undoubtedly, however, the media and the arts were two of the areas where the success of women was most notable.

The best-known women artists of earlier generations, such as the musician

Teresa Carreño (1853–1917) and the novelist Teresa de la Parra (1889–1936), stood out not just because of their talent but also because they accomplished their achievements in a society where women's success in the arts was not widely accepted. Indeed, the fact that both artists received early acclaim abroad, Carreño in New York and Parra in Paris, facilitated their subsequent fame in Venezuela. By the 1990s, however, numerous women had achieved prominence in music, fine art, film, and literature, and many had become media celebrities. Equally significant were those who became promoters of culture, such as María Teresa Castillo, who served as director of the Ateneo in Caracas, and Sofía Imber, director of the Museum of Contemporary Art and a high-profile cultural critic. The trend is set to continue. Whatever the future development of the arts in Venezuela may be, one of the few certainties is that women will have an increasing influence in all of them.

FOREIGN RELATIONS

Venezuelan politicians have often sought ways of exploiting the country's mixed cultural identity and the strategic advantages of its geographical position. During the Pérez presidency in the 1970s, government spokesmen, eager for the country to enhance its relations with neighboring nations and to play a more dynamic role in the region, proudly declared Venezuela to be simultaneously a Caribbean, an Andean, an Amazonian, and an Atlantic nation. Oil wealth seemed to offer the prospect of greater prominence in regional affairs. Although such ambitions receded in the decades that followed, largely due to the mounting economic and political difficulties, closer ties with neighboring countries were actively pursued by later governments. Those relations have been far from easy, however. For a long period they were marred by disputes over frontiers, and in the twentieth century occasional quarrels broke out over specific political issues.

A treaty establishing the frontier between Venezuela and Brazil was signed by the two governments in 1859. Some details relating to the most remote part of the boundary region remained to be settled, but they were finally resolved by an agreement in 1905. There were a few moments of tension later in the century. During the 1960s and 1970s, when Brazil was ruled by a military dictatorship, some Venezuelan politicians expressed fears about Brazilian expansionism, especially when they noted increased Brazilian economic and military activity in the frontier region. Later, there were complaints by Venezuela about incursions into its territory by Brazilian prospectors in search of gold and other precious metals, some of which resulted in violence. Despite these problems, relations between the two countries remained cordial overall. Brazilian popular culture, particularly music and television soap operas, has had a high profile in Venezuela. Wider cultural exchange and cooperation have been limited, however, and for many Venezuelans, Brazil remains, to a large extent, an unknown quantity. Relations also have been generally amicable with the neighbor to the east, English-speaking Guyana, even though the dispute over that border has been the most protracted of all. The frontier was never precisely established at the time of independence, and the matter remains unresolved. Despite the periodic negotiations that have taken place, Venezuela still lays claim to over half of Guyana's territory. Certain communities in the east of Venezuela, close to the border, have a rich body of folk songs sung in a mixture of Spanish and English, the result of the influx of immigrants from Guyana and Trinidad.

It is with Colombia that relations have been most conflictual. Arguments over the border were settled only in 1941, and a dispute over who had sovereignty over the islands known as Los Monjes, north of the Gulf of Venezuela, continued until 1952, when Colombia recognized Venezuela's claim. Disagreements still rumbled afterward, however, particularly with regard to the question of control over the Gulf of Venezuela itself, which is crucial for the transportation of Venezuelan oil. Although outright conflict between the two countries was avoided, there were periodic border skirmishes and moments of high tension, and in the closing decades of the twentieth century, other border issues—illegal immigration into Venezuela, drug trafficking, and the activity of Colombian guerrilla groups close to the frontier—placed further strain on relations. These problems have colored the way Colombians are viewed in Venezuela. It is a sad fact that despite the many cultural similarities between the two countries, anti–Colombian sentiment is strong among many Venezuelans.

The greatest impact on modern Venezuelan culture and lifestyles has undoubtedly been made by relations with the United States. From the 1930s on, as the oil trade tightened the economic and political ties between the two countries, American cultural products, customs, and consumer tastes began to supplant those from Europe, which had tended to dominate in the nineteenth century. Virtually all aspects of life and social behavior in Venezuela have been affected. U.S. influence is seen today in the growing importance of the English language in Venezuelan society; ways of dressing and eating habits; and the recently adopted celebration of Thanksgiving Day and Valentine's Day. (The role of influence on the media and the arts will be discussed in the chapters that follow.)

REFERENCES

Box, Ben, ed. *The 1997 South American Handbook*. Bath, England: Footprint Handbooks, 1997.

Briceño Iragorry, Mario. *Mensaje sin destino*. Caracas: Monte Ávila, 1980.

Brooks John, ed. *The 1982 South American Handbook*. Bath, England: Trade and Travel Publications, 1982.

Caballero, Manuel. *Ni Dios ni federación*. Caracas: Planeta, 1995.

———. *De 'pequeño Venecia' a la 'Gran Venezuela.'* Caracas: Monte Ávila, 1997.

Carrera Damas, Germán. *Una nación llamada Venezuela*. Caracas: Monte Ávila, 1994.

Coronil, Fernando. *The Magical State: Nature, Money and Modernity in Venezuela*. Chicago: University of Chicago Press, 1997.

Cubitt, Tessa. *Latin American Society*. Harlow, UK: Longman, 1995.

Ewell, Judith. *Venezuela: A Century of Change*. London: Hurst, 1984.

Ferguson, James. *Venezuela in Focus: Guide to the People, Politics and Culture*. London: L.A.B., 1994.

Galeano, Eduardo. *Open Veins of Latin America*. New York: Monthly Review Press, 1997.

Lieuwen, Edwin. *Venezuela*. London: Oxford University Press, 1965.

Miliani, Domingo. *Vida intelectual de Venezuela*. Caracas: Ministerio de Educación, 1971.

Pino Iturrieta, Elías, et al. *Historia mínima de Venezuela*. Caracas: Fundación de los Trabajadores de Lagoven, 1993.

Salazar-Carrillo, Jorge. *Oil and Development in Venezuela During the Twentieth Century*. London: Praeger, 1994.

Salcedo-Bastardo, J. L. *Historia fundamental de Venezuela*. Caracas: Ediciones de la Biblioteca, 1993.

Segnini, Y., ed. "Instituciones culturales de Venezuela." In *Conocer Venezuela: Cultura y folklore*, Vol. 4, 447–479. Barcelona: Salvat, 1988.

Vilda, Carmelo. *Proceso de la cultura en Venezuela*. Vols. 1 and 2. Caracas: Centro Gumilla, 1983.

———. *Proceso de la cultura en Venezuela*. Vol. 3. Caracas: Centro Gumilla, 1984.

2

Religion

ACCORDING TO GOVERNMENT figures, as much as 96% of the Venezuelan population is nominally Roman Catholic (website of Venezuelan Embassy, London). Religious faith and practice, however, are much more diverse than that figure suggests. As elsewhere in Latin America, a variety of cultural influences and specific historical factors have merged to produce some original expressions of Catholic belief. Many who consider themselves Catholics are at the same time devotees of popular cults, some of which have been accepted by the Catholic Church. Others have been condemned as deviant practices that undermine fundamental Catholic principles. Whatever their status, these cults are the most distinctive feature of religious life in Venezuela. They have generated a wide range of regularly practiced rituals, and the images and figures associated with them are a common sight in homes, shops, and vehicles across the country.

Waves of immigrants have introduced other major religions into Venezuela; Protestantism, Islam, Judaism, and the Orthodox churches are all represented. However, the number of adherents has remained far too small to challenge the dominant position of Catholicism. Protestantism has the second largest following, though the Evangelical churches that spread throughout Latin America in the latter decades of the twentieth century have not had the same impact in Venezuela as in other nations of the region. Many of the indigenous communities in the remoter areas of the country still preserve their own religious traditions, but they comprise no more than 2% of the population (Ferguson, 1994, 73). The dominance of the Catholic Church must not be exaggerated, however. As will be explained, events and circumstances have considerably limited its social and political influence throughout much of its long history in Venezuela. Today, many Venezuelans are indifferent to it, and only a small minority are regular churchgoers. The struggle to make the Catholic Church a more effective force within society has proved difficult, but its increased activity in the 1980s and 1990s, in response to the mounting economic problems, political uncertainty, and social tension of those decades, presented it with a new opportunity to strengthen its role and extend its influence.

CATHOLICISM

As a major instrument for asserting Spain's control over its American colonies, the Catholic Church played a crucial role in the colonization process in Venezuela. Its representatives were among the first European settlers to establish themselves there. Following Columbus's first voyage, the pope granted the Spanish Crown control over the new lands in return for disseminating the faith among their native inhabitants. From the beginning, the Church was subordinate to the Crown, whose authority was confirmed by papal decrees in the early sixteenth century. It was the Crown, for example, which decided upon senior church appointments and the construction of church buildings. Catholicism was the only authorized religion in the colonies; all others were suppressed. The Inquisition was established in Venezuela for that purpose, though in practice it was largely weak and ineffective. Despite its prominent role in the life of the colony, however, the Church in Venezuela was unable to acquire the same strength and influence that it achieved in Mexico, Peru, and Colombia. There were a number of reasons for this.

To start with, Spain did not consider that Venezuela afforded the same economic potential as those other regions, and allocated very limited resources to it. As a consequence, the Venezuelan Church suffered from a lack of funds and a lack of clergy. Its work was further hampered by the fact that the indigenous population was divided into scattered and largely nomadic groups, a situation impeding the task of conversion and instruction. There was also a lack of unity within the Church itself. There were frequent conflicts between the civil authorities and the clergy, and within the clergy, over questions of authority and division of responsibility. The missionaries sent to Venezuela in the sixteenth century, such as the Franciscans, the Jesuits, and the Capuchins, achieved most in terms of subduing the indigenous communities and consolidating Spanish control, but they, too, were weakened by disputes, not only with the colonial authorities and the secular clergy but also among themselves. The result was that the diffusion of Catholicism in Venezuela was slow, spasmodic, and fragmented. The authority of the Church was constantly undermined, and though it managed to establish a few strong centers, most notably in the Andes region, it had only a minimal impact on large expanses of the country.

After considerable difficulties, the first diocese was founded in Venezuela in 1531, and Venezuela's first bishop arrived there three years later. In the latter decades of the eighteenth century, two further dioceses were established, and the Church was more stable and better organized than it had ever been. The acquisition of land and property had given it a sounder economic base, and the clergy were more numerous. The Church dominated education, administered most hospitals and cemeteries, and controlled the records of births, deaths, and marriages. The progress that had been made, however, was brutally interrupted by the War of Independence, which lasted from 1811 until 1821. Many priests left the Church, fled abroad, or were killed, and the destruction or abandonment of Church property weakened it economically. Equally damaging, the clergy at all levels were bitterly divided into pro–Spanish and pro–independence camps. The archbishop of Caracas, Narciso Coll y Prat, supported independence when it was declared in 1811, but Popes Pius VII and Leo XII condemned it. The divisions persisted long after the war was over and independence was finally secure, for though some clerics reached an accommodation with the new republican government, others resisted its attempt to curb the role of the Church. Tension between the Church and the state characterized much of the nineteenth century.

Many of the leaders of independence were liberals imbued with Enlightenment thought. They regarded the Church as a reactionary institution whose privileges were a vestige of Spanish colonial power. There was thus a strong current within the new republican government in favor of anticlerical legislation. Initially caution prevailed. Bolívar's view, that it was best to enlist Church support for the new political regime which was being established and avoid a backlash against Church reform, was accepted. As the new government secured its position, however, measures to ensure the subordination of the Church were enacted. The most significant for the future was the law of ecclesiastical patronage, approved in 1824, which provided the basis for relations between Church and state until 1964, when it was finally abolished. The provisions of the law served to consolidate the state's control over the activities of the Church, including the appointment of senior clerics and the administration of Church funds. Protests by members of the clergy were easily brushed aside.

However, even stronger anticlerical policies were carried out by the government as the nineteenth century progressed, ensuring as far as was possible the full acquiescence of the Church to the state. Bishops and priests who protested too much were sent into exile; the archbishop of Caracas, Ramón Ignacio Méndez, suffered that fate twice in the 1830s. The question of religious tolerance had been a contentious issue in Venezuela for many years, but in 1834 non–Catholic faiths were officially declared legitimate for the first time through a law permitting freedom of worship. Other acts followed, suppressing the monasteries and requiring obedience from bishops, but it was under the presidency of Antonio Guzmán Blanco (three presidencies 1870–1876; 1879–1882, and 1886–1888) that the attack on the Church reached its height. His wave of anticlerical laws included the closure of all seminaries (1872), the secularization of parish registers and of cemeteries (1873), and the establishment of civil marriage (also 1873). Guzmán Blanco even proposed the separation of the Venezuelan Church from Rome in 1876, but the intervention of the Vatican succeeded in preventing the break. Weakened economically and financially dependent upon the state, its role restricted and tightly controlled, the credibility and influence of the Church fell to their lowest level.

The major elements of Guzmán Blanco's anticlerical laws were retained by twentieth-century Venezuelan governments, and firm control by the state continued. Because the Church no longer posed a serious challenge to those in power, they could afford to make concessions to reduce tension between state and Church, and to allow the Church to strengthen its organization. This was most notable between 1908 and 1935, the years when Juan Vicente Gómez dominated political life in Venezuela. Cool but tolerant toward the Church, he subsidized it and permitted it some institutional expansion, expecting its complete obedience in return. New Catholic schools and seminaries were founded, and churches and Church-run medical centers were constructed. In 1916, Gómez normalized the relations between the state and the Vatican, which had been close to the breaking point a few decades before. Nevertheless, clergy who dared to criticize his regime faced the threat of exile, and the Church was largely compliant and complacent.

Accommodation to the state enabled the Church to improve and expand its organization. By the early 1940s, the number of diocesan priests in office had risen to 664, and 49% of secondary school students were in Catholic schools (*Diccionario de Historia de Venezuela*, 363). Church leaders began to find their voices again and speak out on political issues. In response to the ideological conflict between right and left that became increasingly acute in the mid-twentieth century, they generally adopted a conservative position, condemning what they saw as attacks on Catholic values by the political left.

The most contentious issue was the Church's role in education. The left-of-center Betancourt government, which took power in 1946, drew up legislation for limiting Catholic education, but there was bitter opposition and it eventually backed down. Catholic schools in fact increased during the decade that followed. The Church hierarchy was so fearful of the radical reform program presented by the Betancourt administration that it generally welcomed the military coup which overthrew it in 1948 and opened the way for dictatorship. The military rulers led by Pérez Jiménez did indeed give considerable support to the Church, raising its budget, promoting an increase in Catholic schools and churches, and overseeing an increase in the number of diocesan priest to 1117 by 1958, largely due to clergy coming from overseas (*Diccionario de Historia de Venezuela*, 364). It was not long, however, before elements within the Church, including the hierarchy, began to direct their criticism toward the military rulers, condemning the repression carried out by the regime. Some members of the clergy suffered persecution as a result.

Having contributed to the movement that finally removed the dictatorship in 1958, the Church worked to consolidate democracy and political pluralism. According to Daniel Levine, a greater preoccupation with human rights and social justice explained the change in the Church's attitude (Levine, 1981, 68). An important seed had been sown, and in the coming decades some sections of the Church would address more critical attention to social and political issues. The Church hierarchy, however, settled back into its accommodation with the state and the social order. In return, the Church received increased funding and support from the civilian administrations. This new understanding was consolidated in 1964, when a government led by Rómulo Betancourt, eager to avoid a repetition of past conflicts with the Church, reached an agreement with the Vatican and abolished the law of state patronage.

The 1960s are often seen as a watershed in the history of Catholicism in Latin America. The broadly conservative consensus of the Church began to crack as more radical and politically oriented notions of Catholicism were presented by clerics and theologians. Attempting to address the continuing problems of poverty, underdevelopment, and social injustice that plagued the region, and influenced by socialist thinking, these more combative elements of the Church demanded closer interaction with the poor, and direct action by Christians to help free them from oppression and exploitation. This approach was developed into its most articulate and radical expression by Catholic thinkers in liberation theology, a movement which, fusing Marxism and Christianity, worked for radical social change. It had a dramatic impact throughout Latin America. In Venezuela, however, the influence of its ideas was diluted by the relative social and political stability, and political democracy, that the country enjoyed at the time, largely due to the prosperity brought by oil production. Before long, however, theologians like the Jesuit Pedro Trigo began to debate ways in which liberation theology might be put into practice in Venezuela, and some members of the Church began to campaign for a greater commitment to the poor, and to work with working-class and peasant communities. Divisions within the Church became evident as the hierarchy condemned such politicized activity. It cooperated with the government in the expulsion of radical foreign clergy and purged faculties of theology and seminaries in order to assert ideological control (Levine, 1992, 76).

These conflicts within the Church, acute in the early 1970s, abated over the following decades, but they demonstrated that it was not as complacent and undynamic an institution as it was so often presented. They also had long-term repercussions. Some members of the clergy decided to ignore the disapproval of Church leaders and dedicate themselves to projects in shantytowns, working-class districts, or poor rural communities. This pastoral work gave the poor support in confronting their daily problems, offered them education and instruction, and helped them to campaign for better facilities. In the 1980s and 1990s, such community projects became increasingly important as the country's economic and social problems intensified, hitting the poorest sectors of the population hardest of all. They often represented the only help available to these people. Gradually, the Church hierarchy looked more positively on this work, recognizing its value, and tensions within the Church abated. Some argue that the success of the socially active Catholic groups obliged the hierarchy to adopt a more critical stance toward government policies (Berryman, 1996, 123). Be that as it may, Church leaders were no longer able to ignore the social unrest that was becoming increasingly evident, or the increasingly severe methods the state used to quell it. The dramatic riots against government austerity measures that broke out in Caracas in February 1989, and led to the death of several hundred people at the hands of the military, highlighted the gravity of the situation. Church leaders became more outspoken on social and political issues, often challenging the government on its record on human rights and social justice.

Circumstances at the end of the twentieth century therefore permitted the Venezuelan Church to enhance its moral authority, and it made an active contribution to the debate on a wide range of issues, from the rights of indigenous communities to the problems of urban violence and marginalization. The first visits to Venezuela by a pope, made by John Paul II in 1985 and 1996, generated huge national interest and further stimulated the discussions on the Church's role. Its influence had grown and it had become more socially active, but it still had significant problems. It still suffered some effects of the institutional weaknesses inherited from the past, and it faced competition from other religions, particularly the Protestant Evangelical churches that were spreading rapidly in many parts of Latin America. Furthermore, indifference to all religion appeared to be growing among significant sectors of the Venezuelan population, notably urban youth.

As for those who *are* practicing Catholics, it is important to recognize that the majority have traditionally followed their own forms of popular Catholicism, which differ in significant ways from the institutional Catholicism promoted by the Church hierarchy. As in other Latin American countries, people's needs, customs, and perceptions have produced original expressions of faith that vary in detail from region to region. Communities throughout Venezuela have incorporated into their Catholic worship beliefs and practices drawn from other cultural traditions, including the indigenous and the African. Pagan and magical elements are fused with Christian ritual, without any contradiction as far as the worshipers are concerned. Many examples are seen in the numerous religious festivals celebrated in different parts of the country during the year. The festivities often last for several days, and familiar Catholic ceremony comprises only a small part. They are major social occasions that help to cement the community together, offering enjoyment and entertainment. The festivals held in various parts of Zulia state in honor of one of Venezuela's most popular saints, San Benito de Palermo, are typical. A Mass and religious procession are central to the celebrations, but San Benito is widely believed to enjoy music, drink, and dance, so those elements are crucial to the homage paid to him. There are many hours of singing, dancing, and drum playing, clearly of African origin, brought to Venezuela by slaves during the colonial period. The statue of the saint is often sprinkled with rum when paraded through the streets, amid wild celebration. (These festivals will be discussed further in Chapter 3.)

The veneration of the saints is crucial to popular Catholicism, for they have the power to grant favors to the worshiper. A promise is made to the saint, and must be carried out when the favor is bestowed. This might entail dedicating a Mass to the saint, for example, or making a pilgrimage to a particular shrine. In peasant communities in Yaracuy state, magical ritual is often used to elicit help from the saints, who are not seen as pure and perfect, but rather as human beings with failings and vices (Pollak-Eltz, 1984, 48). Many individuals have their own favorite saint with whom they regularly

Altar of popular religious icons in Sorte, Yaracuy state, dominated by the figure of María Lionza. Photo by Nelson Garrido. Courtesy of the Fundación Bigott.

communicate and from whom they seek assistance. Particular saints are associated with particular powers. San Pedro is linked to good harvests, Santa Polonia is said to cure toothaches, and San Antonio is often called upon to help find lost possessions, and also to help young women find a boyfriend. San Cipriano emphasizes the fusion of magic and religion that lies at the heart of this popular Catholicism, for he is considered to be the protector of practitioners of black magic.

For Catholics throughout Latin America, the Virgin Mary is a figure of special adoration, and Venezuela is no exception. She assumes different guises in different regions of the country. In Zulia she is known as Virgen de la Chiquinquirá, and is patron saint of the state; as Virgen del Valle she

Procession of the Virgen del Valle on the island of Margarita. Photo courtesy of
Archivo El Nacional.

holds the same position in the state of Nueva Esparta. Whatever her local
name, the Virgin is honored once a year in each place by a great festival,
the centerpiece of which is normally the carrying of her statue through the
streets. Huge crowds usually participate. In January 1999, the annual procession of the Virgin who is patron saint of Lara state, known as La Divina
Pastora (the Divine Shepherdess), is reported to have attracted approximately 1.7 million people to the streets of Barquisimeto, the state capital
(*La Nacional*, January 15, 1999). There is often a rich local history associated with these Virgins, usually involving miraculous events. La Divina
Pastora is an example. Her statue was made in Spain and, by request, sent
to the Church of La Concepción in Barquisimeto in 1736. But it was de-
livered to the wrong church, the Church of Santa Rosa, just outside the

city. The parish priest arranged for a group of men to carry it to the right church, but it suddenly became so heavy that it could not be lifted. The priest took it as a sign that the Virgin wished to stay in Santa Rosa, and the statue has been housed there ever since.

Not surprisingly, there are also stories of miraculous appearances of the Virgin in various parts of Venezuela, some of which have become major sites of pilgrimage as a result. The best-known is the basilica in the center of Guanare, capital of Portuguesa state, which contains the image of the Virgin of Coromoto. It is said that this Virgin appeared before a group of Indians in 1651, not far from the town. In 1942 she was officially declared patron saint of Venezuela by Pope Pius XII. A more recent site is Betania, an old plantation south of Caracas, where a vision of the Virgin Mary first appeared in March 1976. She was seen again several times over the following years, and in 1984 she appeared before a group of approximately 150 people. Following an investigation, Church leaders declared the event to be miraculous, and the site to be sacred. A shrine was established; it now regularly receives worshipers, many seeking favors or fulfilling vows for favors bestowed.

Popular Catholicism tends to see the Virgin Mary and the saints as real people with special powers who serve as intermediaries between the individual and God. There are in fact many other figures in Venezuela identified as being able to fulfill the same role because of their supernatural qualities. They, too, are called upon for assistance and become the objects of cult worship, treated like saints. Some, of course, are not accepted by Church leaders, who regard them as non–Catholic cults dominated by idolatry. There are, however, two particular figures who, in very different ways, have acquired a large number of devotees and received recognition from the Church: Madre María de San José, and José Gregorio Hernández.

Madre María was born Laura Evangelista Alvarado Cardozo, in the colonial town of Choroní, close to the Caribbean coast, in 1875. She decided to enter holy orders while a teenager working as a volunteer in a Church-run hospital for the poor in the nearby city of Maracay. She became a nun in 1901, as a founder-member of a new Augustine order, and took the name María de San José. She was soon named Mother Superior. She was instrumental in the foundation of over thirty charitable institutions, mainly schools and hospitals, and became renowned for her work with the poor and the sick. Many stories of the miraculous powers attributed to her circulated during her lifetime. She died in 1967, in the convent at Maracay where she had lived most of her life.

The process of her beatification, the first step toward canonization, was initiated in 1978 and lasted nearly seventeen years. Details of her holy life and charitable work had to be gathered for the Vatican. As proof of her divine powers, evidence was presented of a specific miracle performed by her in 1982, when a sister in the same Maracay convent, who had been ill and unable to walk for several years, was fully restored to health, and walked again, after praying for a cure at Madre María's tomb. The next step in the process took place on January 19, 1994, when her body was exhumed to verify that it was still intact and perfectly preserved. That was confirmed. The coffin had badly deteriorated, but the body was found to be in a perfect state of preservation, as was the sprig of lilies clasped in her hands. Pope John Paul II formally confirmed her beatification in May 1995, and she became the first Venezuelan to attain such status. Madre María's body was placed in a glass sarcophagus so that the faithful could pay homage to her, and a basilica was built opposite her Maracay convent to accommodate it. This has become a major center of pilgrimage, receiving hundreds of visitors each day, many of whom go to ask favors of her or to give thanks for favors received. Though a figure of popular devotion, she also represents orthodox Catholicism, and her veneration is enthusiastically celebrated and promoted by the Catholic Church.

The cult of José Gregorio Hernández is more controversial so far as the Church hierarchy is concerned. He, too, was a devout Catholic who dedicated himself to caring for the poor and the sick, and the campaign to canonize him, which began in 1949, has steadily gathered momentum, especially since the beatification of María de San José. However, his image has also been incorporated into the non–Catholic magical or spiritualist rituals practiced by significant sectors of the population. He was born in 1864, in the small town of Isnotú, in the Venezuelan Andes. Having completed his medical studies in Caracas, he graduated as a doctor in 1888, and a few years later set up his practice in the capital. He gave classes at the Central University there, becoming respected as an academic, but it was as "the Doctor of the Poor" that he achieved celebrity, tending to those with few resources with little concern for payment. He saw it as a Christian duty. He twice attempted to take up religious orders, but was prevented from doing so by ill health. He was killed in 1919, knocked down by a car in a Caracas street.

His fame grew rapidly after his death, and numerous miracles have been attributed to him. Both his birthplace and his tomb, in the Church of La Candelaria in Caracas, are important sites for worshipers, but images and figurines of him typically dressed in black suit, hat, and tie, and holding a medical bag, are found all over Venezuela. He has a far wider following than María de San José, and is even revered in some parts of Colombia and Ecuador. To his devotees, he is already a saint with the power to provide help and protection, above all in matters of health, which is of considerable importance to many unable to afford conventional medical care. Among the José Gregorio artifacts for sale to believers are bottles of medicine with his image on them. To a large extent, his huge popular appeal is explained by the fact that he was an ordinary member of his community, a layman who put his beliefs into practice by using his professional skills to help the poor. Such is his popular following throughout Venezuela that there is now significant support within the Church for his beatification.

POPULAR CULTS AND POPULAR BELIEFS

In a cemetery in Caracas is the grave of a young woman known as María Francia, who allegedly died shortly before her wedding, having been bitten by a snake. Offerings in the form of flowers and candles are placed on her grave by devotees who seek favors. She is believed to have the power to intercede in matters of love, so she is typically asked for help in finding a suitable spouse or in resolving a case of unrequited love.

Such individuals become the focus of cults because their lives have captured the popular imagination, and because in death they are believed to have magical powers to help the living. It is not surprising, therefore, that a number of historical figures associated with political power have become cult figures. An example is the dictator Juan Vicente Gómez, whose tomb in Maracay is surrounded by plaques giving thanks for favors granted by his spirit. This cult worship is not restricted to national figures, for John F. Kennedy is also reported to be the subject of veneration by some in Venezuela. No political leader, however, has been worshiped more devoutly than Venezuela's national hero, Simón Bolívar. Devotees often place an image of him, frequently accompanied by a prayer or a quotation attributed to him, in a prominent place in their home, or carry it in their wallet, purse, or pocket, so that his assistance and guidance are always available. Because he is considered to be wise and astute, his help is often sought for financial ventures, and his spirit is frequently invoked by mediums for consultation on political issues. The popular mythology relating to Bolívar has grown steadily, fed by the divine powers linked to him. It is expressed in many popular songs, prayers, and poems, and in folk medicines that carry his name. Partly through their association with Bolívar, other heroes of the wars of independence are worshiped as well, such as Negro Felipe, who was killed fighting the Spanish in the decisive battle of Carabobo in 1821. His statuette is often found alongside other icons of popular religious devotion.

The most unusual and mysterious of Venezuela's popular cults is that of

María Lionza. Over the years it has attracted considerable attention from anthropologists because of its huge following, its varied rituals, and its being such a striking example of syncretism, fusing Indian legend, African voodoo, and elements of Catholicism. Its precise origins are obscure, but it is a twentieth-century phenomenon, most likely created by rural migrants to the city who merged different types of ritual they knew in order to form a new cult to help them meet the challenges and problems posed by their new environment. There are numerous myths about María Lionza, but it is not known whether a person of that name ever existed. According to popular belief, she was an Indian princess, or perhaps the daughter of an Indian princess and a Spanish conquistador, who was from a mountainous region in the state of Yaracuy, west of Caracas. Popular effigies of her show a pale, naked young woman, a crown on her head, who is riding a tapir. This image was adapted by the sculptor Alejandro Colina for what is one of the best-known statues in Caracas, located on the Francisco Fajardo Freeway not far from the city center. Produced for a major sports meet in 1951, María Lionza is shown, on the tapir, with the Olympic torch raised aloft in her hands.

There is an abundance of myths about her. According to one, she survived an attempt to sacrifice herself to the god of water and became a goddess herself, and the protectress of the natural world around her. Some devotees believe she lives in a palace in the rain forest; others believe she inhabits a cave, protected by a giant snake, where the courageous can seek her, endure the series of trials set by her, and, if successful, obtain supernatural powers in return for their soul (Aretz, 1988, 224). She is venerated in many towns and cities in Venezuela, but the most important site for worship is in her own sacred land, the Sorte Mountain, in Yaracuy state. The faithful congregate regularly there by the thousands. They purify themselves by bathing in the nearby River Yaracuy, and make offerings of perfume, food, and flowers to her. In fact, a whole range of spirits are worshiped, and some devotees climb to the top of the mountain, where the spirits' force is said to be more strongly felt.

Spirit worship is central to the cult, so among the many rituals the most important involve invoking the spirits through a medium, in order to consult them and ask favors of them. The spirits are numerous, with new ones being added regularly, and are organized into "courts." There is a court for African deities, comprised mainly of gods from the Yoruba religion; a court for Indian spirits; one for Catholic saints; and another for the spirits of the sun, the moon, and the planets. There is even one for the souls of deceased villains, whose assistance can be sought by worshipers to save friends or relatives from a life of crime. Bolívar and José Gregorio Hernández also are regularly called upon. As usual, favors granted have to be repaid with an act or offering of thanks. The mediums fall into a trance when possessed by spirits, and their normal sensations are apparently suspended, a state sometimes demonstrated by the eating of live embers or fragments of glass.

Not surprisingly, the Catholic Church has been strong in its opposition to the cult of María Lionza, though many of the devotees still regard themselves as Catholics. Spirit worship and magic are frequently practiced alongside orthodox religious ritual rather than as an alternative to it. Evidence of the mixing of different religious traditions is clearly seen in the small shrines many Venezuelans keep in their homes, where effigies of María Lionza and José Gregorio often stand alongside others of the saints, and portraits of Bolívar are placed next to images of the Virgin Mary. The hybrid culture and particular social conditions of modern Venezuela have given rise to a rich variety of original and highly personalized forms of worship.

Despite the advance of modern influences, belief in the magical remains strong among large sections of the Venezuelan population. Many rural communities, for example, believe in lost souls and other ghostly supernatural beings who either appear in human or animal form, or make their presence felt while remaining invisible. Some are malevolent spirits seeking to harm the living, whereas others are souls in torment who have come to ask for prayers to be said for them so they can obtain absolution. Though many are local, specific to a particular community, some are common to many regions of the country, such as La Llorona, the ghost of a woman said to have killed her child and is heard endlessly weeping, and La Sayona, the wife of the devil, who appears as a beautiful woman dressed in white to tempt men. Many peasant families traditionally placed wooden crosses on or above the front doors of their homes to ward off malignant spirits, and there are numerous prayers still recited for the same purpose (Aretz, 1988, 225–228).

There are many in Venezuela who attribute certain illnesses to *mal de ojo* (evil eye). This is said to be a deep envy transmitted by someone; such a person is often recognizable by his or her large, protruding eyes. He or she causes harm to the object of envy, particularly children, animals and plants, by staring at them. Again, prayers are required to effect a cure, and in some rural areas a local folk healer may be called in to carry out a ceremony of exorcism (Aretz, 1988, 229). Certain items are believed to have properties that protect the individual from the evil eye. In villages in Yaracuy state, peony seeds are used for that purpose, hung around a child's neck like a necklace, as are certain semiprecious stones, especially jet, which are tied around a baby's wrist (Pollak-Eltz, 1984, 91). The wearing of charms for good luck is commonplace, equivalent for some to carrying the image of a saint in their wallet or in their vehicle. A variety of substances, among them quicksilver, tobacco, and magnetic metals, are said to attract good fortune.

The folk healer, or *curandero*, still has a role in many communities in Venezuela, providing alternative medical care through a combination of religious and magical rituals and a knowledge of the curative properties of plants. Folk remedies are regularly sought by many people, who either find orthodox medical treatment beyond their means or have only limited confidence in it. There are herbal remedies for most physical illnesses, and many *curanderos* recite prayers during the various stages of their work, from collecting the plants, to mixing the potion, to administering it to the patient. Disorders with no evident physical cause are often explained as the result of negative influences that bring the patient misfortune, and are said to require special prayers and rituals in order to be cured. Plants play a role here, too. Aloe vera, for example, a plant well known for its healing qualities, is also believed to combat bad luck, serving as a cure when the patient washes in water to which its sap has been added, and for prevention when the plant is picked on Good Friday before sunrise and hung up in the home.

Many of these practices are just as common in the big cities as they are in the rural interior. Indeed, some observers have suggested that magical religious rituals increased in the final decades of the twentieth century as people in the city, particularly the poorest and most vulnerable, sought their own strategies for dealing with daily difficulties. In the 1990s, on the Avenida Baralt, in the center of Caracas, there were many *yerbaterías* (herbalist's shops) selling plants, potions, and essences, as well as plaster effigies of popular saints, and offering advice on the best remedies for all physical and emotional disorders. The most common requests made by customers are for help in resolving problems with a marriage or a love affair; for good fortune in business and matters of money, such as luck in the lottery; and for overcoming vices, especially dependency on alcohol. In addition to the potions that are consumed by the patient, there are specially prepared essences to be used when bathing, again accompanied by prayers, which have to be recited at specifically determined times. To the outsider such beliefs and rituals may seem to belong to an anachronistic folklore rooted in superstition, but to many Venezuelans they form part of everyday life, representing valid ways of coping with emotional and psychological problems, and effective therapies for dealing with ill health.

PROTESTANTISM

The dramatic expansion of the Protestant Evangelical churches, such as has been found in other Latin American countries, most notably in neighboring Brazil, has not occurred in Venezuela. Growth has been slow, and no more than 4% of the Venezuelan population was estimated to be Protestant in 1996 (Berryman, 1996, 125). Other sources put the figure even lower. Some argue that the modern patterns of urban life and consumer culture that have absorbed an ever greater percentage of the Venezuelan population in the latter twentieth century have produced increasing indifference toward all religions.

During the colonial period in Venezuela, the Catholic Church and the military authorities worked together to try to ensure that religions other than Catholicism were not disseminated. Despite these restrictions, however, Protestants based in other parts of the Caribbean, such as Curaçao, and Protestant businessmen from northern Europe with connections in Venezuela, propagated information about their faith. After independence was won from Spain in 1821, conditions became more favorable for non–Catholic religions. Since most of the new political leaders were liberals who wanted to curb the role of the Catholic Church, they were receptive to the establishment of Protestant communities. Bolívar, for example, had attended lectures in London given by the Quaker Joseph Lancaster in 1810, and in the 1820s he invited Lancaster to set up schools in Venezuela (*Diccionario de Historia de Venezuela*, 1988, 364). An Anglican cemetery was established in Caracas in 1832, supported by the British consul, and a chapel was built alongside it the following year. Significantly, the first president of the Republic of Venezuela, José Antonio Páez, attended the inauguration ceremony, and in 1834 his government passed a law formally granting freedom of worship, conferring upon all religions the legal right to be practiced openly.

However, Protestantism made very limited progress in the nineteenth century. The first missionaries arrived from overseas, but most stayed for only a short time, and their work was impeded by the hostility of the Catholic Church. Only at the end of the century were firm bases laid, with the foundation of long-lasting congregations, like those of the Lutherans and the Plymouth Brethren in Caracas around 1894; the construction of the first churches; and the arrival of the first permanent missionaries, mainly from the United States. The work of North Americans and Europeans was crucial for the establishment of Protestantism. The first Venezuelan pastor was not ordained until 1915 (*Diccionario de Historia de Venezuela*, 1988, 365). Over the following decades, however, the involvement of Venezuelans increased.

Their main missionary work was carried out in the countryside, in small towns, and in poor areas on city outskirts; the foreign missionaries operated mainly in the city centers (Sinclair, 1981, 641).

The increased numbers of Venezuelan Protestants in the twentieth century came mainly through conversion of Catholics from the poorer sections of society. The pattern was uneven, however, with churches in some areas registering appreciable growth and others, elsewhere, very little. In Caracas, for example, there were reported to be only four Protestant churches in the 1940s, and it was not until the 1960s and the 1970s—when the number reached fifty-two—that there was a significant expansion (Berryman, 1996, 126). Protestantism had the most success in areas of new urban development in the interior. U.S. Protestants became increasingly influential during the twentieth century, for they not only comprised the considerable majority of foreign missionaries but also provided occasional groups of settlers who boosted congregations, such as a community of Baptists in 1946 and one of Lutherans two years later. The fact that most of Venezuela's Protestant churches are of U.S. origin is reflected in the form of the services and in the architecture of many of the churches.

As elsewhere, Protestantism in Venezuela is very heterogeneous, divided into many different denominations that have differing opinions on religious matters and often have little contact with one another. There has been a greater degree of cooperation since the 1950s, however. In 1959, the Consejo Evangélico de Venezuela (Venezuelan Evangelical Council) was founded in Caracas to promote collaboration. It eventually obtained the affiliation of the majority of the Protestant churches, and had a total of seventy-eight member organizations by the 1990s. Most denominations also participated in the First Venezuelan Evangelical Congress, which was held at Caracas in 1979. To some commentators, however, this cooperation tended to be superficial, and the individualism that has characterized the denominations has hampered the Protestant movement as a whole. By the 1990s, the Baptists and the Presbyterians were the only "historic churches," those established the longest in Venezuela, that had a significant presence. The largest Protestant denominations were more recently founded Evangelical churches, the Assemblies of God and the Light of the World, with estimated memberships of sixty thousand and thirty-five thousand respectively (Berryman, 1996, 125–126).

OTHER RELIGIONS

Several other minority religions have made a significant contribution to Venezuelan history and culture, in spite of having endured centuries of repression. The various indigenous groups, for example, preserve many of their traditional religious practices. In parts of the country, the vestiges of African religious beliefs also are evident. Dating back to the transportation of slaves during the colonial period, African rituals have tended to merge with indigenous and Catholic traditions over the centuries, to create new syncretic forms of worship, exemplified by the cult of María Lionza already discussed.

The history of Judaism and Islam in Venezuela is somewhat sketchy until the twentieth century, partly due to the long period of persecution both religions experienced. The first official report of Jews in the country, dated 1720, states that Bishop Pedro José de Olavarriaga had ordered the destruction of the synagogue in the town of Tucacas, in Falcón state. It is believed that Jews who fled persecution in Spain settled on the Dutch island of Curaçao and then emigrated to Tucacas, seeking to engage in commerce. The greater religious liberty allowed by independence leaders, including the suppression of the Inquisition in 1821, enabled Jewish immigration to increase in the early nineteenth century, though prejudice persisted. A community of Sephardic Jews was established at Coro in 1824, under the leadership of David Hoheb, but it had to endure periodic anti–Jewish attacks and riots in the decades that followed. Numbering approximately 160 people by 1848, it is believed to be the first Jewish community in independent Latin America. The Jewish cemetery that was inaugurated at Coro in 1832, the oldest still in use in South America, was declared a national monument in 1970. By the last decades of the nineteenth century, Jews were playing an important role in the commercial life of such cities as Barcelona, Coro, Caracas, and Valencia.

The Sociedad Benéfica Israelita (Jewish Beneficent Society), founded by Sephardic Jews in 1907, was one of Venezuela's first Jewish associations. The Jewish community steadily became more organized and unified during the course of the twentieth century, its numbers expanded by immigrants fleeing Europe during World War I and, particularly, World War II. Jewish papers such as *El Mundo Israelita* (Jewish World) and *Prensa Judía* (Jewish Press) were founded, synagogues and Jewish schools were opened, and a number of Jewish associations were established, among them the Centro Israelita de Caracas (Jewish Center of Caracas) and the Sociedad Israelita de Maracaibo (Jewish Society of Maracaibo). Today, many Venezuelan Jews maintain only tenuous links with Judaism. Jewish cultural identity, however, remains strong, reinforced through many clubs, schools, associations, publications, and a wide range of cultural activities, including the study of the Hebrew language and Jewish traditions.

It is probable that Muslims also settled in Venezuela during the colonial

The Sheik Ibrahim al-Ibrahim mosque in Caracas. Photo courtesy of Mark Dinneen.

period, though there is no evidence to confirm it. It is known that many left Spain to seek a better life in Spanish America, often having formally converted to Christianity in order to avoid persecution. Not until the early twentieth century, however, is there clear information about the Islamic community in Venezuela, with the arrival of immigrants escaping the upheavals of the Ottoman Empire and World War I. From that point on, the Muslim population grew steadily, with some sources claiming that by the 1990s, as many as forty thousand were living in Caracas alone. There was no mosque in the city, however, and it was decided to construct one close to the city center, so as to provide a focal point for religious and cultural activities. Promoted by an Islamic foundation based in Saudi Arabia, the Sheik Ibrahim al-Ibrahim mosque was completed in 1992. It is one of the most impressive buildings in Caracas, and the largest mosque in Latin America; the intention is to make it the most important Islamic center in the Caribbean region.

Religious groups have multiplied in Venezuela through the impetus provided by diverse influences from overseas. European immigrants have founded Russian, Armenian, and Greek Orthodox churches. *Umbanda* from Brazil and *santería* from Cuba, two cults of remote African origin, have gained followers. Jehovah's Witnesses have become active in various parts of the country, and some Buddhist centers have been established. However, the number of worshipers involved in these religions has been small, and their impact at the national level has been very limited.

REFERENCES

Aretz, Isabel. *Manuel de folklore*. Caracas: Monte Ávila, 1988.

Barrios, Dilia. *La primera beata de Venezuela: María de San José*. Caracas: San Pablo, 1995.

Berryman, Phillip. *Religion in the Megacity: Catholic and Protestant Portraits from Latin America*. New York: Orbis Books, 1996.

Cardot, Carlos F. "La iglesia venezolana entre 1930–1962." In *Historia general de la iglesia en América Latina*. Vol. 7, 552–597. Salamanca: Ediciones Sígueme, 1981.

Diccionario de Historia de Venezuela. 356–368. Caracas: Fundación Polar, 1988.

Levine, Daniel. *Religion and Politics in Latin America: The Catholic Church in Venezuela and Colombia*. Princeton, NJ: Princeton University Press, 1981.

———. *Popular Voices in Latin American Catholicism*. Princeton, NJ: Princeton University Press, 1992.

Micheo, Alberto, and Luis Ugalde. "Proceso histórico de la iglesia venezolana." In *Historia general de la iglesia en América Latina*. Vol. 7, 600–638. Salamanca: Ediciones Sígueme, 1981.

Pollak-Eltz, Angelina. *Maria Lionza, mito y culto venezolano*. Caracas: UCAB, 1972.

———. "Folklore y cultura en los pueblos negros de Yaracuy." In *Montalban*, no. 15, 23–125. Caracas: UCAB, 1984.

Sinclair, John. "El movimiento protestante en Colombia y Venezuela en perspectiva." In *Historia general de la iglesia en América Latina*. Vol. 7, 639–646. Salamanca: Ediciones Sígueme, 1981.

Watters, Mary. *A History of the Church in Venezuela, 1810–1930*. Chapel Hill: University of North Carolina Press, 1933.

Website of Asociación Israelita de Venezuela. http://www.aiv.org/.

Website of Consejo Evangélico de Venezuela. http://www geocities.com/Heartland/ Prairie/3896.

Website of Dr. José Gregorio Hernández. http://www.facilred.com/josé_gregorio/ index.html.

Website of Mezquita Sheik Ibrahim Bin Abdul Aziz Al-Ibrahim. http://www. mezquitaibrahim.org.

Website of Venezuelan Embassy in London. http://www.demon.co.uk/emb-venuk/ V-brief.htm.

3

Social Customs

ALTHOUGH THE PATTERNS and customs of daily life in Venezuela vary greatly according to region and socioeconomic group, for the considerable majority of Venezuelans the extended family continues to play the central role. These permanent and closely knit relationships, incorporating cousins and often more distant relatives, are invariably the main source of whatever support and assistance the individual may require, such as financial aid or help in finding employment, as well as the focal point for much of his or her social life. Kinship ties and *compadrazgo*—the naming of godparents for children in the family, still widely practiced—provide a further layer of relationships, so that most Venezuelans are immersed in a wide network of personal ties throughout their lives. Modern urban patterns of life have obviously affected the way these relationships are conducted, but they remain a vitally important component of everyday life.

Contact between family members is generally very regular, centering on frequent visits, meals, and parties, but it is the big occasions marking the major stages in life, such as weddings, baptisms, and funerals, that bring the extended family together and cement relationships. There are some distinctive rituals attached to these ceremonies, such as the custom of baptizing babies twice. Traditionally, a baby was first baptized informally by family members shortly after birth, with *padrinos de agua* (water godparents) sprinkling holy water over the infant. This was to ensure that should the baby die before formal baptism by the Church, he or she would still have received the sacrament. The formal baptism, sometimes involving different godparents, would take place several months later. Though disappearing in the large cities, this practice is still common in the countryside and smaller towns. Godparents may be either friends or relatives, and in accepting the role they not only undertake to give some degree of support to the child, and take responsibility for him or her if anything should happen to the parents, but also consolidate their relationship with the parents.

For practicing Catholics, the next major celebration in the child's life is his or her first Communion, normally when aged between eight and eleven. It involves most of the family, close family friends, and a new godfather or godmother, chosen for the occasion by the child. It is also common for girls reaching fifteen to be given a coming-of-age party, which may be formal or informal, and varies considerably in its lavishness, according to the family's resources. It is a vestige from a past era, when fifteen was considered to be the age when womanhood began and the girl, now able to dress as a woman and wear makeup, was no longer to be treated as a child, but as a señorita. It is still traditional for the party to open with a waltz, to which the girl dances first with her father, and then with all the other men in turn, representing her entrance into adult society.

There were many formal rituals related to courtship and marriage—such as serenading a young woman, and formally asking her parents for her hand in marriage—that, although now sounding very antiquated, died out in Venezuela only in the latter decades of the twentieth century. Today, informality prevails. The majority of couples still get married in church, though they are also required to register their marriage with the civil authorities in a separate ceremony beforehand. Rice, symbolizing prosperity, is thrown at the newly married couple as they leave the church. The guests then usually form a cavalcade of cars, frequently decorated with ribbons and bows, that drives to the reception, continually sounding their horns.

Customs relating to death also have changed significantly over the decades. Until funeral parlors became major businesses in the mid-twentieth century, offering a full range of services to the family of the deceased, the family itself did most of the work for a funeral, including preparing the corpse and arranging the wake and the burial. The family's role today is much more limited, though in poorer homes in the cities and the interior of the country, funerals continue to be more participatory and communal affairs. Wakes, generally lasting between twenty-four and thirty-six hours, are normal practice in all regions and among all social classes. In some areas, they still take place in the family home, as in years gone by, but now in the cities and towns the "chapels of rest" offered by the funeral parlors have taken over the role. Funerals are important occasions for the family, bringing all its members together in mutual support and solidarity. The *novenario*, praying for the eternal rest of the deceased by reciting the rosary for nine consecutive evenings, is commonly carried out in Catholic households shortly after the burial of a family member. Although available in some areas, cremation is still not widely practiced. Paying respect to the deceased and keeping alive his or her memory is of great importance to most Venezuelans. Regular visits to the graves of relatives generally continue for years and even decades after the burial, and roadside crosses or shrines, marking the spot where someone died in an accident, are a common sight throughout the country.

Despite the huge advances made by women in the last decades of the twentieth century, machismo—patterns of behavior based on the notion of male superiority—still finds expression in various forms in Venezuelan society. Many professional women find that their career development is hindered by prejudice, and in some parts of the interior men continue to consider the fathering of a large number of children, often with several women, to be proof of their virility. Within the Venezuelan family, however, it is more often than not the mother, rather than the father, who is the central figure. It is generally around her that the daily life of the family revolves, and upon her that the day-to-day welfare of its members, and its long term unity, depends. Social changes in the latter part of the twentieth century have tended to consolidate this situation. Urbanization has resulted in new work opportunities outside the home for women, and a greater degree of independence for them, at the same time eroding the male authority that was traditional in many families. An increasing number of households are now headed by women. Divorce was made legal early in the twentieth century and is now very common in Venezuela.

There is little reserve in social relations in Venezuela. Emphasis is on informality and openness. People are generally effusive in their demonstrations of warmth and affection, and physical contact plays a significant part. Even in the case of relatively recent acquaintances, it is usual for women to be kissed on greeting and parting, and men often warmly embrace one another. Emotions are displayed publicly on a regular basis, ranging from the joy expressed in street dancing during festivals and celebrations, to the impatience and aggression frequently evident in the gestures and horn blowing of frustrated motorists in the traffic jams of the large cities.

HOLIDAYS

As in other Christian societies, Christmas in Venezuela is the principal festival for family celebration. Its increasing commercialization in the latter part of the twentieth century has led to more and more manifestations of

American influence, and the results are often incongruous, such as the wintery snow scenes, totally alien to the tropical Caribbean, that decorate many shop windows and apartments. At the same time, however, Venezuela has a number of unique Christmas traditions that remain strong throughout the country.

Certain types of music are played during Christmas time. *Aguinaldos* are traditional songs that have their roots in Spain; their verses, sung alternately by soloist and chorus, are inspired by either the religious significance of Christmas or the celebrations of the period. The melodies vary considerably, but they are always sung to traditional instruments, such as the mandolin, the clarinet, or the accordion, and various types of percussion. Much more popular, mainly because of their fast and vibrant dance rhythm, are *gaitas*, strongly associated with Zulia state, where they originated, but now heard in all parts of the country. The range of themes is enormous. There are "devotional *gaitas*" on religious themes, others of social protest and political satire, and many on lighthearted romantic themes. From late October, it is the *gaita* more than anything else that announces the coming festivities throughout Venezuela, and then provides the music for numerous Christmas parties.

Among the Christmas trees and other decorations introduced from abroad, the nativity scene or crib stands out. The roots of this tradition can be traced to sixteenth-century Europe, and it is still strong throughout Venezuela. Examples ranging from simple mangers with the three traditional figures, to highly elaborate displays involving numerous human figures, animals, angels, and twinkling lights, are commonly seen in homes, places of work, and public spaces such as squares, shopping centers, and subway stations. Money is often left on them by passers-by or visitors, to be used to purchase more figures or lights for the following year, thus ensuring that the tradition continues. It has become common in many towns for competitions for the best nativity scene to be organized. The scenes are constructed and put on display long before Christmas, but the figure of the baby Christ is generally revealed only on the night of his birth, December 24. The making of nativity scenes has long been a popular art form. Mangers in a variety of forms, made from wood, pottery, and other materials, are regularly sold at craft fairs and markets all over the country.

It is on the night of December 24 that the main family celebration of Christmas takes place, and, as elsewhere, the centerpiece of the festivities is a large meal. Most traditional among the food served at this time of year, and more symbolic of Christmas than anything else as far as most Venezue-

Nativity scene in Altamira Square, Caracas. Photo courtesy of Mark Dinneen.

lans are concerned, are the *hallacas*, consisting of chopped chicken, beef, and pork, raisins, tomatoes, and olives, mixed in a corn dough and wrapped in banana leaves. These packets are tied with cord and steamed. Other typical Christmas dishes are roast leg of pork, bread containing ham and olives (*pan de jamón*), and, as a dessert, *dulce de lechosa*, a sweet conserve of pawpaw. Midnight Mass is still attended by a significant number of people. On Christmas morning, children wake up to find presents in their bedroom or under the Christmas tree, left, they are told, by baby Jesus. The figure of Santa Claus was imported only in the final decades of the twentieth century. Christmas Day is normally spent quietly, visiting friends and relatives, and recovering from the celebrations the night before.

Some unusual popular festivities are carried out in certain regions of the country over the Christmas period. One of the most striking is *los pastores* (the shepherds), a mixture of theater and dance that takes place in the states of Aragua and Carabobo, and recounts the role played by the shepherds in the story of Christ's birth. The precise form the ceremony takes varies from one town to another. In San Joaquín, in Carabobo state, the costumed participants playing the shepherds attend Mass, at the end of which they stay behind and pretend to be asleep. An angel enters to waken them and inform them of Jesus' birth. They leave and begin the search for the baby, during which time a statue of the infant Jesus is placed in a crib in the square in front of the church. Finding him there, the shepherds begin a celebration, dancing well into the night.

In many homes in the Andean region, renowned for its deeply rooted religious traditions, another ceremony paying homage to the newly born Christ, called the *paradura del niño* (standing the child on his feet), is carried out in January, or even the first days of February. In front of the nativity scene in a house, members of the family, friends, and neighbors sing to the figure of baby Jesus in his manger, often accompanied by musicians playing guitars and violins. The infant Christ is then taken out of the manger and placed in a scarf or neckerchief, which is held at the corners and carried around the house and the patio. The image of Jesus is then kissed by each participant in turn before being placed back in the manger, this time standing upright. More songs are sung, and a toast, usually with wine, is made to the child. Sometimes, during the Christmas period, the figure of the infant Christ is "stolen" from his manager, and the owners have to search for him in neighbors' houses until he is located and retrieved.

Two other dates during the Christmas period are celebrated in some regions of the country: December 28, the Day of the Innocents, and January 6, Epiphany. The Day of the Innocents commemorates the slaughter of male infants, shortly after Christ's birth, on the orders of King Herod. Traditionally, it was a time when Venezuelan children were given license to dress up in costumes and play practical jokes, but many adults particpated as well. Although not as strong as it used to be, some people still retain the custom. In some towns, a festival is held to mark the day, with dancing the main activity. First, groups of men, called *locainas*, dance together in a circle, each with its own band of musicians playing the drum, guitar, and *cuatro*, and then couples dance, often holding a baby in their arms or dancing round a child, to recall the significance of the ritual. The music and dancing continue in a parade through the streets. In keeping with the jesting and joking associated with the date, the music is lively and joyful, and the dancing is playful. Wearing extravagant costumes and comical masks, the participants attempt to conceal their identity from everyone, even disguising their voices when speaking.

Epiphany, the celebration on January 6 of the arrival of the three kings in Bethlehem to pay homage to the baby Jesus, was traditionally an important date on the Catholic calender, but it is not widely commemorated in Venezuela today. It was a time for giving more gifts, recalling those given to Jesus by the kings, and children used to leave shoes under their bed at night and find presents in them in the morning. This practice, however, virtually died out in the final decades of the twentieth century. There are a few towns, however, that present a religious play recounting the story of the kings, and in San Miguel de Boconó, a village in the Andes, a remarkable and unique pageant takes place. People dance through the streets in extraordinary costumes until, in midafternoon, the three kings ride into town, dressed in crowns and capes. This marks the high point of the celebrations, which continue well into the night at parties celebrated in houses throughout the village.

Almost everywhere in the country, fireworks are set off continually on the night of December 31, reaching a crescendo at midnight. Many observe the old tradition, imported from Spain, of eating twelve grapes, one at each chime as the clock strikes midnight, while simultaneously making twelve wishes, one for each month of the coming year. Embraces and good wishes are then exchanged among all those present, followed by a boisterous party. Other midnight rituals to encourage good fortune have recently become popular, carried out partly in fun but also rooted in age-old superstitions. Eating lentils as the clock strikes twelve is said to bring economic prosperity during the coming year. Anyone wishing to marry stands on a chair and rings a bell at midnight, and those hoping to travel pack a suitcase with clothes and walk around the block.

Traditionally, *parrandas* were a major part of the Christmas and New Year celebrations throughout Venezuela, and they are still carried out in small towns and villages. At night, a group of musicians with drums, and sometimes other instruments, such as violins, goes through the streets, playing and singing seasonal songs, stopping at houses along the way, where they are served drink and food. Virtually the whole village is drawn into the celebration, which often continues until six or seven the following morning, by which time the participants are decidedly the worse for wear. *Parrandas* were common in many neighborhoods in large cities, but they declined there in the latter decades of the twentieth century, largely due the increasingly impersonal nature of relationships and growing concerns about security.

As in other Catholic countries, Masses and processions take place everywhere at Easter, though the way in which they are conducted varies considerably from one area to another. Many in Caracas simply take the week off to go on holiday. The processions in the city tend to be more formal, reserved affairs directed by the Church, whereas in smaller towns they are major community-organized events of mass participation (as are other religious festivals). The culmination of events is the major procession through the town on Good Friday, when a large crowd, praying and singing, follows the image of Christ, and sometimes of saints. In some towns in the interior, such as Tostos, in the Andean region, Christ's passion is acted out each Holy Week, usually on Good Friday. Onlookers crowd into the streets to watch fellow townspeople playing Christ, the Virgin Mary, Pontius Pilate, Mary Magdalene, and other major participants, as they recount Jesus' trial, crucifixion, and death. Although it follows the story as told in the Bible, this popular form of theater always adds new elements and new interpretations by the actors, so that the performance is significantly different each year.

On Easter Sunday a popular celebration known as "the burning of Judas," very different from the solemn religious events of the preceding week, takes place in numerous communities across the country. The betrayal of Christ is symbolically avenged. A dummy much like a scarecrow is made, representing Judas, and paraded through the town during the day. Households and passers-by are asked to contribute money for alcohol for the evening's celebration, when, amid much revelry, Judas, his straw stuffing full of firecrackers, is placed on a bonfire and burned. As in many such festivals, merriment and humor dominate, and the participants invariably use the occasion to poke fun at others. Frequently they prepare a last will and testament for Judas, which is read in public before the burning. In it, Judas gives his opinion of the conduct of various inhabitants of the town, often complete with spicy details, and states what they are to receive as a "reward." It is also common for the dummy to be made to look like a particular politician, even like the president, so that the community can get its own back on unpopular leaders. In fact, according to one observer, virtually every president since the 1930s has been Judas at some burning (Martínez Alcalá, 1990, 104).

A series of public holidays commemorates the officially proclaimed landmarks in Venezuela's history, such as Bolívar's birthday, the battle of Carabobo, and Independence Day. They are marked by formal ceremonies, such as the placing of floral tributes at the foot of Bolívar's statue in main squares and military-style parades. The significance of these occasions is particularly emphasized in schools, where children are involved in a series of related activities before the day in question. There is minimal participation in the ceremonies by the general public, but they serve to reinforce a sense of nationhood and cultural unity.

OTHER TRADITIONAL FESTIVALS

Venezuela has a wealth of popular festivals. Many take place during the Christmas and New Year period, as already mentioned, but throughout the year many others are held in different parts of the country. Most of them have long historical roots, but they are constantly evolving, their precise format changing from year to year, and often varying considerably from one town to another. Popular participation is the essential ingredient. Lively and inventive—incorporating music, dance, theater, and humor in numerous ways—they represent one of the most dynamic and distinctive features of Venezuelan culture.

As in other countries of the Caribbean and in Brazil, carnival is celebrated each year in February or March. The precise origins of this ancient festival are unclear, but for centuries, in Roman Catholic countries, carnival has been a time of wild merrymaking when normal social conventions and constraints are suspended, and people can freely enjoy themselves for several days, dancing and carousing in the street while consuming copious amounts of liquor before the austere forty days of Lent begin. In the colonial period, the religious authorities frequently expressed concern about immoral behavior during carnival, and attempted to impose restrictions.

The festival has steadily evolved through time, and some elements, such as competitions for the best float and best costume, are relatively recent additions. Outrageous behavior continues to be an essential ingredient, however, and pranks are an integral part of the activities. In towns and villages throughout Venezuela, passers-by often get rotten eggs or buckets of water thrown over them during carnival, just as they did centuries ago in Spain, the land to which much of Venezuela's carnival tradition can be traced. For a long time it was one of the most popular festivals in Venezuela, but it faded in many parts of the country in the course of the twentieth century, until in the latter decades there were hardly any organized celebrations in some places. In towns where it does continue, the highlight is always the parade of floats, outlandishly costumed dancers, and bands. The event is particularly large and exuberant in Carúpano, a town in the east of the country, where it has been promoted by the local authorities as a tourist attraction.

There are certain regional variations in the way in which carnival is celebrated. In Naiguatá, a fishing village east of Caracas, the "burial of the sardine" is performed on Ash Wednesday, as carnival ends. In another ritual with Spanish roots, the image of a sardine is symbolically buried while joyful celebrations take place with much alcohol, music, and dance. It signifies the "burial" of another carnival and the start of Lent, permitting one final bout of revelry. The most original carnival in Venezuela is that of El Callao, an old gold mining town in the far east of the country. The British and American mining companies contracted significant numbers of workers from Trinidad and other Caribbean islands, and it is mainly their descendants who maintain the carnival tradition. The West Indian influence is clearly seen in some of the costumes and, most strikingly, in the calypso music played for the parades. The words are sometimes sung in Spanish or French, but English or a regional dialect, the most common languages of the town, are more usual. The parades, their music dominated by traditional Caribbean percussion instruments, continue well into the night, followed through the streets by dancing crowds.

The considerable number and the variety of popular festivals that take place in Venezuela are to a large extent explained by the fact that virtually every city, town, and village has a patron—a virgin or a saint—who is honored once a year in specially organized festivities. As mentioned in Chapter 2, the procession around the town, in which the image of the patron saint is carried, is the focal point, but it is accompanied by secular celebrations. In Maracaibo, for example, the festival for the Virgin of Chiquinquirá, patron saint of the state of Zulia, is celebrated on November 18, though a whole week is normally taken up with dances, street parties, music, and even bullfights. In smaller towns, the feast day of the patron saint is much less grand in scale, but it is often the main community event of the year.

Like many patron saints, the Virgin of Chiquinquirá is associated with miraculous occurrences. The small painted image of her, which is housed in the basilica in the center of Maracaibo, dates from the mid-eighteenth century and is said to have been found by a washerwoman on the shore of Lake Maracaibo. After she hung it on the wall of the humble shack where she lived, a banging noise and brilliant light emanated from it. Many other miracles have since been claimed on her behalf. There are many such stories that explain not only why a particular saint or Virgin is revered in a given locality, but also the nature of the celebrations dedicated to him or her. In Guatire, east of Caracas, a festival to San Pedro is held every year on June 29. According to legend, a black slave called María Ignacia, who lived on a nearby sugar plantation during the colonial period, prayed to the saint, asking him to save her dying daughter, Rosa. She promised that if he did so, she would dance and sing the whole twenty-four hours of his feast day in homage to him. Rosa is said to have recovered, and ever since, the event has been celebrated annually. In addition to the main procession behind the image of San Pedro, a group of individuals goes through the town, singing and dancing. Most prominent among them is a man dressed as a woman, playing the part of María Ignacia; the musicians and other dancers portray her fellow slaves. A black rag doll carried by them as they dance represents her miraculously cured daughter, Rosa.

However, the saints who are subject of the largest and most fervent celebrations are San Antonio, San Benito, and San Juan. The centerpiece of the festivals dedicated to San Antonio, which take place on June 13 in many parts of Lara state, where he is particularly revered, is a suite of dances known as the *tamunangue*. It consists of various musical rhythms, songs, and complex dance steps, and is widely regarded as one of Venezuela's richest folkloric expressions. It begins with a mock battle in which two male dancers fence with sticks, followed by a series of dances in honor of the saint, and finally the procession in which his image is carried aloft. The name of the dance suite is derived from *tamunango*, a drum of African origin that is used to beat the different rhythms.

San Benito, as mentioned in Chapter 2, is particularly venerated in the west of the country, especially among Afro-Venezuelan communities in the state of Zulia. The processions and celebrations for the saint are often frenetic, characterized by the powerful rhythms of a battery of drums of African origin called *chumbángueles*.

The festival of San Juan Bautista (Saint John the Baptist), held on June 23 and 24, is the most widespread of all, celebrated across four states and in many towns around Caracas. It is particularly strong among Afro-Venezuelan communities, for San Juan has for centuries been regarded as the saint of slaves and their descendants. The beating of drums on the night of June 23 announces the start of the festival, in which, like all such celebrations, dance and drink play an essential part. The image of the saint is treated as an active participant. During the day he is not only carried through the streets by dancing and singing crowds—and made to "dance" along by those carrying him—but also is frequently carried into a river, so that he can bathe with his devotees in a ritual of purification. San Juan is considered to be the saint of the water, and in the coastal village of Ocumare de la Costa, his image is taken out to sea on a boat for several hours before being carried ashore for the celebrations in the streets. In some villages, the procession takes the saint to visit outlying houses so that families living in them can receive his blessing. The crowd following along continues dancing to the drums, which go on beating for most of the day. The dancing for this festival is traditionally very sexual, with sensuous movements and provocative gestures.

All these festivals have undergone changes over the years. Efforts by the state to support and promote them as manifestations of national culture, or as tourist attractions, have often led to alterations in the way they are organized or presented. As studies have shown, however, the communities involved have frequently resisted such externally imposed change, and have fought to continue their traditional celebrations in ways that are meaningful to them (Guss, 1998). Many festivals are therefore a compromise between pressures from outside and the needs and desires of the community.

Without doubt, the best-known of Venezuela's many folkloric manifestations are the performances of the devil dancers, which take place in several small towns not far from Caracas to mark Corpus Christi, a festival to honor the Eucharist that dates back to twelfth-century Europe. The practice of dressing up as a devil to pay homage to Christ, thereby symbolically representing the submission of evil to his teaching, was introduced into Latin America by the Spanish, and the dancing has taken place in Venezuela since colonial times. Its ancient roots, its mixture of pagan and Christian ritual, and its extraordinary visual impact explain the widespread attention the festival has received. The dancers are townsfolk who have pledged to dance, often for years or even for life, to fulfill religious promises they have made.

The town of San Francisco de Yare has achieved national, and even international, celebrity because of its devil dancers. A religious ceremony usually takes place the night before, and the next morning, through streets lined with onlookers, the devils dance to the church, where fireworks announce their arrival. They wear grotesque masks made of papier mâché, with horns and exaggerated features, and wear bright red costumes with a rosary or cross pinned to the chest. Each carries a maraca to maintain the rhythm as they dance. They hear Mass in the church, after which any new participants inform the priest of the promises they have made, as a way of making them formal. Among the most common promises is that of dancing in exchange for the restoration to full health of themselves or of a relative (Domínguez, 1984, 19). They then dance through the streets, calling at houses along the way. The final act is an evening procession, with the devils dancing along, at the end of which they kneel in submission before the Eucharist.

All these popular festivals entail considerable organization and preparation by the community. Much of the work has traditionally been done by *cofradías* (brotherhoods) set up by the main participants of the festival, usually those fulfilling religious promises. The origins of these organizations go back to the colonial period, and for centuries they have played an important role in many communities; in addition to preparing for feast days, they served as mutual aid societies. Each member paid an annual subscription, and the funds were used to help a member when he fell ill, or to contribute toward the funeral costs when he died. Many of the brotherhoods have disappeared over time, though some continue to exist, fulfilling the same basic role as in past centuries. San Francisco de Yare's brotherhood of devil dancers is one of the oldest and strongest.

Venezuela's tradition of folkloric and religious festivals remains strong and varied, despite the inevitable modifications that occur from year to year. The

Dancing devil, in San Francisco de Yare, performs for Corpus Christi in one of Venezuela's many popular festivals. Photo by Nelson Garrido. Photo courtesy of the Fundación Bigott.

richness of their music and dance has produced a number of studies by scholars of folklore, such as Luis Arturo Domínguez. The costumes that are made for the occasion are works of art in their own right, as are the masks, which, made of paper, cardboard or cloth, are both decorative and symbolic. The mask of a mule traditionally represents patience and forbearance. That of an old man or woman indicates experience and reflection, and that of a young person stands for audaciousness. For centuries such masks have been an integral part of ancient rituals, and they remind us that underlying many of the festivities, with their exuberant celebration and colorful spectacle, are deeply held beliefs and values.

PATTERNS OF DAILY LIFE

To a large extent, life in the small towns and villages of Venezuela revolves around regular festivals, which give structure to the year and unity to the community while providing breaks from the daily routine that offer involvement and entertainment. Such communities are usually closely knit, and the social interaction between neighbors is still a vital part of daily life. Impromptu visits are frequent, and, in the evening people often sit outside their homes, in chairs placed on the sidewalk, and spend hours conversing. Small towns obviously have their disadvantages limited work opportunities being one of them—but their more leisurely and community-based pattern of life contrasts significantly with that of the city. For many better-off city dwellers, a second home in the countryside or close to the beach is a major aspiration.

Lifestyles in the city vary greatly in accordance with the dramatic differences in income levels between social sectors. For those with the resources to make use of them, there is an ever increasing array of new leisure and shopping facilities available. American influence has become increasingly apparent in middle-class lifestyles—for example, the great esteem in which the automobile is held. High incomes combined with extremely cheap gasoline meant that the number of privately owned cars increased rapidly during the economic boom. Serious problems have resulted in the biggest cities, above all in Caracas, where traffic jams have become a major bane in the life of its inhabitants, whose daily routine often has to be reorganized to take into account blocked roads and long delays. Although the downturn in the national economy in the 1980s and 1990s reduced the budgets of most of the population, ostentatious spending continued to be a key characteristic of the life of the wealthier sectors. Most members of the middle classes get paid every two weeks on a Friday, and many celebrate in style that evening. Packed streets, clubs, and bars on paydays are a regular feature of life in the center of Caracas. Most big cities are located near the coast, so escaping to the beach for holidays or on weekends is a popular pastime for many of their middle-class inhabitants.

Lavish consumption is beyond the means of the majority of Venezuela's urban population, however. Poverty became more widespread in the cities in the 1980s and 1990s, as did violence, in part due to the increased activities of criminal gangs. The fear of crime that has resulted has significantly modified the social life of more and more people in the large cities, such as Caracas, Maracaibo, and Valencia, who have become accustomed to living in houses or apartments protected with railings, bars, or barbed wire, and to taking careful precautions when traveling through some districts of the city. This experience is by no means exclusive to Venezuela, of course. Similar problems, often more acute, exist in many other Latin American countries. It is, however, one more factor in explaining changing customs in the city, and the erosion of many of the community-based activities that took place in many urban neighborhoods throughout much of the twentieth century.

FARÁNDULA

For many Venezuelans, *farándula* is a major interest; for some, it is close to an obsession. The term refers to news and gossip about show business and the media, and more specifically about the professional, public, and private lives of its celebrities, which are followed avidly by a significant proportion of the population. Singers, musicians, television personalities, and actors and actresses, especially from the numerous soap operas, are the principal focus of interest. The phenomenon is a product of the rapid expansion of the media and publicity business. It is often highly intrusive, for scandals and love affairs are particularly prized news items. It is also, however, big business in Venezuela. There are pages dedicated to *farándula* in most major newspapers, several magazines that specialize in the subject (e.g., *Venezuela Gráfica* [Graphic Venezuela] and *Ronda* [The Round]), and television programs that focus on it.

Among *farándula* celebrities, Venezuela's beauty queens attract special attention. Though beauty contests have steadily decreased in popularity in many countries, due to changing tastes and a greater sensitivity toward issues of sexism, they have retained much of their appeal and prestige in Venezuela. This is partly explained by the frequent success Venezuelan women have had in international contests, attracting worldwide publicity to the country, and by the fact that many of Venezuela's beauty queens have subsequently gone on to become celebrities in other fields. Because the rewards for success are high, beauty contests have become an industry. In Caracas, Organización Miss Venezuela, under the management of Osmel Sousa, not only organizes the Miss Venezuela contest but also grooms specially selected young women deemed to have beauty queen potential. Candidates are trained in modeling, social communication, and the English language, and plastic surgery is arranged if it is thought necessary to enhance the chances of success. To its critics the beauty contest business appears puerile, or is politically unacceptable.

Irene Saez on the campaign trail in Caracas. Photo courtesy of Archivo El Nacional.

Nevertheless, there is a significant list of women who have used beauty contests to launch themselves into high-profile careers in Venezuela. The trend was set by Susana Dujim, who in 1955 became the first Venezuelan to win the title of Miss World, and then went on to a prominent career as a television presenter. Many others followed, such as Astrid Carolina Herrera, well known as an actress in television soap operas; Bárbara Palacios, television celebrity and businesswoman; and Maite Delgado, who developed a career in television as a presenter. The most famous example of all, however, is Irene Saez, Miss Universe 1981, who later embarked on a career in politics. For many years she served as mayor of Chacao, one of the central districts of Caracas, and then ran as a presidential candidate in the 1998 elections. Unsuccessful in that venture, she became governor of the state of Nueva Esparta the following year.

SPORTS AND GAMES

Venezuela is unique among South American nations in that baseball is the principal national sport. Playing it is the favorite pastime of many. In all regions of the country youngsters regularly practice or play it in the street, using a stick and a crushed milk carton if no bat and ball are available. The professional clubs are supported by legions of passionate followers. The game was first played in Venezuela in the last decades of the nineteenth century, introduced either by Americans and Cubans living in Caracas, or by young Venezuelans who had studied in the United States. The first Venezuelan baseball club was founded in the capital in 1895, but for several years it had no opposition, so it had to divide itself into two sides in order to have a game. The sport soon began to spread rapidly, however, and clubs proliferated in Caracas and beyond. Visits by teams from overseas increased technical skills and enthusiasm, and expansion continued steadily throughout the 1930s. U.S. oil workers in Venezuela did much to promote the sport in the country. In 1941, Venezuela's first significant international success in the game was achieved when the national team won the fourth World Series of Amateur Baseball. Children were given the day off from school for the final game against Cuba, which gripped the attention of the nation. Baseball's position as the national sport was consolidated, and it has never been seriously challenged since then.

The professional game was established in 1945, when a meeting of major clubs created the Venezuelan League of Professional Baseball. Its first championship series was held the following year, and in time a national league emerged, with the largest cities—Barquisimeto, Caracas, Maracaibo, Maracay, and Valencia—providing the major teams. One of the highlights of each season is the intense rivalry between the two biggest clubs, the Lions of Caracas and Magallanes of Valencia, which dates back to the 1930s, when both were based in Caracas, and played fiercely competitive games against one another. Magallanes eventually moved to Valencia, but the rivalry intensified rather than diminished. The exchange of jokes and jibes between the supporters of each side—for the most part good-natured—has become part and parcel of the game. Top foreign players are contracted to play for the principal clubs, and the standard of the professional league is high, but the main ambition for the most talented players is to play major league baseball in the United States. Alejandro Carrasquel was the first to do so when he played for the Washington Senators in 1939, and many others have followed, often with considerable success. Luis Aparicio, the first Venezuelan to earn a place in the U.S. Baseball Hall of Fame; David Concepción; Antonio Armas; and Andrés Galarraga have become major figures in the sport.

The cultural importance of baseball in Venezuela is clearly shown in the way it has featured in works of literature, paintings, films, television programs, and songs, and there are plans to open a museum of the sport in a shopping center in Valencia. There is not another sport in Venezuela that can compare with baseball in terms of mass appeal, though the number of other sports that are played is considerable. Basketball is the second most

Magallanes baseball team, of Valencia, during training. Photo courtesy of Archivo El Nacional.

popular, helped by the fact that it is played in many schools, by both sexes, and because the national men's team made such impressive progress in international competitions during the 1990s, with a series of headline-making performances. It qualified for a world basketball championship for the first time in 1990; won the South American title in 1992 by beating Brazil; and, in the Americas Cup in 1997, obtained its first victory over the United States. These results were the product of the steady development that basketball, for both men and women, had undergone since the 1930s. The professional game received a major boost with the creation of the "special league" in 1974, which, well supported by the private sector and well covered by the media, raised the game to a new level of professionalism. Top foreign players are contracted to play for the major clubs in the Venezuelan League of Professional Basketball, as the top league became known in 1993, though the country has produced fine players of its own, such as Carl Herrera, who went on to play in the United States.

It is surprising that the development of soccer has been so slow in Venezuela, given the fanatical following for the game in neighboring Brazil and

Colombia, but it has undoubtedly suffered on account of the strong popularity of baseball. It was introduced into the country in the 1870s—by British railway workers, according to one uncorroborated theory. For several decades it was largely confined to Caracas, where the National Football Federation was founded in 1925, but it spread to other regions, such as the Andes and Zulia, in the course of the next decade. It was strictly amateur, and generally considered to be a sport for the well-off. The arrival of European immigrants in the 1950s gave it new dynamism and popularity, and it was the immigrant communities of Italians, Portuguese, and Galicians who provided the major support for many of the first professional teams that emerged in the late 1950s. Major clubs such as Caracas FC and Deportivo Táchira, frequently import players from countries like Brazil and Argentina, but the national team has yet to make any significant impact on world soccer and Venezuela has not qualified for the game's showpiece event, the World Cup finals.

Boxing has spread steadily since the 1920s, and now attracts a large number of followers. Since 1965, when Carlos "Morocho" Hernández became the first Venezuelan to win a world title, many other international successes have played a major part in increasing the popularity of the professional sport. Amateur boxing has brought Venezuela many of its medals in the Olympic Games. There is an even wider following for horse racing, and betting is a major pastime for many, demonstrated by the fact that the most popular racing paper, the *Gaceta hípica* (Horse Racing Gazette), has for many years been the country's top-selling weekly publication. Softball, volleyball, golf, tennis, cycling, and swimming are all well established in the country, as are some ancient blood sports inherited from Spain. Cockfighting, for example, is still widespread in many smaller towns, and bullfights have taken place ever since the colonial era, when they sometimes formed part of popular festivals. There are impressive bullrings in Caracas, Maracay, and Valencia, and some Venezuelan bullfighters, such as César Girón, have achieved international celebrity, although, as elsewhere, there has been mounting pressure from animal rights organizations seeking to outlaw the practice. *Toros coleados*, in which contestants ride after a bull and attempt to grab its tail and pull it to the ground, has an equally long history. Contests are held regularly in many towns in the interior, which have tracks specially built for the purpose, and national championships take place annually. Finally, mention must be made of open-air lawn bowling, called *bolas criollas* in Venezuela, because it is one of the most frequently played games throughout the country. Organized competitions are played in clubs, but it is most commonly played informally, by groups of friends and neighbors, on patches of ground in towns and villages.

A huge *arepa* entices customers to El Arepazo, one of the best-known *areperas* in Caracas. Photo courtesy of Mark Dinneen.

TRADITIONAL FOODS AND DRINK

Nowhere is the hybridity that characterizes Venezuelan culture more evident than in the country's culinary traditions. Common local ingredients, such as corn, potatoes, avocados, and yucca, whose use dates back well before the Spanish conquest, were joined over the centuries by foodstuffs imported initially from Spain, then from other parts of Europe and the Americas. Even during the colonial period the Venezuelan diet was influenced by many different countries, for although Spain prohibited its colonies from trading with nations other than herself, illegal trade was rife in Venezuela. The majority of the ingredients used in Venezuelan cooking today—including rice, wheat, sugar, many meats, and spices—were introduced via Europe, as were the methods of cooking now most commonly employed. Frequently, however, these imports have been used to produce new recipes, in accordance with local conditions and preferences, thus generating dishes that can be said to be distinctly Venezuelan.

The most common food, consumed by all sectors of the population, is the *arepa*, a doughy roll made of corn flour and then fried or baked. It is frequently eaten for breakfast or as a snack, stuffed with cheese, meat, or chicken; it also sometimes accompanies main meals, much as the tortilla is served with Mexican meals. Among the most popular snack bars in towns and cities throughout Venezuela are the *areperas*, which specialize in *arepas* with a variety of different fillings. Also popular, though consumed much less regularly, are *cachapas*, flat, sweet pancakes of corn flour, usually eaten with soft white cheese, and *cazabe*, a crisp, flat, starch-free bread made of yucca.

Venezuela's national dish, *pabellón* consists of the country's most popular foods: shredded beef, rice, fried plantains, and black beans with grated cheese. Venezuelan beef is widely recognized for its high quality, and is by far the most frequently consumed meat, although growing concern for a healthy diet led to increased consumption of fish and chicken in the last decades of the twentieth century. The religious tradition of not eating meat on Fridays is still observed by a small percentage of strongly Catholic families. As a replacement, they eat fish and, particularly during the Easter period, capybara, the world's largest rodent, known in Venezuela as *chigüire*, which is not counted as meat because it is aquatic. Naturally, different regions of Venezuela have their own specialties, such as the fish dishes prepared in many towns on the coast, the trout served in the Andes, and the goat cooked in various forms in states such as Lara and Yaracuy. The wildlife of the Amazon region provides its indigenous communities with some highly distinctive foods, including tapir, turtle, ants, and various species of birds. The traditional Christmas dishes referred to earlier remain extremely popular across the country.

Venezuela produces some of the finest coffee in the world, and for a while in the nineteenth century it was the country's major export commodity. Along with other sectors of agricultural production, coffee declined appreciably as oil came to dominate exports, but it has remained important for the domestic market. As in virtually all Latin American countries, the café is an important institution in Venezuela, playing a major role in daily social life almost everywhere. So varied are the forms in which coffee is served that a large vocabulary has developed in Venezuela to describe the variations in color and strength. The abundance of tropical fruit available, such as papaya, mango, and guava, means that natural fruit juices are sold in cafés and restaurants everywhere. Other popular drinks are coconut milk; *chicha*, which may be made from rice or corn; and *papelón*, a mixture of water, raw sugar, and lemon juice. Consumption of these has declined, however, as the sale of commercially produced soft drinks and beer has expanded. As far as liquor is concerned, rum has a long history in Venezuela, as it does throughout the

Caribbean. Some Venezuelan varieties are of high quality, but the country's middle classes have increasingly turned to imported whiskey, regarded as having greater cachet.

A variety of factors, such as the desire or need to spend less time preparing meals, and the availability of so many tinned and prepared foods, have undermined many of Venezuela's traditional meals and eating habits in recent decades. The culmination of this process, as in so many other countries around the world, has been the rapid spread of fast-food chains, both national and foreign-owned, in towns and cities throughout the country. Yet, as in all the other areas of daily life, the national continues to coexist with the cosmopolitan, albeit in changing forms. And despite the ever increasing variety and availability of international cuisine, local foods remain popular and firmly established components of the Venezuelan diet.

REFERENCES

Alemán, Carmen Elena. *Corpus Christi y San Juan Bautista: Dos manifestaciones rituales en la comunidad afrovenezolona de Chuao.* Caracas: Fundación Bigott, 1997.

Domínguez, Luis Arturo. *Diablos danzantes en San Francisco de Yare.* Los Teques: Biblioteca de Autores y Temas Mirandinos, 1984.

Domínguez, Luis Arturo, and Adolfo Salazar Quijada. *Fiestas y danzas folklóricos en Venezuela.* Caracas: Monte Ávila, 1992.

Guss, David M. "The Selling of San Juan: The Performance of History in an Afro-Venezuelan Community." In *Blackness in Latin America and the Caribbean.* Ed. Norman E. Whitten and Arlene Thomas, 244–277. Bloomington: Indiana University Press, 1998.

Klein, Elizabeth. *A Traveler's Guide for Venezuela.* Caracas: Armitano Editores, 1994.

Lovera, José Rafael. *Historia de la alimentación en Venezuela.* Caracas: Monte Ávila, 1988.

Martínez Alcalá, Adolfo. *Esta tierra mía.* Caracas: Procter and Gamble de Venezuela, 1990.

Pollak-Eltz, Angelina. *Vestigios africanos en la cultura del pueblo venezolano.* Caracas: Universidad Católica Andrés Gello, 1972.

4

Broadcasting and Print Media

PRINT MEDIA

AS ELSEWHERE in Latin America, the press in Venezuela has had a turbulent history. Not only has it frequently suffered from unstable economic conditions in the country, but it also has been particularly vulnerable to political pressures, with publications often facing censorship, or even shutdown, by hostile governments. Despite the difficulties, however, the newspaper and magazine industry was consolidated in the course of the twentieth century. New production techniques were steadily incorporated, high standards of professionalism were set within the industry, and a significant number of high-quality publications was launched.

The emergence of newspapers in Venezuela coincided with the arrival of printing presses in the early nineteenth century. Although presses operated in Mexico and Peru relatively early in the colonial period, other parts of Spain's American empire, including Venezuela, were frustrated in their attempts to develop the same facilities. In the early 1800s, the propaganda war in Venezuela between the Spanish authorities and the independence fighters made access to printing presses increasingly important. Revolutionary leaflets and papers did circulate in the country during those years, but they had to be printed overseas, mainly in Trinidad. Finally, toward the end of 1808, the Spanish authorities in Caracas ordered a printing workshop to be set up in the city, and it was transported from Trinidad by two British printers, Matthew Gallagher and James Lamb. Within a few weeks, on October 24, 1808, Venezuela's first newspaper was produced. Called *Gazeta de Caracas*

(Caracas Gazette), it proclaimed support for the Spanish Crown and dismissed the independence cause. The timing was significant, for only months before, Napoleon's armies had occupied Spain and deposed the Spanish king, creating a crisis for Spanish authority that would be a vital catalyst for the independence movement across the empire.

The Venezuelan press thus began life as a political instrument, during a period of great turmoil and conflict. The independence fighters eventually took control of the *Gazeta de Caracas* and used it to promote their own cause, but other papers were soon created by both sides. The royalists produced such publications as *El Celador de la Constitución* (Monitor of the Constitution) and *El Farol* (The Lantern), and the independence cause had suitably named papers like *El Patriota de Venezuela* (Venezuela Patriot). The most significant newspaper of the time was undoubtedly the *Correo del Orinoco* (Orinoco Post,) founded in the town of Angostura (today Ciudad Bolívar), on July 27, 1818. Angostura was a stronghold of the independence cause, and the paper played a major role in propagating its ideas, both in Venezuela and overseas. It carried many reports and declarations by Simón Bolívar, who clearly recognized the political value of the press. The historical significance of the paper continues to be commemorated each year in Venezuela; the date of its foundation, July 27, is celebrated as the "day of the journalist." The paper lasted only four years, closing in March 1822, some nine months after Venezuelan independence had finally been sealed by the defeat of the Spanish armies at the battle of Carabobo. Many of the papers of the time had even shorter lives, reflecting the fact that they were published to meet specific objectives which arose at a particular point in history.

Gradually, printing presses were established in towns other than Caracas, and a pattern soon emerged: the setting up of a printing workshop was quickly followed by the creation of a newspaper. Maracaibo, Puerto Cabello, and Guanare, for example, each launched its first paper within a year or so of the arrival of printing in those towns in the early 1820s. Political objectives continued to dominate the press even after independence from Spain. The majority of papers were founded to represent a political party or one of the regional political leaders known as caudillos. Rather than to convey news, the papers existed first and foremost to express opinion and galvanize public support for political programs, and they were characterized by impassioned argument, satirical attacks on political opponents, and, not infrequently, personal insult. *El Venezolano* (The Venezuelan), for example, was one of the main papers that served as a campaign instrument for the Liberals in the 1840s; the Conservatives had their own papers, one of the most notable of which was paradoxically titled *El Liberal* (The Liberal).

The political conflicts and instability of the decades following independence largely explain the rapid proliferation of papers in the 1830s and 1840s. They also explain why so many of them were ephemeral, for as political circumstances changed, some papers disappeared and new ones were launched. Most circulated in a very restricted area because transport was still extremely limited. Subscriptions were their main source of income, for advertising was insignificant. Although no reliable circulation figures are available, they were clearly small in every case, for the rate of illiteracy was high. Most of the papers were published irregularly, weekly at most; it is believed that the *Diario de Avisos* (Daily News), launched in Caracas in 1837 to convey business and commercial news, was the first daily publication. Nevertheless, despite these limitations, the press was firmly established as a vital means of communication, stimulating debate, and coordinating campaigns on political and social issues.

Production techniques modernized as the nineteenth century progressed, especially during the Guzmán Blanco regime (1870–1888), which placed economic growth and modernization at the heart of its agenda. The government's main paper was *La Opinión Pública* (Public Opinion), which, published over a twenty-year period, introduced new printing techniques to enhance visual appeal, and was the first paper to be printed on a steam-powered press. Inevitably, the opposition eventually established papers, too, though they were subjected to government repression. Some were closed down completely, a demonstration of the political importance that the authorities attached to the press. The shadow of repression would hover over newspapers for many decades to come, but the last years of the nineteenth century still produced some significant publications. One was *La Religión* (Religion), the paper of the Catholic Church, which, founded in 1890 and still being published today, is Venezuela's oldest existing newspaper. Another was *El Cojo Ilustrado* (The Enlightened Cripple), published from 1892 to 1915, the best of the literary journals that became popular at the time, with a very high quality of production and contributions from internationally famous writers. The most advanced newspaper of the time, however, was *El Pregonero* (The Town Crier). Founded in 1893, it was produced by the most modern machinery available and was the first Venezuelan paper to use advertising as a major source of income. It was also one of the first papers to shift the emphasis to news reporting and away from the expression of political opinion.

The editor of *El Pregonero*, Rafael Arévalo González, was imprisoned on numerous occasions because of the paper's criticism of the government, and it was finally closed down in 1913, as repression reached its height under the dictatorship of Juan Vicente Gómez. New papers were founded, among them the Caracas daily *El Universal* (The Universal) in 1909, but they were obliged to toe the government line. Technological advances brought steady improvement in the quality of production, clearly seen in some of the magazines of the era, such as *La Gaceta Médica* (Medical Gazette) and *Élite*, a cultural journal founded in 1925 and now Venezuela's oldest magazine.

At the same time, the appearance of papers changed radically with the introduction of photographs, arguably the most significant innovation of the period. However, the lack of freedom of expression severely limited both the role of the press and the further improvement of the professional standards of journalists, for reporters and writers were frequently arrested and imprisoned. The publications that were most successful in defying the harsh censorship of the Gómez era were humorous journals, such as *Pitorreos* (The Teaser) (1918–1919) and *Fantoches* (Loud-Mouth) (1923–1941), which used satire, jokes, and cartoons to challenge the regime, though they, too, suffered government intervention. Indeed, *Pitorreos*—so popular that people reportedly lined up to buy it—was closed down by the dictatorship, and its editors were imprisoned.

The death of Gómez in 1935 heralded a new era for the Venezuelan press, and editors and journalists immediately sought to take advantage of the new liberty. Press freedom, however, still had to be won. In February 1936, the new government of President López Contreras, faced with riots as crowds ransacked and set fire to the property of known Gómez supporters, repressed civil liberties again and censored the press. Huge demonstrations, more rioting, and well organized public pressure succeeded in getting the measures reversed. It was a significant moment because popular action had achieved an important advance for press freedom, though conflicts over the issue of free expression would continue to flare up periodically in the following years.

The 1940s was an important decade in the history of the Venezuelan press as the country readjusted to democratic life. A number of new newspapers were created in response to the more open political conditions, the majority expressing the desire for radical social change that had long been oppressed, such as *Aquí Está* (Here It Is), a paper created by the Communist Party in 1944. At the same time, other entrepreneurs and editors sought to produce publications that were in line with the most modern examples overseas, easy to read, and attractive in design. Two papers proved to be landmarks in the development of the modern Venezuelan press: *Últimas Noticias* (Latest News), founded in 1941, and *El Nacional* (The National), which followed in 1943, both of which are still published in Caracas. *Últimas Noticias* was the country's first tabloid. The aim was to produce a newspaper that was attractive to a wide readership, with striking headlines and photographs, and lively, easy-to-read reports. The new style achieved considerable success—the paper quickly attained high circulation figures, with the urban working class forming a significant percentage of its readers.

El Nacional was similar in its innovative approach to presenting and discussing news items, and in its layout and its organization, though it retained standard size. It was launched by Miguel Otero Silva, already well known as a journalist and novelist, with the financial backing of his father. It was distinctive in its layout, for in order to facilitate reading and make it as attractive as possible, large lettering, clearer headlines, and bigger illustrations were used. A less cluttered appearance was created by reorganizing space, and the paper was divided into sections according to subject, with more pages devoted to political debate and cultural news. The editorial, a traditional element in Venezuelan papers, was replaced by a box with a much briefer and more direct statement of opinion about a current issue. Many of these changes were soon adopted by other newspapers. Otero Silva obtained the services of many talented and experienced writers, which enabled the paper to develop a reputation for high-quality journalism and debate. It was of left-wing orientation in its early years, and supported many progressive movements within the country and overseas. It faced serious problems as a result, however. In 1962, the National Association of Advertisers, to which many large international companies belonged, imposed an ad boycott on the paper because of its support for the Cuban Revolution. *El Nacional* was saved from bankruptcy by a radical shake-up of personnel and a move toward the political center. By the closing decades of the century it had established itself as one of Latin America's leading newspapers, largely because of its responsiveness to new opportunities—taking advantage of new technology, for example, and introducing its popular weekend magazines *Feriadao* (Day Off) and *Pandora*.

The modernization of the press in the 1940s led to new levels of professionalization and specialization among journalists. They began to organize with the aim of strengthening their profession, and in 1941 they formed the Venezuelan Association of Journalists, which expanded rapidly. Its success generated other associations, such as "circles" of specialized journalists, like the Circle of Sports Journalists, and in 1946, a union, which was initially called the National Union of Journalists, but later became the National Union of Newspaper Workers. Recognition of the specialized skills that journalism now required was demonstrated by the foundation of the School of Journalism in 1946. It produced its first graduates in 1949, and later became part of the Central University of Venezuela in Caracas, with the title of School of Social Communication.

Although solid foundations for a modern newspaper industry had been laid, political events again disrupted the process. A military coup in 1948 installed another dictatorship, eventually under the presidency of General Pérez Jiménez, and the media were subjected to increasingly strict censorship. Many papers were temporarily closed down on more than one occasion, including *El Universal* and *El Nacional*, and some were silenced completely, such as the *Tribuna Popular* (Popular Tribune) which had become the official paper of the Communist Party. A large number of journalists faced imprisonment or exile. Only progovernment papers such as *El Heraldo* (The Herald) continued unimpeded, though an alternative press emerged to keep dissenting opinion alive. A number of clandestine papers circulated, with such titles as *Resistencia* (Resistance) and *Libertad* (Liberty), and *Tribuna Popular* went underground as well. Venezuelans exiled by the regime established newspapers overseas, and student organizations and trade unions launched alternative publications, most of which were quickly repressed.

When the regime was overthrown in January 1958, and democracy was restored, the newspapers brought out special editions to celebrate the event. *El Nacional*'s ran to 160,000 copies, which it claimed was a record number for a Venezuelan daily newspaper. The basic strength the newspaper industry had developed in the decade before the dictatorship meant that it was able to recover relatively quickly in the new era of democracy. To assist the process, the major newspapers organized themselves into the Bloque Venezolano de Prensa (Venezuelan Press Bloc), to coordinate demands and policy. A new phase of renewal began. Existing newspapers increased their print runs and their pages, and new papers were launched. New magazines flourished, too, and the strength of the market permitted the gradual appearance of specialized journals, exemplified by literary magazines, such as *Poesía Venezolana* (Venezuelan Poetry), and scientific journals like *Acta Científica* (Scientific Record) and *Tierra y Hombre* (Land and Man).

There would be reminders in subsequent decades of the vulnerability of the press to political turbulence. In the 1960s, the guerrilla activity in the country led the government to impose restrictions on the press again, and when the attempted coup to overthrow president Pérez took place in February 1992, the government temporarily shut down certain papers, including *El Nacional*. However, the last three decades of the century were relatively stable for Venezuela, politically and economically, and those conditions enabled the press to continue its consolidation and expansion. Caracas was obviously the focal point of the industry, and new, modern, and well produced dailies were established, such as *2001* (1973) and *El Diario de Caracas* (Caracas Daily; 1979), the latter launched by an exiled Argentine newspaperman, Rodolfo Terragano. However, there was notable development across the rest of the country, too, with papers being produced in all regions. Some of the major regional daily papers had long traditions, such as *Panorama*, established in Maracaibo in 1914, and *El Carabobeño*, (The Caraboboan), in Valencia, which dates from 1933. The growth of the provincial press led to the formation of the Venezuelan Chamber of Regional Newspapers in 1986, with forty daily papers as members.

As the industry has grown, the system of financing and patterns of ownership have inevitably become more complex and diverse. The days of one or two individuals producing a paper by themselves from a simple print shop have long passed. Some major papers, such as *El Universal* and *El Nacional*, are owned by families with a long history in the newspaper industry. Others, however, belong to huge corporations, like 1BC, which owns *El Diario de Caracas* in addition to radio and television stations, a recording company, and publishing companies. Though the circulation figures of many publications have risen, so have the costs of production. More skilled and specialized labor is required, and the publications have become more sophisticated and larger—for instance, the supplements that now accompany many newspapers. The large and secure financial base now required has been provided by advertising, an industry that expanded rapidly as a result of the consumerism generated by the oil boom. This has raised concern in some quarters that the press, and other sectors of the media, have become too dependent on powerful commercial interests, which can have a strong influence on the way news is presented and on the editorial line.

Another indication of the growth of the industry was the increased diversity of magazines available in the latter decades of the twentieth century. New titles appeared in response to specialized areas of interest, such as *Computer World Venezuela* and *Estilo* (Style), a journal of graphic art and photography, which seeks to promote young experimental artists. Among the journals with the longest tradition, however, are those of humor and satire, whose role during the Gómez period was mentioned earlier. Many titles have appeared in Venezuela over the decades, most of them short-lived. Their sharp social and political criticism in an accessible, enjoyable format has long had a popular following. The most notable figure in this type of press is Pedro León Zapata (b. 1928), well known as a painter but also Venezuela's most renowned cartoonist. In 1978 he founded *El Sádico Ilustrado* (The Illustrated Sadist), offering a highly irreverent view of contemporary Venezuelan society. Uniting outstanding illustrators and major writers such as Salvador Garmendia and Luis Britto García, it brought unprecedented quality to humorous journalism. Like so many similar journals before it, it soon ceased publication. Zapata's work, however, remained firmly in the public eye, through his striking and often caustic cartoons that appeared regularly in *El Nacional*. The tradition of such journalism was continued in *El Camaleón* (The Chameleon), a satirical supplement that for many years appeared weekly in the same paper.

In the last decades of the twentieth century, two large corporations dominated the publication of magazines in Venezuela, between them producing a large proportion of the country's most popular titles. Cadena Capriles was responsible for such publications as *Élite*, a current affairs journal, the women's magazines *Página* (Page) and *Kena*, and others on horse racing and show business, as well as the newspapers *El Mundo* (The World) and *Últimas Noticias*. Bloque De Armas produced rival magazines in every area, numbering nearly thirty titles in total. These included its own current affairs magazine, *Bohemia*; magazines for women such as *Variedades* (Variety) and *Mujer de Hoy* (Today's Woman); and others on horse racing, cooking, and pop music, as well as the newspapers *Abril* (April), *Meridiano* (Meridian), and *2001*. However, their markets had become increasingly competitive, with Spanish editions of major foreign magazines, such as *Time, Cosmopolitan*, and *Buen Hogar* (Good Housekeeping), attracting a significant readership.

In 1990, there were estimated to be sixty-seven provincial daily papers, and twelve in Caracas (*Gran enciclopedia de Venezuela*, 1998, vol. 8, 292). *El Universal* and *El Nacional* are the two best known internationally. Both use the most modern production techniques and, with several other Venezuelan papers, are available on the world wide web. Despite the economic difficulties of the 1990s, the press remained reasonably buoyant, receptive to innovation, and highly organized. It is now linked to international associations. The Venezuelan press is a member of the InterAmerican Press Society, and the main professional body for journalists in Venezuela, now called the Colegio Nacional de Periodistas (National College of Journalists), is linked to the Latin American Federation of Journalists.

RADIO

The first experiments with radio in Venezuela took place in Caracas in the mid-1920s. In 1926 two businessmen, Roberto Scholtz and Alfredo Moller, established the country's first radio station, AYRE, using equipment from the Western Electric Company; they began broadcasting in May of that year. The programs were very limited, a mixture of news and music, and reception was often poor. It was not a commercial station, and relied on subscriptions. A combination of financial difficulties and political problems—President Gómez was generally hostile to the project—led to the closure of the station in 1928.

Two years later, a more successful attempt was made. Edgar Anzola, a radio enthusiast, had studied the way stations operated in the United States, and was determined to establish one in his native Venezuela. He decided that advertising would have to provide the financial basis for radio. Anzola is now recognized as the founder of commercial radio in the country. With financial support from the American businessman William H. Phelps, and technical help from some talented engineers, he launched Broadcasting Caracas in the capital in December 1930. When the Gómez dictatorship ended in 1935, it was decided to change the name to Radio Caracas, which it has kept ever since. From the outset, it was well organized and offered varied and good quality programs, including opera, orchestral music, performances by such international stars as Carlos Gardel and Arthur Rubinstein, and the first radio soap operas. At first, there were no serials written especially for radio; instead, plays for the theater were adapted, with additional words in the dialogue to clarify to the listener the actions and positions of the characters. Eventually, however, the first Venezuelan radio serial was produced. Written by Alfredo Cortina and titled *La comedia Santa Teresa* (The Story of Santa Teresa), it followed the daily life of a middle-class Caracas family. Listeners easily identified with the problems of city life and the economic conditions the family faced, as well as the neighborhood gossip. The program achieved a large following during its four years of existence and paved the way for the radio soap operas that were so successful in later years.

Other radio stations were soon launched in competition with Broadcasting Caracas, the first being Radiodifusora Venezuela (Venezuela Broadcasting), founded in 1932. Like other stations of the early 1930s, it was subjected to strict censorship by the Gómez dictatorship; when the dictator died in 1935, it was the first to introduce political criticism into its programs. Caracas obtained its third radio station in 1935, with the foundation of Ondas Populares (Popular Airwaves). The 1930s saw the proliferation of stations in many other parts of the country, such as Valencia, where La Voz de Carabobo (The Voice of Carabobo) was created in 1934, and Barcelona, where Emisoras Unidas (United Broadcasting) began broadcasting in 1935. By 1936, Maracaibo had four stations, with Radiodifusora Maracaibo dating from 1934, the earliest. The government of López Contreras, in power from 1936 to 1941, recognized the growing importance of radio. In July 1936 it passed a decree to establish a state radio station, which would become known as Radio Nacional (National Radio).

In 1934, the same year the first regional station was created in Valencia,

Alfredo Cortina and Mario García Arocha founded a company in Caracas called Estudios Universos (Universe Studios), which produced a variety of programs and bought time on Radiodifusora Venezuela to broadcast them. The custom-built studios they used were the most modern available and, according to Cortina, only Radio Excelsior in Mexico City and La Voz de la Víctor (Voice of Victor) in Buenos Aires had studios of equal size in Latin America (Cortina, 1995, 107). They included an auditorium for 130 people, so the public could watch programs as they were recorded. It even participated actively in some, such as *The Cases of Inspector Vat*, in which the audience was asked to play the role of the detective and solve the case. A prize was awarded to the winners. The name of the inspector is explained by the fact that the whiskey company Vat 69 sponsored the program, a system of financing firmly in place by that time.

The number of radio listeners increased further during World War II, when numerous stations kept the public informed of events through popular news programs. The period from the early 1940s through the mid-1950s, before television had firmly established itself in the country, represented the golden age of radio in Venezuela. Audience figures remained consistently high. Sports programs were among the most popular, with regular commentaries presented on baseball, horse racing, boxing, soccer, and bullfights. There were many musical shows, like *Fiesta Fabulosa* (Fabulous Fiesta), broadcast by Radio Caracas, that included performances by international stars such as Pérez Prado and Pedro Infante, and national singers like Alfredo Sadel, whose career was effectively launched by the show. It also included comedians, and comedy programs soon achieved great popularity. One of the most successful was *Frijolito y Robustina*, also on Radio Caracas, a program that gave a humorous and satirical view of national life. The scripts were by Carlos Fernández, not only one of the most talented writers for radio during the period but also a producer and an actor. It was in fact common for major radio personalities of those years to have experience in a range of different activities. Another well-known example is Adolfo Martínez Alcalá, a producer, director, actor, and popular presenter who had begun his radio career in the late 1940s and was still presenting programs on Radio Capital in the 1990s.

However, it was the radio soap operas that attracted the biggest audiences during those years. One of the best known, *El derecho de nacer* (The Right to Be Born), broadcast on Radio Continente in 1949 and 1950, established a new record for the largest number of listeners. Such success meant that soap operas became the most attractive programs for companies wishing to advertise their products. They would buy time on the major stations and then contract staff and artists to produce a soap opera. The popularity of these programs, and the involvement of big corporations like Procter and Gamble and Colgate Palmolive, intensified competition between the radio stations.

The 1940s and 1950s produced a wave of talented writers, producers, actors, and presenters, many of whom eventually moved into television. The best-known personalities quickly became household names, and radio often launched them on long and wide-ranging careers in the media. Víctor Saume, for example, a popular presenter of musical shows on radio, later became the first director of Radio Rumbos (Radio Pathways), one of the most popular stations of the early 1950s, before taking up a career in television. Another case was Amador Bendayán, who began broadcasting on Ondas Populares in 1937, presented a series of successful shows on various stations, acted in several films, and finally became one of Venezuela's best-known television personalities of the 1960s and 1970s.

Besides providing entertainment, the radio stations strengthened their news coverage and cultural programs during those years. News reporting reached new levels of professionalism with such programs as *Panorama universal* and *El repórter Esso*. During World War II, the latter had become the most listened-to program on the radio. One of the best-known news readers of the time, Pedro José Fajardo, of Radio Caracas, went on to work as an announcer with the BBC World Service in London. Venezuelan arts and culture were also promoted through such programs as *El torneo del saber* (Tournament of Knowledge), on which a panel, including the writers Arturo Uslar Pietri and Alejo Carpentier, discussed a wide range of cultural issues.

The great years of radio ended in the mid-1950s, when its popularity and growth were severely undermined by the spread of television. Radio audience figures dropped, and many of the most talented technicians and artists left to work in television. Furthermore, television steadily drew vital advertising revenue away from radio. In 1972 radio in Venezuela received 18% of the advertising money invested in the media, compared with 35% for television. By 1980, radio's share had fallen to 6% and that of television had risen to 51%. By 1986, radio was down to 3.9%, compared with television's 67% (*Enciclopedia temática*, 1993, vol. 7, 27). The great years of radio were also the years of the Pérez Jiménez dictatorship (in power 1949–1958) and, like other sectors of the media, radio had to contend with the restrictions imposed by censorship.

Radio stations sought different ways of arresting the decline. Some of those in Caracas merged with others in the provinces to form networks that would be larger and more cost-effective. New opportunities were also exploited.

One station, Radio Aeropuerto (Airport Radio), specialized in giving flight information; others, notably Radio Caracas, used reporters on motorbikes, or in airplanes or helicopters, to gather up-to-date traffic information, which soon became a standard feature on the radio in the capital. The radio also found some important new outlets. Cheap gasoline meant growing traffic in the big cities, and more and more cars, taxis, and buses became equipped with radios. The spread of portable radios also helped, enabling listeners to tune in whenever they went.

Inevitably, the content of what was broadcast underwent changes. In the 1960s, directors of radio stations radically altered the style of their programs, presenting a more modern, youthful image that would attract more young listeners. Disc jockeys emerged, presenting shows of pop music such as *Hit Parade de Venezuela* and *Desfile de éxitos* (March of Hits). Both were on Radio Caracas, one of the first stations to revise its programming by dropping such traditional features as soap operas and sports coverage. The culmination of this process came in 1968, when Radio Capital was formed, the first station specially aimed at the young age group, with slick presentation, jingles, and guest appearances by internationally known pop artists. This was the most striking characteristic of commercial radio of the period, but the end of the 1960s also saw the state-run station, Radio Nacional, extend its coverage across the country, concentrating particularly on educational and cultural programs.

The major development in the final decades of the twentieth century was the emergence of FM stereo radio. It became available in the 1970s, but its impact became really significant in the late 1980s and 1990s. New FM stations emerged, each tending to specialize in a certain type of music. They were popular with advertisers because they were now able to target their products at specific types of audiences. As a result, AM stations were obliged to change as well, tending to move away from music to more talk and news programs. There was another significant innovation during the same period: programs with public participation were developed, with listeners phoning in to discuss topics or answer a quiz. The success of one of the most popular shows of the time, *A Full Chola* with Juan Manuel La Guardia, broadcast on Radio Capital, is explained by the variety of fare offered, mixing listeners' calls with music, comedy, discussion, interviews, and information on events, political developments, and traffic problems in Caracas. Also in the 1990s Radio KYS FM become the first station available on the Internet, twenty-four hours a day, making it accessible to a new, highly dispersed audience. Such adaptability has helped the radio to compensate for the growing number of television channels that have become available. In the 1990s, there were over one hundred FM radio stations broadcasting in the country and approximately two hundred AM stations (*Gran enciclopedia de Venezuela*, 1998, vol. 8, 310).

TELEVISION

On November 22, 1952, Venezuelan television was launched, promoted by the state. There had been experiments in previous years, but on that date the first television company was inaugurated, the state-run Televisora Nacional (National Broadcasting Company), which gave the general public access to the medium for the first time. The Venezuelan president, government ministers, and other dignitaries attended the ceremony in Caracas, and television sets were located in public view. Anticipation of the event caused a considerable stir among the capital's inhabitants, though it proved to be an anticlimax. Following a blessing by the archbishop, an electrical fault ended the transmission, and further broadcasting was delayed for nearly six weeks. Nevertheless, television had been established in Caracas, and it expanded rapidly over the following decades.

Televisora Nacional stopped broadcasting in 1974, largely because much of its equipment had become outdated. As part of a policy of modernizing and expanding state broadcasting, a new state-controlled company, Venezolana de Televisión (Venezuelan Television), was established that same year. It was in the private sector, however, that the development of television was most dynamic. The first commercial channel, Televisa, had been launched in Caracas in May 1953. The driving force behind it was Gonzalo Veloz Mancera, a well-known figure in the world of broadcasting, who had been the owner of the radio station Ondas Populares for many years. A number of its programs in the early years, such as *Tío Tigre y Tío Conejo* (Uncle Tiger and Uncle Rabbit) and *Los casos del Inspector Nick* (The Cases of Inspector Nick), were developments of successful radio programs, and, most significant as far as the future was concerned, television soap operas were created on the basis of their radio counterparts. There was also a considerable number of cultural programs.

Whereas Televisora Nacional could be seen only in the capital, Televisa attempted to extend its broadcasts beyond Caracas, and within a few years it had established relay stations so that its programs could be seen in La Victoria and Valencia. This process was continued in 1956 when the company set up a subsidiary in Maracaibo. Called Televisora del Zulia, it was that region's first television channel. However, by 1960 Televisa had run into serious financial difficulties, and it was bought by the huge Venezuelan-owned Cisneros Corporation, with the help of the U.S. network ABC, whose investment provided 43% of the funds (Sinclair, 1999, 80). With the help of Cuban TV professionals who left their country after the 1959 revolution, the Cisneros Corporation modernized the company and relaunched it as Venevisión. It eventually became the country's largest and most financially successful television company.

The development of television in the 1950s was very much centered in Caracas. Radio Caracas Televisión, founded there at the end of 1953, became the country's third television company. The parent company was CORA-VEN, which also owned Radio Caracas. (In the 1960s, the American company NBC owned a stake of Radio Caracas Televisión, but it was bought out by Venezuelan shareholders and thus returned to total Venezuelan ownership.) During the 1950s, Radio Caracas Televisión spread its coverage across a large part of the country, taking in such states as Zulia, Falcón, Lara, and Carabobo. Attempts to establish television companies in the provinces proved to be more difficult, mainly because of problems with attracting the advertising revenue needed to secure them financially. Most advertisers were more attracted to the large companies based in the capital. As a result, Ondas del Lago Maracaibo, founded in Maracaibo in 1957, had to close down in the early 1960s because of financial difficulties. The same happened to Radio Valencia Televisión, which was launched in Valencia in 1958 and stopped broadcasting in 1962. Only in later decades, after the major national networks like Radio Caracas Televisión and Venevisión had consolidated their coverage across most of the country, were smaller regional channels able to establish themselves.

The advances in television technology were quickly incorporated by the major Venezuelan companies, whose expanding revenues from advertising enabled them to increase their investment. Equipment for filming and transmitting was steadily updated, and the introduction of videotape in 1961 facilitated the recording of programs and opened the way for their sale abroad. Equally significant was the live broadcast of the U.S. moon landing in July 1969 by Radio Caracas Televisión. A major technical achievement, it initiated a new era of international transmissions via satellite. Venevisión also attempted to broadcast the event, but failed, losing out to their rivals. The fierce competition between Radio Caracas Televisión and Venevisión was a key feature of commercial television in Venezuela for the rest of the century.

The late 1960s also saw the appearance of color television in Venezuela, but several different systems were available and the government took considerable time to decide which should be adopted in Venezuela. While the government deliberated, color sets were smuggled into the country in the early 1970s, forcing the Pérez government to issue a special presidential decree suspending all transmissions in color while a new commission continued to consider the matter. It was not until January 1979 that the U.S. system was finally selected. The following year regular broadcasts in color began, starting on the state-run channel in January, and then on the other channels in the following months.

With regard to the programs produced in Venezuela, the most striking feature since the early years has been the huge number of *telenovelas* (soap operas) that have been created, many achieving immense popularity both in Venezuela and beyond. Television was only in its first year of existence in the country when the first *telenovela* was shown. Titled *La criada de la granja* (The Farm Maid), it was broadcast by Televisa in 1953 in fifteen-minute episodes. It established a romantic theme that would become popular in early soaps: the poor peasant girl whose sufferings are finally alleviated when she finds love. It was not surprising that the *telenovela* should make such an early appearance on Venezuelan television, for it had been a highly popular genre on radio for many years, and was easily transferred to television. Indeed, a few *telenovelas*, like *El derecho de nacer*, broadcast on Radio Caracas Televisión in 1965, were adaptations of successful radio soap operas.

Telenovelas proliferated rapidly in Venezuela. In 1954, a total of twenty-three were shown. A regular pattern was set in those years, with most being shown in half-hour episodes each weekday, usually in the early evening. In addition to drama and love stories in local settings, there were some, such as *La juventud de Bolívar* (Bolívar's Youth), that had a historical base, and others that were adaptations of well-known novels, such as *Cumbres borrascosas* (Stormy Heights), a version of Emily Brontë's *Wuthering Heights*. The censorship imposed by the Pérez Jiménez dictatorship made overtly social themes impossible during most of the 1950s. Soaps adapted from novels were likely to be prohibited if their writers were known opponents of the regime. However, even after the fall of the dictatorship in 1958, social and political topics were generally avoided. Radio Caracas Televisión did broadcast *Doña Bárbara*, a *telenovela* based on the novel of the same name by Rómulo Gallegos, a sworn enemy of the dictatorship, but this was an exception.

Instead of national issues, stories of love, treachery, and individual struggle were the preferred themes, and the large viewer figures suggested to producers that that was in line with audience preference. Romance was the most essential ingredient, as indicated by many of the titles of popular series, such as *Tú eres mi vida* (You Are My Life) in 1963, and *Milagro de amor* (Miracle of Love) and *El amor tiene cara de mujer* (Love Has the Face of a Woman), both in 1966. In the early years many soaps were in fact based on, or adapted from, scripts written by Cubans, for Cuba had a particularly strong tradition in the genre, and Venezuelan television companies were eager to tap that expertise. It was not until well into the 1970s that serious attempts were made to produce soaps based on the realities of the nation.

Because of the growing number produced in the 1960s, and their continuing popularity, *telenovelas* began to attract increasing critical attention. Many writers and TV critics argued that the plots were puerile and too sentimental, and Church representatives criticized them for conveying values of materialism and self-indulgence. Educators expressed particular concern about the effects that the constant repetition of such values had on children (Colomina de Rivera, 1968). Others pointed to the increasing length of many soaps and argued that more attention was given to quantity than to quality. It became a common practice among television company directors and producers to spin out *telenovelas* by adding more episodes as they went along, if the audience figures were good. The derogatory term *culebrón* (long snake) became a popular word to refer to soaps regarded as too long and meandering. One, entitled *Raquel* (1973–1975), set a new record when it stretched to 642 episodes. Such were the complaints from educators and other groups about the negative effects of such extended series, that the government took the extraordinary step of issuing a decree in 1976 which stipulated that 180 episodes of no more than one hour each should be the maximum for soap operas transmitted on evening television, and that more attention should be paid to the cultural content.

The decree was only partially effective and was eventually abolished, but for a while it did make television company directors reassess the type of soap operas they presented, and reconsider the question of quality. The result was a series of what were described as "cultural soap operas" produced in the 1970s. Some, like *La trepadora* (The Social Climber) and *Pobre negro* (Poor Black Man), were adapted from works of literature (both from novels by Gallegos), but others were written as soap operas, such as *La hija de Juana Crespo* (The Daughter of Juana Crespo; 1977), one of the first to offer a portrait of contemporary Venezuelan life. Some talented writers began producing scripts conceiving the *telenovela* as a form of artistic expression rather than as pure entertainment. One was Salvador Garmendia, the highly acclaimed novelist and short story writer, and another was José Ignacio Cabrujas, whose *La señora de Cárdenas* (Mrs. Cardenas), one of the most successful soap operas of 1977, used the relationship between a middle-class couple in Caracas to raise questions about aspects of national social and political life.

Somewhat ironically, the government, having played a significant part in stimulating the production of series that confronted social and moral issues, now became so alarmed at such critical investigation of national life on mainstream television that it censored a number of soap operas in the late 1970s and early 1980s. Meanwhile, the traditional *telenovelas* of romance and intrigue continued to be broadcast to large audiences, unimpeded by the state.

Though the debate over quality has continued up to the present, it is undeniable that Venezuelan soap operas have sold well abroad and have achieved a popular following in many parts of the world. Few of the country's other cultural expressions have become so well known internationally. They have been shown in most other Latin American countries, Spain and other parts of Europe, and the United States and Canada. Even more remarkable has been their popularity in such different cultural environments as China, the Middle East, India, and Japan. The biggest international success of all was achieved by *Cristal*, a soap opera produced by Radio Caracas Televisión in the 1980s, which recounts the highly romantic life story of a young Venezuelan woman. It established new viewing records for an entertainment program in several countries besides Venezuela. *Telenovelas* have become a big industry throughout Latin America, and Venezuela has established itself as one of the major producers, along with Brazil, Colombia, and Mexico. Indeed, in 1990 Venezuela produced more soap operas than any other nation in the region, and by 1994 they were being sold in almost one hundred countries worldwide.

Obviously, such success represents significant earnings for the companies and networks that produce *telenovelas*, such as Venevisión and Radio Caracas Televisión. On the other hand, producing series with the international market in mind can lead to standardization, avoiding references to specifically national situations and issues not likely to be understood overseas. For some critics, this reinforces the repetition of stereotypical situations and characters that typify the most trite and superficial *telenovelas*. It is not always easy to strike a balance between national interest and international appeal. The most successful soap in Venezuela in the 1990s, *Por estas calles* (Along These Streets), broadcast by Radio Caracas Televisión, serves as an example. It was a portrait of urban life in modern Venezuela, exposing dishonesty, corruption, and immorality at all levels. For Venezuelans, the clinical analysis of their society with all its tensions and conflicts was absorbing, and audiences were huge, yet the series was a failure overseas, presumably because the viewers were unable to relate to the themes covered. Some soap operas are in fact edited in order to provide separate versions for overseas markets, a process that entails removing sections regarded as too specific to Venezuela.

The *telenovela* has become an integral part of life for a huge percentage of the Venezuelan population. The fact that in the 1990s soap operas occupied approximately a quarter of all program time on national television Monday through Saturday testifies to their appeal. No other type of program produced in the country has attracted so much attention or generated so much debate, but mention must be made of other significant shows and broadcasts. As elsewhere, there is a large audience for sports coverage, especially of the major baseball games. There have long been high-quality discussion-based programs, such as *Primer plano* (Close-up), shown on Sundays, in which presenter Marcel Garnier interviews politicians and personalities about a range of social and political issues. Variety shows have always been popular, typified by the long-running *Sábado sensacional* (Sensational Saturday), a program mixing music with other acts, which was presented for many years by Amador Bendayán, and continued throughout the 1990s with other presenters. One variety show that had a particularly significant impact in the 1960s and 1970s was *El show de Renny*, in which the presenter, Renny Ottolina, interposed incisive comments on the state of the nation in the program of entertainment. It soon had a huge following and Ottolina was given a Sunday series as well, a musical show titled *Renny presenta*, which became the first Venezuelan television show to be exported. It made Ottolina a well-known figure in several Latin American countries. He was Venezuela's most respected and admired television personality during those decades, and he used that base to run as a candidate for the presidency. He was killed in a plane crash while campaigning in 1978.

Foreign influence on Venezuelan television, above all that of the United States, has long been a major area of concern among commentators, critics, and politicians. Congressional debates on the issue took place in the 1970s, discussing reforms to strengthen public broadcasting, but no clear policies were implemented as a result. Since then, condemnation of North American cultural domination has continued to be voiced. For some, the implantation of the American model of commercial television, and the propagation of American values, has meant that the prime function of Venezuelan television has been to encourage consumerism and to provide entertainment, with its educational role considerably diminished (Wells, 1972). As to the percentage of foreign programs imported, statistics vary. Some sources argue that, from a very high figure in the 1950s and 1960s, imported programs declined in number in the 1980s and 1990s. Nevertheless, according to one source, in 1991 close to 60% of the programs shown were made outside Venezuela, most of them films or entertainment shows (Ferguson, 1994, 62). Although that includes programs from Europe and elsewhere in Latin America, the considerable majority were from the United States, and the issue is likely to remain contentious for some time to come.

During the closing decade of the twentieth century, Venevisión consolidated its position as Venezuela's biggest television station, with an estimated 50% of the audience, followed by its great rival, Radio Caracas Televisión, which had 30%, and then the other channels, including the state-owned Venezolana de Televisión, sharing the rest (Sinclair, 1999, 83). In addition to the major networks, there were a number of smaller, regional companies. There also were some new, more specialized channels transmitting on UHF, such as CMT (1993), which focuses on cultural programs; Globovisión (1995), which concentrates on news reports twenty-four hours a day; and Puma TV (1996), founded by the singer José Luis "El Puma" Rodríguez, a station dedicated exclusively to popular music and pop videos. Advances in technology mean that numerous channels from all over the world are now available to Venezuelan viewers. Satellite dishes have become a common sight in the large cities, and one satellite system, Direct TV, offers as many as ninety different channels. There are also a number of cable systems available.

The consumer society that emerged from the oil boom has generated a large advertising industry, and the rapid expansion of that industry largely explains the dynamism of television in Venezuela in recent decades. It is perhaps most clearly demonstrated by the international importance of Venevisión and Radio Caracas Televisión, two of the largest exporters of programs in Latin America. Some individuals and groups, such as church organizations, have criticized television companies for being too obsessed with profit, interested only in increasing their ratings and advertising revenue, and neglecting their role as a vehicle for information and education. Seeking a solution, many politicians and intellectuals have argued for the need to reinforce state broadcasting, supported and regulated by new, more vigorous legislation, so that it can provide a wider range of programs as an alternative to the fare offered by the private channels (Hernández Díaz, 1992, 88). Such arguments are likely to continue well into the twenty-first century. Venezuela has the highest per capita access to television of any country in Latin America, and it would be foolish to underestimate the influence the medium has on social attitudes and patterns of behavior within that country.

REFERENCES

Alinsky, Marvin. *Latin American Media: Guidance and Censorship*. Ames: Iowa State University Press, 1981.

Colomina de Rivera, Marta. *El huésped alienante: Un estudio sobre audiencia y efectos de las radio-telenovelas en Venezuela*. Maracaibo: Universidad de Zulia, 1968.

Cortina, Alfredo, *Historia de la radio en Venezuela*. Caracas: Fundarte, 1995.

Enciclopedia temática de Venezuela. Vol. 7, 13–32. Caracas: Venelibros, 1993.

Esteva-Grillet, Roldán. *Medios de comunicación y lucha ideológica en la Venezuela del boom petrolero*. Caracas: Ediciones Metropolitanas, 1990.

Ferguson, James. *In Focus: Venezuela. A Guide to the People, Politics and Culture*. London: LAB, 1994.

Gran enciclopedia de Venezuela. Vol. 8, 283–329. Caracas: Editorial Globe, 1998.

Hernández Díaz, Gustavo. "Situación de la radiotelevisión en Venezuela, para el año 1991." *Anuario inicio*. Vol. 4, 85–104. Caracas: UCV, 1992.

Sinclair, John. *Latin American Television: A Global View*. Oxford: Oxford University Press, 1999.

Vilda, Carmelo. *Proceso de la cultura en Venezuela (1935–85)*. Caracas: Centro Gumilla, 1984.

Wells, Alan. *Picture-Tube Imperialism?: The Impact of U.S. Television on Latin American Television*. Maryknoll, NY: Orbis, 1972.

5

Cinema

ESTABLISHING A VIABLE and stable national film industry in Venezuela has proved to be a long and difficult process, and one that is still continuing today. The Venezuelan cinema has developed spasmodically, constantly oscillating between the notable achievements of certain producers and directors, on the one hand, and the frequent setbacks resulting from adverse economic or political circumstances, on the other. As will be seen in this chapter, films of high quality and considerable critical acclaim have nonetheless emerged, many of them debating vital, and often controversial, national issues.

As in other areas of Venezuelan cultural and artistic life, oil has played a crucial role in defining the nature of national film production. Indeed, many would argue that it has had an even greater impact, both negative and positive, on the nation's cinema than on other forms of artistic expressions. The huge oil revenues have provided successive governments with the means to fund and promote national filmmaking, which has so often had to depend on state support. It is also true, however, that the influx of petrodollars has increased the influence of U.S. culture and lifestyles throughout the country, reflected in the great popularity of the numerous American films that are imported. Venezuelan filmmakers, generally with very limited resources, have found it difficult to compete against the powerful, prosperous and high-tech Hollywood film industry. They have frequently complained that the large corporations which dominate the distribution and showing of films in Venezuela have persistently favored American imports while treating their own films as an inferior product, failing to promote them adequately, consigning them to inferior theaters, and even charging audiences more to see them. As a result, domestic film production has been inhibited, according to many of those involved, and the only solution is to introduce legislation to protect and support the national film industry.

THE EARLY DECADES

Although not as strong or internationally acclaimed as the Argentine, Brazilian, or Mexican cinema, the Venezuelan film industry has an almost equally long history. The first film showing in the country, organized by an entrepreneur named Manuel Trujillo Durán, took place in 1896, the year following the world's first public showing of a motion picture by the Lumière brothers in Paris. In 1897, in Maracaibo, Trujillo Durán showed two documentary shorts he had produced himself, the first films known to have been made in Venezuela. Other documentaries followed, recording carnival in Caracas, for example. Most were financed and strictly controlled by the government of Juan Vicente Gómez. In 1913 the first Venezuelan fiction film was made. Titled *El fusilamiento de Pilar* (The Shooting of Pilar), it was produced by a group of Spanish actors. The authorities confiscated it because they considered it to be disrespectful.

Political and economic obstacles made filmmaking extremely difficult in those early years, but gradual progress was nonetheless made, thanks to the often remarkable efforts of a handful of enthusiastic pioneers. Prominent among them was Amábilis Cordero (1892–1974), who in Barquisimeto produced, directed, filmed, and distributed a series of documentary and fictional films in the 1920s and 1930s. Active at the same time was Edgar Anzola (1893–1981), among whose films was *La trepadora* (The Climber), dating from 1925. Based on a novel by Rómulo Gallegos, it has the distinction of being Venezuela's most successful silent film, as well as the first Venezuelan film to be shown abroad. In 1935 came the country's first sound film: *El milagro del lago* (The Miracle of the Lake), a documentary made by Efraín Gómez. Despite these achievements, however, film production was slow, hampered by the high costs involved. It was mainly foreign films, especially American and French, that were shown as the cinema spread to cities across the country in the first decades of the twentieth century. Indeed, in 1935, 91% of the films projected in Venezuela were from the United States (Marrosa, 1996, 58).

Attempts were made in the 1930s and 1940s to establish private film companies in Venezuela, but their existence was precarious. The relationship between the cinema and the state was significant even at that early stage, for state propaganda and government sponsorship provided filmmakers with their main stable source of income. Efforts to produce films with a strong popular appeal for Venezuelan audiences met with very limited success. Many were sentimental melodramas, modeled on the radio soap operas that attracted large numbers of listeners at the time, but the Venezuelan public showed a marked preference for foreign films, which were generally better produced and technically more sophisticated. Arguably the only Venezuelan film of the 1940s that was of lasting significance was *Juan de la calle* (Juan of the Street), made in 1941 by Rafael Rivero from a script specially written by Rómulo Gallegos. Relating the story of a group of young delinquents, and arguing for reform to rectify the situation, the film was an early example of the cinema of social criticism that would become such a strong current in Venezuela two decades later. Gallegos's keen interest in the cinema led him to found a film company called Estudios Ávila, but it soon failed, overcome by financial problems. Its work was continued, however. An astute businessman, Guillermo Villegas Blanco, bought its assets in 1942 and created Bolívar Films, Venezuela's first financially successful film company.

CONSOLIDATION

The formation of Bolívar Films was a landmark in the development of the Venezuelan cinema. Steadily expanding into an efficient and profitable concern, it put the film industry on a solid commercial footing. It made lucrative publicity shorts, documentaries, and, through government commissions, news and information films. By 1946 it was in a position to produce full-scale feature films. Little attempt was made to express national concerns, however. With profitability the key objective, commercially successful models from abroad were imitated, especially films from Mexico and Argentina, which had the strongest film industries in Latin America in the 1930s and 1940s. Melodrama and comedy were two of the preferred types. Most of the cinematographic techniques employed were imported, as were numerous directors, actors, and technicians, for in a precarious market untapped local talent was more often than not considered too risky. Bolívar Films produced eight feature films between 1949 and 1953, several of which enjoyed significant box office success. Most notable among them was *La balandra Isabel llegó esta tarde* (The Yacht Isabel Arrived This Afternoon), made in 1950, a romantic comedy adapted from a story by Guillermo Meneses and directed by the Argentine Carlos Hugo Christensen. Its photography won an award at Cannes. These were films of light entertainment, often of limited originality, generally with only token reference to the cultural and social realities of the nation. Nevertheless, the commercial viability of the company's activities, combined with the spread of television and the expansion of the advertising industry in Venezuela, stimulated the formation of other film companies in the early 1950s, most of them producing publicity films and documentaries, and providing technical services.

Under these conditions, the cinema began to attract directors interested in developing its capacity as a medium of personal and national expression. Many had considerable experience in radio or in the theater, and some had studied film production abroad. Though varied in their approach and style, they shared a new conception of the cinema. Earlier, with the prevailing concern to create a solid and profitable film industry, it was most frequently the producer who initiated and developed the project, and selected and brought together the necessary personnel to work on it. These new directors were determined to take greater initiative, seeing themselves more as creative artists with the responsibility for developing the full potential of film. The exploration of Venezuelan society, with all its contradictions and inequalities, was an important aspect of their work. César Enríquez Ludert, a director who had studied at the IDHEC (Institut des Haütes Estudes Cinématographiques [Institute of Advance Film Studies]) in Paris, set the pattern in 1960 with *La escalinata* (The Stairway), a film notable for its strong condemnation of the poverty and exploitation suffered by the most deprived sectors of Venezuelan society.

Another product of the Paris Institute, Margot Benacerraf, born in Caracas in 1926, became the first woman to have a lasting impact on the Venezuelan cinema. She demonstrated the full potential of the documentary with two remarkable films: *Reverón* (1952), on the life of the famous Venezuelan painter Armando Reverón, and *Araya* (1958), showing the resilience of a poor coastal community scraping a living from the salt mines and from fishing on the remote Araya Peninsula in the east of the country. *Araya* won the FIPRESCI (The International Federation of Film Critics) Prize at the 1959 Cannes Film Festival. Though a commentary emphasizes the grueling daily routine of a family, working from dawn to dusk, it is not social criticism that dominates the film but the beauty of its presentation, with its dramatic black-and-white photography of land, sea, and salt, and its evocative sounds and songs. Benacerraf refused to compromise with the commercial cinema, and dedicated herself to the development of film as a means to explore national life and culture while remaining sensitive to its aesthetic dimension. Her films have been few, but she has remained an influential figure in the Venezuelan cinema, campaigning for greater support, and founding, in 1966, the Cinemateca Nacional (National Film Library), one of the country's most important film institutions.

Another major cinema career began at the end of the 1950s when Román Chalbaud, arguably Venezuela's best-known director of the century, made his first film, *Caín adolescente* (Adolescent Cain) in 1959. Like some of his later films, it was adapted from a stage play he had written—he already had several years of experience working in the theater, and later worked in television as well. Chalbaud's career therefore highlights the ongoing interaction of the Venezuelan cinema with other cultural and artistic forms. *Caín adolescente* follows the migration of a poor family from the countryside to the slums of Caracas. Few films of the 1950s were as memorable. Most of them, varying in quality, were musicals or comedies meant simply to entertain. The following decade, however, would see the Venezuelan cinema become a major instrument of social exploration, and often denunciation.

CINEMA OF SOCIAL COMMITMENT

The political ferment throughout Latin America in the 1960s provided the context for a cinema of radical social commitment in many countries of the region, and Venezuela was no exception. With the overthrow of the ten-year dictatorship of Pérez Jiménez in 1958, a new era of democratic politics and open debate began, and the Cuban Revolution the following year galvanized political and cultural activity by Venezuela's radical left. Guerrilla armies became active in both the cities and countryside. The short, both documentary and fictional, became the preferred form for Venezuelan moviemakers to record and debate the political struggles of the time. The costs were low, and the universities provided regular and receptive audiences, as well as part of the funding. The shorts that resulted were often highly emotive denunciations of poverty and exploitation, or somewhat ingenuous presentations or protest movements of guerrilla activity, but they represented an important stage of development for the country's cinema. Much was learned about the value of film as an instrument for social investigation and political combat, and such themes continue to form a major current in the Venezuelan cinema. A number of the directors who began their careers with short films, such as Ivork Cordido, César Cortez, and Fernando Toro, went on to make a major contribution to the "new Venezuelan cinema" of the 1970s, the most fertile period of film production the country has had to date.

On the other hand, many of the political films of the 1960s were ephemeral, responding to the conditions of the moment, and attempts to widen their audience among the working classes produced very limited results. The experience of Jacobo Borges, well known as a painter as well as a filmmaker, was typical. Seeking to make cinema more popular and accessible, he took his films to working-class areas of Caracas, where he also held workshops on filmmaking, but the project remained small-scale, carried out in isolation and limited in its influence. Nevertheless, political objectives of this kind produced a number of films of lasting significance. *La paga* (Wages), for example, made in 1962, is a medium-length film about the struggle of rural workers by the Colombian-born director Ciro Durán. Clear in its socialist orientation and produced by a cooperative, it epitomizes the idealism of the period, but because of its questioning tone and aesthetic quality, it is now recognized as a pioneering film that points the way toward the New Latin America Cinema established at the end of the 1960s.

In contrast, the mainstream commercial cinema continued to produce feature films, often with overseas collaboration, that offered nothing new or original. There were the usual romantic comedies, such as the 1965 film *Loco por ellas* (Crazy About Them), directed by Mauricio de la Pedrosa, and dramas like *Acción en Caracas* (Action in Caracas), made in 1966 by Mueller y Xiol, which repeated well-worn plots. These strictly commercial productions contributed little to the development of national filmmaking.

The Venezuelan universities played a major role in the socially oriented cinema. A research project on film at the Universidad Central in Caracas, for example, led to the production of two significant documentary shorts: *La ciudad que nos ve* (The City That Watches Us), from 1966, directed by Jesús Enrique Guédez, focusing on the growing shantytowns of the city, and *Estudio 1* (Studio 1), an experimental film that launched the career of director Julio César Mármol. Most significant of all was the work of the Department of Cinema in the Universidad de los Andes, which from the late 1960s to the mid-1980s produced over one hundred newsreels, documentaries, and feature films. Well equipped and with excellent teachers, it became a major focus for noncommercial film production and experiment. Numerous aspects of Venezuelan cultural, social, and, above all, political life were covered by the new directors who emerged. Donald Myerston's *Renovación* (Renewal), of 1969, documented the struggle for university reform, and Jorge Sole's *T.V. Venezuela*, from the same year, investigated the dependency of Venezuelan television on multinational information networks.

Parallel to this increased level of film production, the 1960s saw the formation of important new organizations that would support the future development of the medium. As already mentioned, in 1966 the Cinemateca Nacional was founded, an institution dedicated to the promotion and exhibition of new films and to research on the cinema. Also in 1966 the annual meetings of filmmakers called Encuentros del Cine began. They became a major forum for the discussion of issues relating to, and problems facing, the cinema. Those who gathered at that first Encuentro, in Ciudad Bolívar in 1966, demanded legislation to protect the national film industry, so that it could compete on a more equal basis with the giant foreign companies whose films continued to dominate the commercial cinemas in Venezuela. It was an issue that would remain at the top of the agenda of filmmakers in the country for many years. A further indication of the increased interest in film that Venezuela experienced in the 1960s, was the founding in 1967 of the country's first magazine dedicated exclusively to the cinema, *Cine al día* (Cinema Now).

The Cuban Revolution of 1959, and the subsequent efforts there to develop a popular, nationalist, and anti-imperialist cinema, was a vital focal point for many Venezuelan filmmakers, as it was for filmmakers all over Latin America. Cuba in the 1960s appeared to be at the forefront of a major movement throughout the developing world that sought radical political change in order to break the economic and cultural dependency of the countries involved. They were years of optimism for those on the radical political left, and for many Venezuelan filmmakers there seemed to be real possibilities of creating within the country the conditions for a national cinema oriented toward social and cultural transformation, in opposition to the U.S. mainstream cinema. They saw their work as closely linked to that of like-minded counterparts elsewhere in Latin America, and there was an important international dimension to Venezuela's cinema of political commitment. Radical filmmakers throughout Latin America, eager to join together to share ideas and experience, formed a continentwide film movement known as the New Latin American Cinema. It was launched in 1967, at the Festival of Latin American Cinema in Viña del Mar, Chile. Venezuelan filmmakers were among the participants at the event, where screenings were followed by roundtables that discussed the ways the cinema could work toward raising political awareness across the region and combating cultural imperialism.

In 1968 the project was continued at another festival in Venezuela. The First Meeting of Latin American Documentary Cinema, held in Mérida and organized by ULA, gave further impetus to documentary film production in the country; and the subsequent work of the Cinema Department at ULA was a direct result. The New Latin American Cinema went on to generate many memorable films and produce critical studies, research work, and manifestos while encouraging debate across national borders. There is no doubt that Venezuelan filmmakers seeking a cinema of national expression benefited considerably from the exchanges with their counterparts from countries where the cinema was particularly dynamic, such as Brazil and Argentina, in addition to Cuba. Many of the ideas and techniques assimilated would put them in good stead as new opportunities for film production opened up in the 1970s.

Before the close of the 1960s two more events took place that would prove significant for the development of the national cinema. In 1968, to celebrate the fourth centenary of the founding of Caracas, a huge exhibition titled "Imagen de Caracas" (Image of Caracas) was opened, sponsored by the city authorities. Over one hundred artists spent two years preparing it, under the direction of Jacobo Borges. Avant-garde film was given a privileged role, with experimental documentaries on city life and striking images of the city's varied architecture, which were blended with painting and photographic exhibitions, music, and theater performances. The whole event highlighted new possibilities for filmmaking, though the City Council closed it after two months because of its high costs. The artists responded with demonstrations in the streets.

By this time, state protection for the national cinema had become the crucial issue for many filmmakers. Film distributors and exhibitors in Venezuela made good profits on the films they imported from the United States, and had little interest in national film production. Filmmakers saw legislation as vital if their work was to be able to compete with foreign films, and petitioning for that was a major objective in the foundation of the National Association of Cinematographic Authors in 1969. It was another important stage in the campaign by filmmakers to obtain ongoing and large-scale state support for their industry. Over the following years, the government responded with a number of ministerial resolutions on a state film policy, but they fell far short of the legislation demanded by filmmakers and, in any case, the principles established were rarely converted into practice.

THE BOOM YEARS

Government financial support and credit provision gave rise to the cinema's most productive period in Venezuela. In 1973, following the Arab-Israeli war, the Organization of Petroleum Exporting Countries, which includes Venezuela, increased the price of a barrel of oil from U.S. $1.76 to U.S.$10.31. As a result, Venezuela's national income rose by 40% and government revenues by 170%. A series of government projects was launched, often lavishly funded, including many in the arts and the media. The debate within the film industry shifted from the issue of protective legislation to the question of government funding. The cinema had advanced steadily over the previous two decades, and there were now significant numbers of experienced and talented directors, plus technical support, ready to take advantage of new opportunities for filmmaking.

Many critics also see 1973 as the beginning of the New Venezuelan Cinema, for it was the year *Cuando quiero llorar no lloro* (When I Want to Cry, I Can't), the film that set the trend, appeared. It was directed by Mauricio Wallerstein, born in Mexico but best known for his work in Venezuela. Based on a novel by Miguel Otero Silva, it follows the story of three young men from different social classes, all named Victorino, who are born on the same day and die on the same day. It criticizes Venezuelan society through contrasts drawn between their experiences of both life and death. The film's combination of social analysis with a high degree of technical quality attracted large audiences. Its success provided the incentive for many other adaptations of literary works over the years that followed, a form of film production that has proved to be particularly fruitful in Venezuela. In 1974 Chalbaud's *La quema de Judas* (The Burning of Judas) was released, focusing on the daily struggles of the marginalized sectors of the city population. Both these films were produced without government support but had considerable box office success, and were heralded by many film critics as signaling a new era of the Venezuelan cinema.

The following years indeed saw a boom in film production, for in 1975 the government began a system of subsidy and credit payment to support it. The state financed twenty-nine feature films between 1975 and 1980 (King, 1990, 157), many of which combined a high degree of aesthetic quality with the exploration of national social and cultural life. Production increased further in the early 1980s. This change was remarkable. Between 1946 and 1970, an average of just over two feature films were produced per year in Venezuela, most privately funded, and from 1971 to 1986 the number reached almost ten a year, the vast majority with state funding (Marrosa, 1996, 52–53). The government also sought to facilitate distribution by stipulating that every exhibitor should show at least twelve Venzeuelan films a year. In fact, most of those produced in the 1970s and early 1980s attracted good audiences anyway, and filmmakers no longer had difficulties in getting their films screened.

Three names stand out in this great period of productivity of the Venezuelan cinema: Román Chalbaud, Mauricio Wallerstein, and Clemente de la Cerda. All had established their reputations as directors in the 1960s, and were among the first to benefit from government support. Chalbaud's *Sagrado y obsceno* (Sacred and Obscene), of 1976, a study of the frustrated guerrilla movement of the 1960s, was the first result. It tells of a former guerrilla who returns to Caracas after an absence of ten years, to hunt down and kill the police chief responsible for the death of some of his former comrades. A commentary on the struggles of the present, complete with humorous characters and dialogue drawn from everyday city life, runs alongside reflections on the struggles of the past. The great strength of Chalbaud is his ability to continue the social themes of the 1960s, frequently conveying acute social criticism, in forms capable of engaging and captivating a wide audience. His 1977 film, *El pez que fuma* (The Smoking Fish), is a notable example. The Smoking Fish is a brothel through which Chalbaud studies the solitude, corruption, and brutality of modern urban life. Though the underworld of crime and prostitution breeds increasing violence, with tragic consequences, the film makes striking use of popular song, dance, and music.

What most characterizes Chalbaud's work is its sympathetic focus on the marginalized sectors of Venezuelan society—prostitutes, petty criminals, disaffected youths, and shantytown dwellers—extolling their resilience in the face of adversity, and exploring their culture as well as their material existence. Like many other directors of the period, Chalbaud is intent on reminding his audience of the conflicts that lie at the heart of Venezuelan society even as oil revenues are modernizing the economy and are producing a huge rise in consumer spending and a construction boom in the cities. *El rebaño de los ángeles* (The Flock of Angels), made in 1978, alternates between two Caracas settings that highlight the problems which blight the lives of so many of its inhabitants from their earliest years: a secondary school, where underfunding and lack of organization generate a series of problems, and the shantytown in which some of the pupils live, where violence and squalor form a part of everyday life. In *La oveja negra* (The Black Sheep), released in 1987, a band of homeless people move into an abandoned ship and develop their own unique style of communal life, resisting all attempts by the police to remove them. A prolific director, Chalbaud was still producing films with the same successful formula in the late 1990s. *Pandemónium*, released in 1997, again explores the poverty, disorder, corruption, and violence of life in modern Caracas, mixing touches of comedy, grotesque scenes, and social comment. Chalbaud has won numerous prizes for his work, both in Venezuela and overseas, and no other Venezuelan filmmaker has earned such international recognition.

The work of Wallerstein also grew out of the cinema of social protest of the 1960s, and in the course of the 1970s, he became the best-known political filmmaker in the country. *Cróncia de un subversivo latinoamericano* (Chronicle of a Latin American Subversive), from 1975, is based on a real event that

Román Chalbaud (center) during the filming of *La oveja negra* in the 1980s. Photo courtesy of Archivo El Nacional.

took place in Venezuela in 1964. It recounts the kidnapping of an American military official by political militants seeking to exchange him for a revolutionary facing execution in Vietnam. *La empresa perdona un momento de locura* (The Company Will Forgive a Moment of Madness), released in 1978, deals with class struggle through the story of a factory worker who has to choose between solidarity with his coworkers and distancing himself from them for the sake of his own social advance and material gain. Wallerstein has since explored further dimensions of social struggle, such as environmental issues and women's rights. *Eva, Julia, Perla* (1980), for example, examines the lives of three sisters frustrated by the suffocating social conventions of middle-class society. Issues of sexuality and sexual relations became an increasingly dominant theme in Wallerstein's later work, as in his 1983 film *Máxima felicidad* (Maximum Happiness), focusing on the complex relationship between a homosexual man, a bisexual youth, and a heterosexual woman.

De la Cerda, who died in 1984, produced ten feature films. He, too, concentrated on the poorest sectors of Venezuelan society, seen as constantly struggling to survive in a hostile environment or trapped in a spiral of crime, violence, and drug addiction. His fourth film, *Soy un delincuente* (I'm a Delinquent), from 1977, made him one of the best-known filmmakers in Latin American. It was more commercially successful in Venezuela than the Hollywood blockbusters *Jaws* and *E.T.*, and broke all box office records in the country (King, 1990, 219). For many critics, it was the long awaited proof that, under the right conditions, national films could compete favorably with foreign imports. Opening with shots of a poverty-stricken shantytown in Caracas, the film follows the effects of the brutalizing environment on a youth who, increasingly involved in crime and drugs, is eventually killed in a shoot-out with police. The protest against social injustice and inequality is driven home at the end of the film when a written statement informs the viewer that revenue from oil sales has risen once again. De la Cerda was a controversial director, accused by some of exploiting sensationalism, but his films are powerful and provocative, raising questions about the underlying tensions and divisions in society. *Campañero de viaje* (Traveling Companion), from 1977, is about a village in the Venezuelan Andes where conflict between a landowner and rural workers leads to violence. In *Los criminales* (The Criminals), released in 1983, social inequality is again emphasized through the story of an upper-class Caracas family visited by a down-and-out intent on pillaging their luxurious home.

Undoubtedly the most memorable and most popular films of the 1970s were explorations of political and criminal violence conveying strong denunciation. Guerrillas and delinquents became the most familiar protagonists on the cinema screen. Many images and thematic elements became repetitive in the extensive series of films that emerged, and the struggles of the characters were often romanticized rather than analyzed critically, but the overall result was a strong body of work that brought unprecedented international recognition to the Venezuelan cinema, and a new solidity and dynamism to its activity. There were also directors who attempted to give new insight into the subject of violence. An example is Enver Cordido's film from 1976, *Compañero Augusto* (Comrade Augusto), which follows the release from prison of an ex-guerrilla, and his inability to settle back into society. It is notable for its psychological analysis of the character, who, finding it impossible to come to terms with his lost ideals, descends into increasing cynicism. *País portátil* (Portable Country), a 1977 film directed by Ivan Feo and Antonio Llerandi, is one of the most powerful films made about Venezuela's political conflicts, deep in its analysis and broad in perspective. Another adaptation of a literary work—this time by the novelist Adriano González

León—it relates the guerrilla battles of the 1960s to earlier periods of violence and oppression in Venezuelan history.

Despite the large number produced during these years, Venezuelan films still constituted only 3% of those shown in the country between 1976 and 1985. The fact, however, that in that period an average of two Venezuelan productions each year were among the ten most watched films is testimony to the popularity the national cinema had achieved (Martínez, 1996, 73). Social themes continued to prevail, and as authoritarian regimes curtailed freedom of expression in Brazil, Argentina, and Chile, the Venezuelan cinema gained importance in the region as an outlet for political criticism and controversial issues. There is no doubt that this oppositional character—the belief that critical social inquiry is a major function of film—has produced some of the most memorable work by Venezuelan directors. Inevitably, some moments of tension have resulted between filmmakers and the state, their main sponsor. The most notorious example occurred in 1981, with Luis Correa's documentary *Ledezma, el caso Mamera* (Ledezma, the Mamera Case), which not only investigated a highly sensitive case of police corruption but also exposed the attempts made by the authorities to prevent the production of the film. Correa was imprisoned and the film was banned; however, when the matter was taken to court, the director won.

It is important to recognize the differences between the social films of the 1970s and 1980s and the highly political work produced in the 1960s. Anxious to avoid a dogmatic approach and produce films of wide appeal, directors sought new forms through which to tackle issues of national concern. Humor, for example, is used in films such as *Canción mansa para un pueblo bravo* (A Gentle Song for an Angry People), dating from 1976, by Giancarlo Carrer. It looks at the question of rural migration by telling the story of a young man from the interior who goes to the city in search of work, only to experience a series of misfortunes and end up making a living from crime. *(Alias) El rey del Joropo* (Alias the King of Joropo), produced in 1977 by Carlos Rebolledo and Thaelman Urguelles, makes use of the vitality of Venezuelan popular culture. Looking at the life of a well-known Venezuelan dancer (but also a criminal) of the 1950s, Alfredo Alvarado, it highlights contradictions that exist in the relationship between forms of popular expression, represented by Alvarado's world of music and dance, and the expanding mass media, represented by the television corporation that hires him and then decides he is unsuitable for the image required. Alvarado wants to be recorded in the program as a human being, and objects to the sensationalism with which he is portrayed.

It was not only the production of feature films that boomed during this period. A number of directors continued with more experimental work, often filming in Super 8, a low-cost type of film preferred by many amateur filmmakers. Best known of those working in this area is Diego Rísquez, whose ability to create maximum effect from scant resources has made his work extremely influential. Instead of dialogues and plots, Rísquez relies on visual impact and dramatic music. He uses *tableaux vivants* (staged scenes where actors neither speak nor move) in his films to evoke moments of the country's past, and he invariably relies on nonprofessional actors. His Super 8 productions were later blown up to 35mm for wider distribution. *Bolívar, sinfonía tropikal* (Bolivar, Tropical Symphony), from 1980, investigates the inconography of Venezuela's independence leader through an allegory of his life and dreams, and Risquez's 1984 film, *Orinoko—nuevo mundo* (Orinoco—New World)) narrates a mythical journey along the river that serves as an allegory for the history of Venezuela.

The expansion of the national cinema led the government to create the Fundo de Fomento Cinematográfico (Cinematic Development Fund; FOCINE), a new agency through which to channel state support. It began its work in 1981 and became the chief government organization through which credit was offered to filmmakers (though now state funding was mixed with private funding). Other ways of encouraging national film production were also sought, such as permitting filmmakers to import equipment at a favorable rate of exchange for the dollar. Most notable, however, were the measures introduced to deal with the country's cinema chains, which generally favored the more profitable foreign films over national productions. Initially, a percentage taken from box office receipts was distributed to local filmmakers by FOCINE. The funds acquired were limited, however, because the government had frozen cinema ticket prices for many years. In 1984 the policy was changed. An increase in ticket prices was approved on the condition that the exhibitors pay 6.6% of their profits from foreign films to the government; the money would be used, via FOCINE, to finance national films. At the same time, exhibitors would receive an extra 6.6% of box office receipts for showing Venezuelan productions.

The work of FOCINE appears to have had some effect, for national film production increased still further after 1981. An average of twelve films a year were made from 1981 to 1986, with a notable widening of thematic content as directors attempted to deal with new aspects of human experience. Against the background of the rapid urbanization that Venezuela had experienced in recent decades, and the urban problems that had resulted, a number of films examined issues of alienation and the failure of human communication. *Agonía* (Agony), a 1985 film by José Novoa, for example, studies the marriage of a wealthy couple that gradually disintegrates as their lives become increasingly empty and devoid of meaning, and *Reflejos* (Reflections), by César Bolívar, made in 1988, follows the story of a group of people who attempt to overcome their feelings of alienation by receiving therapy at a psychiatric center.

THE GROWING INVOLVEMENT OF WOMEN

Until the 1970s, the participation of women filmmakers was very limited in Venezuela, but it increased significantly as a result of the expanding opportunities for film production in that decade. Two women in particular made their mark: Solveig Hoogesteijn and Fina Torres. Heralded as two of Venezuela's most talented new directors of the period, their work introduced new themes and prioritized the point of view of the female characters.

Having begun with documentaries in the 1970s, Hoogesteijn (b. 1946) went on to produce full-length feature films in the following decade, most notably *Macu, la mujer del policía* (Macu, the Policeman's Wife), dating from 1987, which was well received by critics and public alike. In fact, it became the biggest box office success the Venezuelan cinema had produced until then, shooting Hoogesteijn to prominence. Based on a real event—the Ledezma case mentioned earlier—it highlights the degradation suffered by a twelve-year-old girl who marries a policeman and comes face-to-face with a hostile world of police corruption, machismo in its most acute forms, and the abuse of power by the authorities. It is a disturbing film in which all the participants are shown to share a degree of responsibility for events. Macu, however, grows in strength as she comes to an understanding of the abuse and oppression she has suffered.

It is not only women's issues and experiences that characterize Hoogesteijn's films, however. The cultural and social contrasts of modern Venezuela also are clearly a major concern. For some critics, her own experience—she was born in Venezuela of a European immigrant family—helps to explain her sensitivity to such matters (Kringer and Portela, 1997, 461). It is clearly evident in her 1996 film *Santera*, which relates the story of a black woman from the coast who has obtained supernatural powers through her practice of Afro-Venezuelan spirit worship. When she is arrested and accused of using her "witchcraft" to commit murder, a white woman doctor from middle-class Caracas attempts to prove her innocence. Through the contrasts drawn between social classes, and between the urban and the rural, the two different worlds of the women are brought into direct confrontation.

Hirma Salcedo (left) and Laura del Sol, principal actresses in Solveig Hoogesteijn's 1996 film, *Santera*, during a break in filming. Photo by Rafael Salvatore. Courtesy of CNAC.

Fina Torres (b. 1951) established her reputation with *Oriana*, a sensual and evocative film focusing on the repressed desires of women. Highly acclaimed for its originality, it won a prize at the Cannes Film Festival of 1985, the year it was released. It recounts how María returns to Venezuela to sell the house she has inherited from her aunt Oriana. The approach is unusual, for, unlike the vast majority of Venezuelan films made until then, it is the interior world of the characters that predominates rather than the social world. The past, highlighting women's resistance to the oppressive social and sexual conventions imposed by the patriarchal order, is reconstructed through the memories of the protagonist. Torres's second film, *Mecánicas celestes* (Celestial Mechanics), appeared in 1994 and was favorably received by critics. A lighthearted look at Latin Americans living in Europe, it tells of a young woman's escape from a life of routine and drudgery in Venezuela. Ana suddenly decides to stand up her fiancé at the church on the day of their wedding, and sets off for Paris to pursue her singing career. There she has various adventures before finally achieving both success and happiness. Reference to Venezuelan social and cultural reality is minimal in the film, for Torres made a conscious decision to break with the tradition of social commitment that had dominated the Venezuelan cinema for decades. Her objectives contrast with the combative style of Hoogesteijn, but the success of both directors gave women's concerns unprecedented prominence in the Venezuelan cinema, and provided much encouragement for other women filmmakers.

THE 1980s AND 1990s

The vulnerability of the cinema's dependence on the state became clear in the late 1980s, when severe economic difficulties, aggravated by a fall in oil prices, led to cutbacks in government spending. The cinema was inevitably affected. The credit offered by FOCINE continued, though it was significantly reduced. Whereas fifteen feature films had been made in 1985, only three were produced in 1988. As the industry gradually began to stabilize again in the 1990s, the question of film funding was debated again. Many argue that more private financing must be encouraged, and others see coproductions as offering a solution, believing that under present conditions very few national cinemas can continue to be economically viable by themselves. Nevertheless, it is clear that much of the responsibility for the survival of the Venezuelan film industry will reside with the state. The limitations of the national market and the distribution monopoly still held by the giant Hollywood concerns make the film business a risky proposition for private investors. Recognizing this, a new government-sponsored agency was launched in 1994, to help revitalize film production after the years of economic difficulty. The Centro Nacional Autónoma de Cinematografía (Autonomous National Cinematographic Center; CNAC) sought a new approach to funding. Instead of direct subsidies or loans, it sought to link state finance to private funding or coproductions with foreign firms, and to attempt to recover the capital it invested in a film by taking a percentage of the income it made. Gradually, film production did recover, and between 1994 and 1997 CNAC cofinanced twenty-six feature films and twenty shorts.

The new generation of directors tended to move away from the well-worn studies of social marginality, and films of the 1990s were characterized by their diversity of theme. Comedies became popular, typified by Alejandro Saderman's 1998 film *Cien años de perdón* (100 Years of Forgiveness), a humorous investigation of the much debated question of corruption that relates how four middle-class friends, feeling the effects of Venezuela's economic crisis, decide to rob a bank. Other filmmakers turned to the thriller, one of the best examples being Fernando Venturini's *Tres noches* (Three

Fernando Venturini directs his 1997 film *Tres noches*. Photo by Lisbeth Salas. Courtesy of CNAC.

Nights), of 1998, in which the murder of a gangster leads the investigating detective into the dangerous world of drug trafficking. Venturini was one of several new directors oriented toward issues of concern to youth. Other notable examples were Carlos Oteyza, who produced two powerful ecological films; Gustavo Balza, whose 1998 film *El valle* (The Valley) examines the moral conflicts that arise from a teenage pregnancy; and Mariana Rondón, whose work explored human relationships under strain, eroded by misunderstanding and failed communication.

The most common criticism of Venezuelan films of the 1980s and 1990s was that too much emphasis was placed on technical and formal quality, at the expense of argument and thematic content. The country was experiencing its most serious economic, political, and social crisis for many decades, but relatively few filmmakers examined the consequences in their work. The desire to break with earlier tradition and the pressure to make commercially viable films help to explain this move away from a cinema of social exploration.

There were, however, notable exceptions. Carlos Azpúrua is perhaps the best representative of filmmakers who explored overtly political topics in the period. In the 1980s he made several documentaries on sensitive social prob-

Scene from Fernando Venturini's 1997 film *Tres noches*. Photo by Lisbeth Salas. Courtesy of CNAC.

lems, such as the destruction of the Amazon rain forest and of the indigenous peoples that inhabit it, and the question of press censorship. His first feature film, *Disparen a matar* (Shoot to Kill), was released in 1991; confronting the issue of human rights violated because of official corruption, it became one of the most talked-about films of the period. The winner of eleven national and international prizes, it deals with the killing of an innocent man by the police, and the efforts made by his mother to break through the official cover-up that follows. Azpúrua's next film, *Amaneció de golpe* (Day of the Coup), of 1997, set against the background of the first of the attempted coups d'états of 1992, had an equally dramatic impact on the Venezuelan public. It narrates the stories of four different sets of people, whose experiences expose the social injustices afflicting the country, as they live through the political drama of the moment.

The films that investigated the problems confronting the nation tended to attract large audiences and considerable critical attention. It is significant that the most talked-about film of 1999 was the hard-hitting *Huelepega, ley de la calle* (Glue-sniffing, the Law of the Street), by Elia Schneider, which, following the fortunes of homeless street children condemned to a world of violent crime and substance abuse, deals with one of the most distressing social ills of the time. Arguably the most acclaimed director in the 1990s was Luis Alberto Lamata, whose work sought new ways of examining the country's cultural formation, focusing particularly on the role played by the conflicts and legends of Venezuela's past. He won numerous international prizes for his films exploring the struggles of individuals during critical moments of the nation's turbulent history, most notably *Desnudo con naranjas* (Nude with Oranges), of 1995, in which an art collector's search for a painting takes us back to a period of civil war that provides the setting for an extraordinary love story.

For many critics, however, it is the documentary cinema that has produced the films of highest and most consistent quality in Venezuela. The firm foundations laid in the 1960s—when the desire to use film as a means of radical critical inquiry, combined with a greater degree of technical awareness and artistic awareness, produced many striking results—were steadily built upon in the decades that followed. Given the near impossibility of screening them in mainstream cinemas, or of showing them on television, the number of documentaries produced has been remarkable. Many of them are part of the prolific output of such directors as Jesús Enrique Guédez and Manuel de Pedro, whose numerous films examining living conditions, social conflicts, and cultural expression in various regions of the country are both investigative journalism and a historical record.

As with fiction films, themes became ever more diversified in the documentaries of the 1980s and 1990s. Carlos Oteyza, for example, examined the behavior of wealthy Venezuelans holidaying in the United States in his 1981 film *Mayami nuestro* (Our Miami). Sexual orientation and behavior was covered in documentaries such as *Trans* (Transvestites), made in 1982 by Manuel Herreros and Mateo Manaure, and the fight for women's rights in Venezuela was traced by Mónica Henríquez's *Crónicas ginecológicas* (Gynecological Chronicles), of 1992. Recording the experiences of the poorest and most marginalized sectors of Venezuelan society—increasingly numerous as economic problems mounted—continued to be a prime objective for many documentary filmmakers, but there was a noticeable shift away from the forthright condemnation of their suffering that prevailed in the films of the 1960s and 1970s, to an emphasis on their creativity and resilience. Jacobo Penzo became the major representative of that approach, leading the way with films such as *El afinque de Marín* (Music Sessions in Marín), made in 1979, in which Caracas shantytown dwellers find fulfillment and pride through their music.

At the close of the century, the Venezuelan film industry remained fragile, with the question of distribution outlets still problematical and funding still precarious. Only a minority of Venezuelan films earned enough at the box office to cover the investment made in them. Nevertheless, considerable development had taken place, especially through state promotion, since the 1970s. Today the country has good facilities for film production and continues to seek alternative strategies for financing it. Directors have demonstrated that, given the opportunities, they can produce work of high quality, on a par with the best films of any other Latin American cinema.

REFERENCES

Acosta, José Miguel, et al. *Panorama histórico del cine en Venezuela, 1896–1993*. Caracas: Cinemateca Nacional, 1997.

Aguirre, Jesús M., and Marcelino Bisbal. *El nuevo cine venezolano*. Caracas: Ateneo de Caracas, 1980.

Izaguirre, Rodolfo. *Cine venezolono: Largometrajes*. Caracas: Cinemateca Nacional, 1983.

King, John. *Magic Reels*. London: Verso, 1990.

Kringer, Clara, and Alejandro Portela. *Cine latinoamericano*. Vol. 1, *Diccionario de realizadores*. Buenos Aires: Jilguero, 1997.

Marrosa, Ambretta. "Cine en Venezuela." Part 1 in *Encuadre* 59 (1996): 55–65. Part 2 in *Encuadre* 60 (1996): 47–57.

Martínez, P. *Cronología del cine venezolano*. Caracas: Cinemateca Nacional, 1996.

Miranda, Julio E. *Palabras sobre imágenes: 30 años de cine venezolano*. Caracas: Monte Ávila, 1994.

Newman, Kathleen, ed. *Latin American Cinema-Le Cinéma latino-americain*. Bloomington: Indiana University Press, 1994.

Trujillo, Antonio D. *La censura cinematográfica en Venezuela*. Mérida: ULA, 1988.

Zambrano, Ivan. *Cine venezolano: Cortometrajes*. Caracas: Cinemateca Nacional, 1984.

6

Literature

VENEZUELAN LITERATURE has not received the international recognition, or even the attention, that has been accorded to that of other major Latin American countries. In part this is explained by the fact that in the 1960s, when the "Boom" propelled Latin American fiction onto the world stage and saw it gain unprecedented international acclaim, Venezuelan literature remained on the margins of the phenomenon. None of its writers attained the world celebrity achieved, for example, by Colombia's Gabriel García Márquez, Argentina's Julio Cortázar, and Mario Vargas Llosa of Peru. Writing in their countries, and in some others, continued to enjoy a high profile worldwide for decades afterward because of the critical and commercial success provided by the Boom. The attention of international critics and readers was uneven, however, and Venezuelan literature enjoyed little of the limelight. The situation has been slow to change. Nonetheless, work of outstanding quality has been written; and several writers, such as Rómulo Gallegos, Guillermo Meneses, and Arturo Uslar Pietri, have rightly won praise abroad and have become major figures in Hispanic literature. It is also true that Venezuela, though not prominent at the time of the Boom, has had a major impact on Latin American literature at other times in its history.

For most literary historians, the independence movement at the beginning of the nineteenth century generated the first significant works of literature in Venezuela, with the pre–Hispanic and colonial periods that preceded it generally considered devoid of worthwhile literary production. It is undoubtedly true that pre–Hispanic Venezuela, comprised of scattered, nomadic indigenous communities, did not produce a rich body of literature comparable with that of the Maya or Inca societies, and that the writing of colonial Venezuela, for much of its history a neglected backwater of the Spanish Empire, did not match in either quantity or quality that of Spain's major centers in the Americas: Colombia, Mexico, and Peru. That does not mean, however, that pre–Independence literature can simply be discounted. The various indigenous groups in Venezuela, for example, expressed their vision of the world and explained their history through their oral tradition, with myths, stories, poetry, and legends whose value has only belatedly been recognized. For centuries they were dismissed as primitive or puerile expressions unworthy of the attention of literary scholars, and it was not until the 1920s and 1930s that research into indigenous oral forms, and their transcription into Spanish, were taken seriously, a change in which missionaries played a major role. Later decades saw the publication of many collections of literature from such indigenous groups as the Warao, the Guajiro, and the Pemón.

As in other parts of Spanish America, the first works written in colonial Venezuela were chronicles recording the geography and social life of the region, and the imposition of Spanish domination over it. Generally written in a highly florid baroque style, their main interest today lies in their historical value rather than their literary qualities. The best-known example, dating from 1723, is *Historia de la conquista y población de la provincia de Venezuela* (History of the Conquest and Population of the Province of Venezuela), by José de Oviedo y Baños, which stands out because it conveys its detailed historical narrative through lucid yet colorful prose. Other genres had very little impact. Documents from the colonial era frequently refer to poetry and plays written at the time, often produced for formal ceremonial occasions, but no outstanding names emerged.

This somewhat barren period was brought to an end by the fight for independence from Spain. In an atmosphere of growing rebellion, a new generation of political activists and intellectuals emerged who were imbued with the ideals of the European Enlightenment. They laid the basis for the literary culture of the new republic that eventually emerged. Since the writing they produced had clearly defined practical aims—seeking to raise awareness, educate, and argue a cause—the preferred forms were the essay, the treatise, letters, and speeches. Those written by Simón Bolívar (1783–1830) were among the finest. His major works, such as *Manifiesto de Cartagena* (Cartagena Manifesto), of 1812, and the *Carta de Jamaica* (Letter from Jamaica), from 1815, are among Latin America's most important political statements of the era. However, Simón Rodríguez (1771–1854) was perhaps the most original of those voices. A revolutionary, utopian thinker on a wide range of matters, for a time he served as Bolívar's tutor, and education was his main concern. He proposed radical educational reform in order to provide a state system of education that could lead to the transformation of society. He spent much of his life in poverty and insecurity, traveling through Europe and South America. Only a small percentage of his writing was published, such as *Sociedades americanas* (American Societies), produced in various versions between 1828 and 1842, and *Defensa de Bolívar* (Defense of Bolívar), in 1830.

ANDRÉS BELLO

Given that most of the writing of the time was produced in response to monumental political upheaval, it is not surprising that creative literature was consigned to a secondary role. When it was written, poetry was the preferred genre, particularly in the 1820s, when it was used to extol the virtues of America and its peoples in the wake of independence. Its main exponent, Andrés Bello (1781–1865), is recognized not only as the principal founder figure of Venezuelan literature but also as one of the most influential intellectuals in nineteenth-century Latin American culture.

Although born in Caracas, Bello lived most of his life in England and Chile, and his most important writing was published in those two countries. The breadth of his intellectual activity is extraordinary. He wrote articles on philosophy, history, the sciences, and the arts; published poetry and major studies on linguistics; and, as an expert on jurisprudence, wrote Chile's Civil Code, which was copied by several other countries of Latin America. During his professional life, he worked as a journal editor, a university rector, held government and diplomatic posts, and served as a senator in Chile.

Bello was a committed supporter of the independence cause, but he had no desire for military or political leadership within it. He sought to look beyond the immediate conflicts of the day, to the longer-term struggle for literary and cultural independence for Spanish America. That was a key theme within his poetry, which, though strongly influenced in form by the great classical writers Virgil and Horace, looks to America for its thematic content. In "Alocución a la poesía" (Address to Poetry), published in a London journal in 1823, he celebrates the geography and history of the region, and its newly won freedom. It is in America, the poem argues, that literature must seek inspiration, not in Europe. The unique and awe-inspiring natural environment of the New World can provide artistic regeneration. This idea is continued in Bello's best-known poem, "Silva a la agricultura de la zona tórrida" (Ode to the Agriculture of the Torrid Zone), of 1826, which praises the fertility of tropical America, and presents life in the countryside and work on the land as the basis for true liberty, prosperity, and spiritual well-being. This, of course, is a poetry of Romantic inspiration, but it is expressed in neoclassical style. Bello's lifetime covered the transition from neoclassicism to Romanticism in Latin America, and the way his poetry brings together the two contrasting tendencies is one of the most striking features of his work. He was a craftsman who worked meticulously at his writing, and few other writers of the period could match the power of his descriptive poetry.

Bello also excelled in other disciplines. He produced some outstanding translations and some important literary criticism. His highly original studies on language culminated in a book that virtually revolutionized the field, *Gramática de la lengua castellana destinada al uso de los americanos* (Grammar of the Spanish Language for the Use of Latin Americans), published in 1847. Many of Bello's views on politics and culture were cautious and conservative, and he faced frequent criticism from more radical intellectuals of the period. They were angered, for example, by his concern to identify positive aspects of the Spanish cultural legacy in America, which they so fervently rejected. Bello believed that Latin America's cultural development was best served by cultivating links with the classical traditions of European civilization, yet he worked tirelessly to promote an independent Spanish American literature existing in its own right, no longer just an adjunct of Iberian culture. It was a task that would be taken up by later generations of writers throughout Latin America, many of whom acknowledged the influence of Bello's work.

THE NINETEENTH CENTURY

Romanticism dominated Latin American literature for much of the nineteenth century, but it was slow to exert its full impact in Venezuela. One reason was the long-lasting influence of neoclassicism, which, emphasizing restraint, balance, and harmony, served to delay the advance of romantic writing with its very different values of sentimentality, passion, and individual inspiration. The social and political conditions prevailing in the country also played their part. The eleven-year war of independence, which ended in 1821, was followed by decades of political strife that at times exploded into civil war. As a result, many writers continued to concentrate on the discussion of national political realities, curbing their literary creativity and invention.

The political and cultural developments of Venezuela after independence are clearly embodied in the work of its major writers. Most cultivated a variety of genres—combining, for example, poetry or narrative fiction with political and historical studies—that reflected the diversity of their professional careers, which often embraced journalism, scholarship, politics, and public office as well as literature. Fermín Toro (1807–1865) is one of the most representative writers of the period. He wrote poetry, several works of political thought, and articles on such disparate topics as botany, geology, philosophy, history, and linguistics. Arguably his best-known work is *Los mártires* (The Martyrs), published in 1842, which is regarded by some literary historians as Venezuela's first novel. Denouncing the poverty Toro saw in London, albeit with excessive sentimentality, it presages the narratives of social protest that, many decades later, became so prevalent in Latin America. Toro was also one of the founders of *costumbrismo* in the country. This form, consisting of short prose sketches recording daily life and customs, thrived in nineteenth-century Venezuela, perhaps because it permitted writers to develop their penchant for fiction while focusing firmly on national reality.

Costumbrismo represents an important phase in the development of Venezuelan literature. Its texts are brief and often superficial, and are extremely limited in terms of literary technique. However, as the most popular form of prose fiction of the time, they played a valuable role documenting and discussing the political and social changes taking place in the new republic. They also paved the way for the more sophisticated forms of narrative that emerged later and debated the problems facing the nation in much greater depth. The list of Venezuelan *costumbrista* writers is extensive, but arguably the form attained its maximum expression in the work of David Mendoza (1823–1867), who gave particularly incisive insight into the customs of the day, both in the city and in the rural interior. His essays were characterized by social criticism, a major ingredient in the best *costumbrista* texts. For all its limitations, *costumbrismo* was a durable form of writing, for it remained vigorous until the last decades of the nineteenth century, when it was gradually superseded by the novel.

While *costumbrismo* flourished, romanticism was making gradual advances in Venezuelan letters, though it still encountered resistance from some prominent writers who staunchly defended neoclassical principles. Most notable among them was Rafael María Baralt (1810–1860), who, having settled in Madrid in 1843, became a literary celebrity with an international reputation, and was the first Latin American to be elected a member of the Spanish Royal Academy. He advocated the need to retain the purity of the Spanish language, to give pride of place to formal elegance in writing, and to combat what he perceived to be the extravagance and effusiveness of Romanticism. Those conservative beliefs were put into practice in his own poetry and prose. Of the writers who actively sought to propagate the ideas and values of romanticism, Juan Vicente González (1810–1866) stands out. His writing on history is significantly different from that of Baralt. Instead of precision and propriety in the narration of events, González concerns himself with atmosphere, sentiment, and drama. His major work, *Biografía de José Félix Ribas* (Biography of José Félix Ribas), of 1858, which focuses on one of the heroes of independence in order to capture the epic struggle against the Spanish, fuses historical study with literary creativity. All his writing was characterized by a lyrical, romantic style. Individualistic, freethinking, and rebellious, González epitomized the romantic temperament.

Relatively little of Venezuela's romantic writing is as memorable as that of González. Much of it slavishly copied French or Spanish models, and both poetry and prose frequently suffered from artificiality, excessive sentimentality, and superficial exoticism. The finest romantic works were produced in the closing decades of the nineteenth century, represented by the prose of Eduardo Blanco (1839–1912) and the poetry of José Antonio Pérez Bonalde (1846–1892). Blanco was a prolific writer. His best-known novel is *Zárate*, published in 1882, which narrates the story of a bandit in colorful, grandiloquent language. For some critics it represents an important landmark in national literature, for they consider it to be the first fully Venezuelan novel in terms of theme, action, characters, and atmosphere. However, it was for his 1881 study of the wars of independence, *Venezuela heroica* (Heroic Venezuela), that he achieved lasting fame. The book, which exalts the events narrated to give them epic grandeur, was regularly taught in Venezuelan schools throughout much of the twentieth century. Pérez Bonalde is widely acknowledged as Venezuela's most talented Romantic writer. His combination of sincerity of expression and sensitivity to language distinguishes him from other poets of the period. The sadness that dominated his life—much of which he spent in political exile, afflicted by broken health—is powerfully conveyed in much of his work, exemplified by "Flor," a moving poem about the death of his daughter. The echoes of Romanticism would continue to be heard well into the twentieth century, but at the time of Pérez Bonalde's death in 1892, Venezuelan writing was already seeking new directions, influenced by a wave of new ideas about literary creativity.

Two authors illustrate the new tendencies emerging. Manuel Vicente Romero García (1865–1917) and Gonzalo Picón Febres (1860–1918) both show vestiges of romanticism in their work, but the influence of realism and naturalism is far stronger, and faithfully portraying Venezuelan society is a major objective of their writing. The plot of Romero García's *Peonía*, of 1890, which tells of a love affair tragically doomed to destruction, is clearly based on earlier romantic models, but the naturalistic depiction of rural life and the work's political satire are its salient features. Central to the narrative is the conflict between enlightened progress, on the one hand, and backwardness, on the other; this theme would recur in many subsequent Venezuelan novels. The description of regional environment, customs, and characters, and the inclusion of local colloquialisms, mark the work as an early example of *criollismo*, a term that refers to literature which seeks to affirm national identity by emphasizing distinctly Venezuelan geographical, social, and cultural characteristics. Picón Febres, best known for his 1899 novel *El sargento Felipe* (Sergeant Felipe), condemning the civil wars that frequently wreaked havoc throughout the country in the nineteenth century, demonstrates the same concern to highlight national customs and environment, and the same employment of realist elements in much of his writing.

Among the new influences at the end of the nineteenth century, none had a greater impact in Venezuela than *modernismo* (modernism), which renovated literature across virtually the whole of Latin America. Arguing that art had value in its own right, for the creation of beauty was a supreme human achievement, it stressed formal and technical perfection in writing, with particular attention given to symbolism, imagery, and musicality. In fact, *modernismo* assimilated elements from a variety of sources. Its cosmopolitanism and elitism would appear, at face value, to be at odds with the *criollismo* being pursued by many Venezuelan writers. There were certainly some who turned their backs on national realities to concentrate on matters of form, but the majority sought to combine modernist formal innovations with their own social and political concerns. As a result, Venezuelan *modernismo* produced texts of considerable thematic diversity. It also produced its most memorable expressions in prose, whereas throughout most of Latin America it was modernist poetry that predominated. Two literary journals, *El Cojo Ilustrado* (The Enlightened Cripple) (1892–1915) and *Cosmópolis* (Cosmopolitan City) (1894–1895)—widely considered to be the two most significant in Venezuelan literary history—played a major role in diffusing the work of the writers of the period, both established and emerging. All the major modernist authors published in them at one time or another. The eclecticism of the journals was one of their main strengths, however, and all aesthetic tendencies were represented.

Manuel Díaz Rodríguez (1871–1927) was the outstanding figure of Venezuelan *modernismo*. He published his first stories, of which the refined poetic language is the most striking feature, in *El Cojo Ilustrado* in the 1890s. He went on to write three novels that brought him international recognition. The first, which dates from 1901, was *Ídolos rotos* (Broken Idols), which conveys a satirical and pessimistic view of Venezuelan society. Alberto, a young sculptor, lives and studies in Paris, where he receives acclaim for his work. He is required to return home to Venezuela for family reasons, and the novel recounts how his lofty ambitions and ideals are frustrated in a country where political instability seems endemic, and the culture of the privileged classes is narrow, pretentious, and superficial. The "broken idols" are his sculptures, which are smashed by soldiers following a military take-over, after which Alberto resolves to abandon Venezuela for good. It is impossible, it appears, for the refined, elitist ideals of artistic creativity that he espouses to be realized in such an environment. Díaz Rodríguez's reputation was established upon his polished, elegant prose style, though for some critics his aesthetic concerns so predominated that plot and characterization suffered as a consequence.

Several of the most talented writers who began their careers under the influence of *modernismo* soon moved away from its cultivation of formal and technical excellence, and were drawn into the examination of national political and social issues. Modernism's renovation of literary language enriched many of the *criollista* novels that resulted. Rufino Blanco Fombona (1874–1944), for example, began as a modernist poet but went on to write prose of political protest. The experience of living in perpetual conflict with dictatorial regimes in Venezuela led him to see literature as a weapon with which to attack corruption and authoritarianism. The bitter and cynical view of early twentieth-century Venezuelan society that is conveyed in his work contrasts with that of Luis Manuel Urbaneja Achelpohl (1875–1937), who sought to highlight positive qualities in national culture and customs. Most of his short stories and novels focus on rural life, and are replete with colorful details of regional traditions. Despite some traces of his early modernism, realism comes to prevail in his writing. Like Blanco Fombona, Urbaneja reacted against certain aspects of modernist aesthetics. Too often, preciosity and pretentiousness were felt to have taken precedence, with preoccupations about form relegating thematic content to secondary consideration. With the country still struggling to find political stability, modernize the economy, and achieve a sense of national cultural identity, the analysis of all aspects of Venezuelan life was paramount. That task was the prime objective of the generation of novelists who dominated Venezuelan literature in the first half of the twentieth century. With them, the reaction against *modernismo* was completed and realism was consolidated as the dominant literary current.

JOSÉ RAFAEL POCATERRA

An uncompromising social critic, Pocaterra (1888–1955) wrote works of caustic satire and vehement denunciation. Virtually all his writing was motivated by the desire to expose the harsh realities he identified in Venezuelan society: oppressive and corrupt dictatorial regimes; unscrupulous dominant classes; a middle class that was still small, weak, and largely ineffectual; and poverty-stricken masses suffering callous exploitation. His bitter and pessimistic vision of his country is understandable, given his own experience of the political conditions of the period. He was twice imprisoned for his opposition to dictatorship, and was obliged to spend over a decade in exile. One of his novels, *La casa de los Ábila* (The House of the Abilas), was produced in the early 1920s while he was in prison—on cigarette paper, written with a pencil stub. To document his environment and the lives of the various social classes within it, Pocaterra employed a stark, unembellished narrative style drawn from European realism and naturalism. His break with the modernists' aesthetic approach to literature was emphatic.

Pocaterra received most praise as a short story writer, and the collection he published in 1922, *Cuentos grotescos* (Grotesque Stories), critically examining a wide range of social and cultural characteristics in vigorous, direct prose, did much to inject new life into the genre in Venezuela. He also produced a powerful testimony, *Memorias de un venezolano de la decadencia* (A Venezuelan's Memoirs of the Period of Decadence), recording the oppression, torture, and imprisonment suffered by opponents of the Gómez dictatorship. Of his novels, arguably the one that most successfully combines all his attributes as a writer is *Vidas oscuras* (Dark Lives), of 1916, which contrasts the fortunes of two brothers. The ruination of Crisóstomo, an honest cattle rancher, and the success enjoyed by the opportunistic and manipulative politician, Juan Antonio, dramatically represent the decline of the old agricultural order of the interior, and the rise of modern, and more unethical, forms of commerce and social behavior in the cities. In a society dominated by false values, hypocrisy and greed triumph. Pocaterra's powers of description, convincing dialogue, and incisive satire are at their best in this work. At times his portrayal of characters and social situations in his novels is oversimplified or exaggerated. Nevertheless, he succeeded in developing a form of documentary realism that raised numerous moral issues which earlier *criollista* writers, for all their determination to focus on national reality, had ignored.

TERESA DE LA PARRA

Born Ana Teresa Parra Sanojo, Teresa de la Parra (1889–1936) is Venezuela's best-known woman writer. Her premature death, following several years of ill health, limited her output to three novels and some short stories, but it is work of exceptional originality. Her examination of female subjectivity was new to Venezuelan literature, for example. Indeed, Parra has been credited with being the first Venezuelan writer to introduce psychological analysis into the novel. She was essentially a realist writer, but her particular brand of realism reveals certain elements of the vanguard prose that was being produced elsewhere in Latin America in the 1920s.

Her first major work, *Ifigenia: Diario de una señorita que escribió porque se fastidiaba* (Ifigenia: Diary of a Young Woman Who Wrote Because She Was Bored) was published in 1924. It is a first-person narrative in an intimate, colloquial style, recounted in the form of a long letter and a diary. In it, the independent-minded María tells of the stifling social conventions of which she and other young women of upper-class Caracas society are victims. Her family wants her to marry César Leal, a rich, respectable doctor whom María finds repellent. She plans to rebel and run away with another man, to whom she is attracted, but she weakens, bowing to family pressure and social expectations, and ends up accepting Leal. The introspection that characterizes the novel sharply differentiates its social criticism from that of Pocaterra and other overtly political writers of the period. Parra's second novel, *Memorias de Mamá Blanca* (Mamá Blanca's Memoirs), of 1929, recalls the childhood years she spent on a Venezuelan sugar plantation. With affection, but avoiding sentimentality, the work evokes the characters and events of an age now past, but whose inequalities and injustices are nonetheless recorded.

Opinion on Parra's work was sharply divided at the time it appeared. Many critics recognized its merits, and *Ifigenia* won first prize in a literary competition in Paris when it was published there in 1924. However, it was strongly attacked by others, though undoubtedly much of the criticism stemmed from the prejudice of male critics against the feminism evident in the work. That prejudice also helps to explain why Parra's writing was for several decades largely ignored in Latin American literary studies. In the 1980s, however, feminist critics began to give it the attention it deserved, leading to new readings and new appreciation.

RÓMULO GALLEGOS

There is no doubt that Gallegos (1884–1969) is the most celebrated figure in Venezuelan literature. He taught a school for seventeen years, and then had a distinguished career in politics, briefly serving as president of Venezuela in 1947–1948. All his work is linked by the fundamental aim of exploring the nation's geography, culture, and social conflicts in greater depth than ever before, and of constructing a new vision of its future based on democ-

Rómulo Gallegos. Photo courtesy of Antonio Barragán Burgos.

racy, justice, and economic progress. Vast in their scope and rich in ideological debate, his novels represent the high point of social realism and of
criollismo in Venezuelan literature.

Gallegos's fame rests largely on his 1929 novel, *Doña Bárbara*. A huge
success when published, and later made into a film and an opera, it is perhaps
the most significant and influential work of fiction produced in Spanish
America before the Boom novels of the 1960s. The tyrannical landowner
Doña Bárbara ruthlessly extends her territory and power until she is successfully resisted by Santos Luzardo, owner of neighboring lands and the
embodiment of enlightenment, justice, and progress. The struggle between
the two characters dramatically represents the ongoing conflict that Gallegos
perceived in Latin America between the forces of barbarism, associated with
backwardness, ignorance, and despotism, and those of civilization, which
carried the promise of economic advance and political democracy. It is significant that the novel was written in the 1920s, against the background of
the repressive Gómez dictatorship, the epitome of barbarism as far as Gallegos
was concerned. The success of Luzardo signifies the symbolic victory of Gallegos's own liberal reformist politics and, at the universal level, the victory

of positive human values over barbaric behavior in all its manifestations. Such an optimistic view of the nation's future, envisaging the triumph of modernization and justice, was extremely rare among writers of the era. Later critics saw it as naive, but it was very appealing to readers at the time.

Doña Bárbara is a novel of impressive breadth. Numerous aspects of Venezuela's sociopolitical reality are referred to through a series of symbolic characters, such as the corrupt Colonel Perñalete, who perverts the law he is supposed to represent, and Mr. Danger, the symbol of U.S. imperialism. The setting of the work—the vast central plains of Venezuela, the llanos—enables Gallegos to develop a long established theme in Latin American literature: the struggle of humans to tame the region's inhospitable natural environment. The legacy of *costumbrismo* is clearly evident in the detailed documentation of the patterns of life and folklore of the plains. This same thematic material forms the basis of his other major novels: *Cantaclaro*, of 1934, a more lyrical narrative about llano life, highlighting its rich folklore, and *Canaima*, of 1935, investigating the social relations and mestizo culture of the Venezuelan jungle. Environment and atmosphere take center stage in these works.

Gallegos's vision of Latin America was eventually challenged by many who saw it as oversimplified and dualistic, and his literary technique, inherited from the nineteenth-century realist tradition, was soon regarded as outdated by writers anxious to introduce the technical innovations evident in other literatures in the early twentieth century. Yet Gallegos's novels represent such a landmark in Venezuelan literary history that they have been a vital point of reference for virtually all the country's subsequent writers. In recognition of his achievement, the Rómulo Gallegos Literary Prize, one of the most prestigious in Latin America, was created by the Venezuelan government in 1964.

MARIANO PICÓN SALAS

Although the fiction of Picón Salas (1901–1965) has clear limitations—interesting in its discussion of ideas and of social problems but lacking in real creative imagination, as far as one critic is concerned (Liscano, 1995, 222)—his role in Venezuelan cultural life was too fundamental to be ignored. It was in other genres that he excelled and established his reputation as one of Latin America's outstanding twentieth-century intellectuals, matched only by Arturo Uslar Pietri in terms of international recognition. He was a pioneer of the study of the region's cultural history, and wrote some of the most lucid and probing studies produced on the subject—for example, his influential 1944 work, *De la conquista a la independencia* (From the Conquest to Independence). His biographies, literary criticism, and autobiographical writings were also outstanding, and for many he was Venezuela's best essayist of the century.

VANGUARD LITERATURE

Avant-garde tendencies were slow to have an impact in Venezuela. Social and cultural conditions in the early twentieth century were not conducive to literary experiment (Liscano, 1995, 37). Documentary realism continued to dominate prose writing during the 1930s, frequently producing highly political investigations into Venezuelan society. Notable examples from the period are *Mene*, a novel from 1936 by Ramón Díaz Sánchez (1903–1968), which denounces exploitative practices by the U.S. oil companies, and *Puros hombres* (Only Men), of 1938, a stark documentary novel by Antonio Arráiz (1903–1962), recording life in Gómez's prisons.

There were, of course, writers who attempted to break away from the prevailing format and revitalize literature, but they received little recognition at the time and were not widely read. Often regarded as eccentric and self-indulgent, too wrapped up in their own concerns to pay attention to the problems of the nation, they saw their work marginalized. Only decades later did the best of these writers receive acclaim for the originality of their contribution. Such was the experience of short story writer Julio Garmendia (1898–1977), whose 1927 collection, *La tienda de muñecos* (The Doll Shop), was unlike any short prose fiction published previously. Turning away from realism, Garmendia wrote stories of fantasy that were more cosmopolitan in outlook and were characterized by irony and humor. Philosophical ideas and suggestion predominate, rather than social comment, and the more fragmented narrative structure presages the sophisticated Latin American fiction of the 1960s. A similar example is Enrique Bernardo Núñez (1895–1964), who wrote a highly innovative novel titled *Cubagua* in the 1920s. It went virtually unnoticed when finally published in 1931. Written in poetic prose and experimental in its treatment of time, the novel entwines Venezuela's colonial past with the Gómez period.

The year 1928 is seen by many literary historians as initiating a new phase of literary development in Venezuela. It was the year that saw the first major public demonstrations, spearheaded by students and young intellectuals, demanding an end to the Gómez dictatorship and a return to democracy. Demands for political change were accompanied by attempts at artistic renovation. The desire to propagate the aesthetic ideas of the international vanguard brought together a group of young writers, known as the "1928 generation," who between them would produce much of the most significant and original prose writing in Venezuela over the following decades. Among the major writers involved were Guillermo Meneses, Miguel Otero Silva, and Arturo Uslar Pietri.

Arturo Uslar Pietri

Uslar (b. 1906) has won most recognition for his short stories. The experiments in his first collection, *Barrabás y otros relatos* (Barabbas and Other Stories), of 1928—involving, for example, psychoanalytical elements, subtle use of metaphor, and the development of cosmopolitan subject matter— clearly reveal the influence of the avant-garde and the desire to take short prose fiction beyond the confines of the *criollismo* that had long dominated it. A later collection, *Red* (Net), published in 1936, is one of the earliest examples in Latin America of the magical realism that would have such an impact on the region's literature over the coming decades. Using innovative techniques and themes, Uslar is widely credited with laying the basis for the modern short story in Venezuela.

He was also one of the first Venezuelan writers to apply vanguard ideas to the novel, as is evident in the first he published, in 1931, titled *Las lanzas coloradas* (The Red Lances). Vividly recounting the most violent years of Venezuela's war of independence (1812–1814), it is innovative in its use of language, which ranges among dramatic description, powerful imagery, and lyrical passages. Subsequent works like *El camino de El Dorado* (The Road to El Dorado), of 1947, about the conquistador Lope de Aguirre, and *La isla de Robinson* (Robinson's Island), published in 1981, which focuses on the writer Simón Rodríguez, were less experimental but consolidated his reputation as Venezuela's foremost historical novelist. He also has published numerous collections of essays covering many aspects of the country's social, economic, cultural, and literary development. Over almost eight decades, Uslar has contributed so much high-quality writing to so many different fields that he has become one of the most respected figures of twentieth-century Latin American literature.

Miguel Otero Silva

Otero Silva (1908–1985) was another writer who contributed to Venezuelan cultural life in various capacities. He was an avant-garde poet, an essayist, a novelist, and, as a journalist, was responsible for founding the country's best-known newspaper, *El Nacional*. His first novel, *Fiebre* (Fever), published in 1939, provided literature's most dramatic expression of the political resistance of the 1928 generation and its repression by the Gómez regime. The author drew on his personal involvement to write the work. The documentation, in gruesome detail, of the torture and imprisonments of the era is counterbalanced by the assertion that the dream of liberty remained alive and could never be destroyed. Both the style and the structure are orthodox, but years later Otero Silva wrote other novels notable for their use of modern literary techniques. *Casas muertas* (Dead Houses), of 1955, uses poetic prose to examine the decline of an agricultural community on the Venezuelan plains as the axis of the national economy moved to the oil industry. *Oficina no. 1* (Office Number 1), published in 1961, continues the theme, following the steady expansion of oil exploitation and its social effects. Political violence and the chronic inequality of wealth distribution were major themes developed in subsequent novels. Otero Silva was a politically committed writer, and all his work focuses on national social issues. However it is the techniques of the modern novel, such as interior monologue and flashback, that distinguish his best fiction from the politically oriented novels produced in the country earlier in the century.

Guillermo Meneses

Of the 1928 generation, it was Meneses (1911–1978) who did most to fully assimilate modern literary tendencies into Venezuelan prose. He was highly acclaimed for both his short stories and his novels; and the sophistication of his writing, with its audacious experiments with narrative structure and language, had a huge influence on the generation of writers who emerged in the 1960s and 1970s. He began by writing works about the country's urban poor, exemplified by his 1934 novelette *La balandra Isabel llegó esta tarde* (The Yacht Isabel Arrived this Afternoon), recounting in lyrical prose the frustrated love of a black prostitute for a sailor. In such texts, Meneses produced vivid portrayals of the failed aspirations of working-class characters overwhelmed by the miserable, exploitative conditions in which they live, but he broke with the established tendency of writers to moralize and denounce, leaving it to the readers to reach their own understanding of events and situations.

In later decades, Meneses's writing became more technically polished, characterized by greater introspection and structural complexity. Abandoning the representative types or symbolic characters common to earlier Venezuelan fiction, he made full use of devices such as interior monologue to deepen the psychological analysis of the protagonists of his stories, and the subconscious became a regular element. The culmination of this process was the publication in 1952 of his major novel, *El falso cuaderno de Narciso Espejo* (The False Notebook of Narciso Espejo). One of Venezuela's best twentieth-century novels, it narrates the autobiography of a young man while raising questions about the nature and function of fiction itself. Much of Meneses's writing is open to diverse interpretations. There is no doubting the historical significance of his work. More clearly than any other writing of the period, it represents a break with the tradition of documentary literature with a social message, and points the way toward the more complex, self-referential, and ambiguous fiction associated with the modern novel.

PROSE OF THE 1960s AND 1970s

The literature produced in these years was largely shaped by two basic tendencies: the desire for continued experimentation and the need to respond to the political turbulence of the period. In 1958, the brutal Pérez Jiménez dictatorship was overthrown, opening the way for a new period of democratic government and free expression, yet political violence continued for most of the 1960s. The mild reformist position of the new civilian government under President Betancourt, and its strongly pro–U.S. stance, split the political left; and guerrilla organizations, influenced by the success of the Cuban Revolution, were soon operating in several regions of the country. So traumatic was this prolonged period of strife and bloodshed that it was the dominant theme of Venezuelan literature until the early 1970s.

Nowhere are political events more dramatically documented than in the work of Juan Vicente Abreu (1927–1987), largely because of his direct personal involvement in them. *Se llamaba S.N.* (It Was Called National Security), published in 1964, is a testimonial novel recounting his experience of torture and humiliation at the hands of Pérez Jiménez's security forces. *Las 4 letras* (The Four Letters), of 1969, is based on his subsequent participation in the frustrated guerrilla movement known as the Armed Forces of National Liberation. The succinct and direct language conveys atmosphere and events with maximum force. Other political militants of the period produced similar testimonies, though rarely of equal quality. Social documentation and social analysis were the prime objectives of such works, and the aesthetic element was generally of secondary concern. The majority of Venezuelan writers, however, were anxious to incorporate into their work the technical innovations that were then being consolidated in the Boom novels which were receiving such high acclaim elsewhere in Latin America. For some, the new, more sophisticated fictional techniques offered the opportunity to explore deeper and more complex dimensions of Venezuelan political and social reality. Foremost among them was Adriano González León (b. 1931).

González León's first work, *Las hogueras más altas* (The Biggest Bonfires), published in 1957, was a collection of short stories that, although still referring to the social environment, emphasized the inner world of a series of characters. Their fears, obsessions, and dreams give the narratives a fantastic or magical atmosphere. The work conforms closely to the objectives of the Sardio literary group, of which González León was a member. Between 1958 and 1961, as democracy was restored to Venezuela, the group sought to revitalize cultural creativity, advocating the incorporation of universal themes into literature in order to extend its parameters beyond the regional and the national. However, it was for his prize-winning novel of 1968, *País portátil* (Portable Country), that González León achieved international recognition. Its main action takes place in a period of twenty-four hours, during which the protagonist, a young urban guerrilla named Andrés, travels across Caracas to carry out a secret assignment. The narrative moves between the present, with Andrés sensing the alienation and political tension of the metropolis as he passes through it, and the past, as his memories take him back to the distant history of his family in the rural interior. Through powerful images, interior monologues, and the exploration of the protagonist's subconscious, the novel creates a complex vision of a country that is deeply divided and where violence remains pervasive. The fusion of the social and the psychological, and its penetrating insight into the fragmented and violent life of the modern city, made *País portátil* an extremely influential novel among young Venezuelan writers. Its major achievement was to take the theme of violence from the rigid format of political testimony and give it new artistic expression.

For some critics, the work of another, more prolific member of the Sardio group, Salvador Garmendia (b. 1928), is the most significant of the 1960s, for it is the first to fully explore the effects on human beings of the mid-twentieth-century consolidation of the modern capitalist economy in Venezuela. It thereby establishes a new phase in the history of Venezuelan literature (Hidalgo de Jesús, 1995, 117). Garmendia concentrates particularly on the new patterns of urban life that were absorbing an ever increasing percentage of the country's population, and presents a disturbing picture of solitude, alienation, unrewarding work, and fragmented, impersonal existence in the city. Many of his characters are drawn from the lower middle class, which was expanding rapidly in the wake of economic expansion, as in his first novel, *Los pequeños seres* (The Little Beings), published in 1959, in which an office worker comes to recognize the utter emptiness of his life.

The common factor in Garmendia's technically sophisticated and psychologically probing novels is the alienation suffered by the characters, who frequently are driven to despair by their sense of mediocrity and unfulfillment. *Día de ceniza* (Day of Ashes), of 1963, focuses on the frustrated attempts of a failed writer to escape the tedium of city life, and in his 1968 novel, *La mala vida* (The Bad Life), a particularly squalid urban environment provides the setting for more degraded lives. Influenced by the themes, forms, and style of Garmendia's writing, other Venezuelan novelists further investigated the problems of urban Venezuela. Garmendia himself explored new themes in later novels. In *Memorias de Altagracia* (Altagracia Memoirs), of 1974, and *El Capitán Kid* (Captain Kid), of 1988, the provincial life of a neighborhood in Barquisimeto is re-created through the imagination of a child.

Some writers who emerged during this period were concerned principally with the aesthetic aspects of literature, rather than with how it might be used to discuss social or political matters. Steeped in the legacy of the avant-garde, they were self-consciously experimental, seeking to create work that was far removed from traditional realist writing. The stories and novels of José Balza (b. 1939), for example, show constant experimentation with narrative structure and language. The interior world of the characters takes precedence over the social world. In his 1965 novel, *Marzo anterior* (The Previous March), the monologue of the protagonist reveals his deepest thoughts, memories, and anxieties, and in *Setecientas palmeras plantadas en un mismo lugar* (Seven Hundred Palm Trees Planted in a Single Place), of 1974, the narrator, embarked on a journey back to his origins, gradually recalls the experiences that have marked his life. Balza's vast and varied output, which includes literary theory and criticism, made him one of the dominant figures of Venezuelan literature in the late twentieth century.

Experiment is taken even further in the work of Oswaldo Trejo (1928–1996) and Luis Britto García (b. 1940). Trejo dispenses with plot and argument to concentrate almost entirely on the form, structure, and language of the text itself. His 1968 novel, *Andén lejano* (Distant Platform), deliberately seeks to destroy the familiar structure of the novel and makes the exploration of the meaning of words its main objective. Constant linguistic experiment, stretching the flexibility of language to the maximum, was the key characteristic of his subsequent work, as colorfully illustrated by the title of his 1980 collection of stories, *Al trajo, trejo troja trujo treja traje trejo*, a tongue twister based on his surname. In the development of Venezuelan literature, Trejo's prose represents the most radical break with the realist tradition. The inventive use of language is also central to the writing of Britto

García, and is evident in his early work dealing with the theme of political repression and violence. It is developed further in his highly acclaimed novel of 1979, *Abrapalabra*, an ambitious, wide-ranging work exploring the cultural and political development of Venezuela in the course of the twentieth century, through the experience of various different eras. It is recognized as one of the major achievements of modern Venezuelan fiction. Britto García has also established himself as one of the country's best essay writers through perceptive studies on political and cultural issues.

The audacious experimentation of such authors attracted much attention and provoked considerable debate, and many critics identified it as the most notable feature of Venezuelan fiction during the 1970s. In fact, it was only one of many currents. The decade saw the publication of historical novels, both by established authors like Otero Silva and Uslar Pietri, and by some new novelists, such as Francisco Herrera Luque (1927–1991), whose 1972 work, *Boves, el urogallo* (Boves, The Capercaillie), about the Spanish guerrilla leader who fought against Bolívar, was one of the best-selling novels of the period. There were also writers who returned to the topic of political violence and student rebellion in the 1960s, notable among them two women novelists who would become major names in later years, Antonieta Madrid (b. 1939) and Laura Antillano (b. 1950). Greater originality in theme and approach was provided by the 1973 novel *El mago de la cara de vidrio* (The Magician with the Glass Face), by Eduardo Liendo (b. 1941), a humorous and satirical work dealing with the effects of the expansion of the mass media. The narrator, confined in a mental hospital, related how his life was destroyed by the television installed in his family home.

PROSE AT THE END OF THE TWENTIETH CENTURY

Liendo shows little inclination to experiment in his work, concentrating instead on narrating events and situations as clearly and succinctly as possible. This was a common trend among writers in the closing decades of the century. Many reacted against what they regarded as the excessive aestheticism of earlier experimental writing, and sought a more straightforward narrative style, one more accessible to the reader. This did not mean a return to the social realism of previous decades. Most writers attempted to balance formal sophistication, assimilating many of the literary techniques developed by previous generations, with the exploration of new themes, such as the role of the mass media in society, questions of sexuality, and the experience of Venezuelans abroad, as exiles, immigrants, or students. Perhaps the most successful author who emerged in this period was Ednodio Quintero (b. 1947), who won several national prizes for novels and stories that were wide-ranging in both narrative form and thematic content.

The 1980s also saw women writers in Venezuela at last move to center stage. Although many women had published work in previous decades, few had received significant recognition. By the final decades of the century, however, female writers, their output far greater than ever before, were enjoying unprecedented critical acclaim and success with the reading public. Ana Teresa Torres and Milagros Mata Gil (b. 1951) were two of the major authors, both offering a female perspective on Venezuela's difficult and at times painful process of modernization. These and other writers of the period embarked on a new phase of critical examination of national reality, prompted largely by the severe economic, political, and social problems that confronted the nation in the 1980s and 1990s. Among the most notable results were works of fiction reviewing Venezuela's historical development, and others focusing on the social decay in the cities, seen as epitomizing the crisis confronting the country.

TWENTIETH-CENTURY POETRY

From 1918, there were clear signs of a reaction against the *modernismo* that dominated Venezuelan poetry at the beginning of the twentieth century, and which was most clearly represented by the work of Rufino Blanco Fombona (1874–1944), mentioned earlier. A group of poets emerged, collectively referred to as the "1918 generation," who, though quite varied in terms of style and thematic content, shared a common desire to break with the precedence given to form that was central to *modernismo*. Major poets of this generation were Fernando Paz Castillo (1893–1981), who wrote philosophical, intimate reflections prompted by the natural world, and Andrés Eloy Blanco (1897–1955), who used the formal legacy of *modernismo* but stressed themes from Venezuelan folklore. This group's efforts at poetic renovation were soon given additional dynamism by the incorporation of avant-garde currents, seen most clearly in the highly original poetry produced by José Antonio Ramón Sucre (1890–1930), which is characterized by its evocative use of imagery and symbols, and its carefully worked form, including poems in prose. Sucre was the poet of the period who had greatest impact on later generations.

Cultural and literary developments elsewhere in the world were steadily incorporated into Venezuelan poetry over the following decades. The poets associated with the *Viernes* (Friday) group, active between 1936 and 1941, were determined to open up literature to European artistic currents, above all to surrealism. The group's outstanding figure was the prolific Vicente Gerbasi (1912–1991), who preferred universal themes and forms. Later, in the 1940s, the *Contrapunto* (Counterpoint) group of poets attempted to increase writers' interest in theories such as psychoanalysis and existentialism. The diversity of influences is reflected in the diversity of poetic production in the 1950s and 1960s, with myriad tendencies evident. Two of the major poets of the period were Juan Liscano Velutini (b. 1915), also one of Venezuela's finest literary critics, and Juan Sánchez Pelaez (b. 1922), who wrote a profoundly subjective poetry marked by surrealism.

The 1960s saw the emergence of several new groups of poets who, in response to the political conflicts in the country, produced an aggressive, antiestablishment poetry. Typical was the group named *El Techo de la Ballena* (The Abode of the Whale), whose writers aimed to promote combative literature, using satire, black humor, and surrealism to attack the cultural norms associated with the state. The poems about guerrilla struggle by Rafael Cadenas (b. 1930) and the irreverent, derisive verse of Caupolicán Ovalles (b. 1936) exemplify the work that resulted from this current. In the following decades numerous writers' groups and literary journals, often short-lived, provided outlets for the work of new poets. Tendencies were more diverse than ever before, including different forms of poetry of social commitment, experimental poetry, and metaphysical poetry.

A new phase of Venezuelan poetry was launched in the 1980s with the creation of two new groups, Tráfico (Traffic) and Guaire, which rejecting both politically committed verse and elitist, hermetic poetry, argued for a poetry based on the concrete and the everyday, using colloquial language for direct communication. Some talented young poets emerged from those groups, such as Rafael Arráiz Lucca (b. 1959) and Yolanda Patin (b. 1955). As in other arts, women's participation in poetry grew appreciably in the closing decades of the twentieth century, Patin being just one of many women who published major collections. The production of poetry in the 1980s and 1990s, though varying greatly in terms of quality, was relatively buoyant, stimulated by the opportunities for publication offered by universities, cultural centers, and national publishing companies, and by the many poetry prizes created.

REFERENCES

Araújo, Orlando. *Narrativa venezolana contemporánea*. Caracas: Editorial Tiempo Nuevo, 1972.

Díaz Seijas, Pedro. *La antigua y la moderna literatura venezolana*. Caracas: Ediciones Armitano, 1970.

Dimo, Edith, and Amarilis Hidalgo de Jesús. *Escritura y desafío. Narradoras venezolanas del siglo XX*. Caracas: Monte Ávila, 1995.

Hidalgo de Jesús, Amarilis. *La novela moderna en Venezuela*. New York: Peter Lang, 1995.

Lewis, Marvin. *Ethnicity and Identity in Contemporary Afro-Venezuelan Literature*. Columbia: University of Missouri Press, 1992.

Liscano, Juan. *Panorama de la literatura venezolana actual*. Caracas: Alfadil Ediciones, 1995.

Márquez Rodríguez, Alexis. *Historia y ficción en la novela venezolana*. Caracas: Ediciones La Casa de Bello, 1991.

Medina, José Ramón. *Noventa años de la literatura venezolana*. Caracas: Monte Ávila, 1993.

Navarro, Armando. *Narradores venezolanos de la nueva generación*. Caracas: Monte Ávila, 1978.

Osorio, Nelson. *La formación de la vanguardia literaria en Venezuela*. Caracas: Biblioteca de la Academia Nacional de la Historia, 1985.

Picón-Salas, Mariano. *Formación y proceso de la literatura de Venezuela*. Caracas: Monte Ávila, 1984.

Rama, Angel. *Ensayos sobre literatura venezolana*. Caracas: Monte Ávila, 1990.

Ratcliff, Dillwyn F. *La prosa de ficción en Venezuela*. Caracas: UCV, 1966.

Santaella, Juan Carlos. *Manifiestos literarios venezolanos*. Caracas: Monte Ávila, 1992.

Uslar Pietri, Arturo. *Letras y hombres de Venezuela*. Madrid: Editorial Mediterráneo, 1974.

Venezuelan Works of Literature Available in English Translation

Fombona, Rufino Blanco. *The Man of Gold*. Trans. by Isaac Goldberg. New York: Brentano's, 1920.

Gallegos, Rómulo. *Doña Bárbara*. Trans. by Robert Malloy. Magnolia, MA: Peter Smith, 1948.

Gallegos, Rómulo. *Canaima*. Trans. by Jaime Tello. Norman: University of Oklahoma Press, 1988.

———. *Canaima*. Trans. by Will Kirkland. Pittsburgh: University of Pittsburgh Press, 1996.

Parra, Teresa de la. *Mamá Blanca's Memoirs*. Trans. by Harriet de Onís. Pittsburgh: University of Pittsburgh Press, 1993.

Parra, Teresa de la. *Iphigenia: The diary of a young lady who wrote because she was bored*. Trans. by Bertie Acker. Austin: University of Texas Press, 1993.

Pietri, Arturo Uslar. *The Red Lances*. Trans. by Harriet de Onís. New York: Alfred A. Knopf, 1963.

Zacklin, Lyda Aponte de, ed. *Venezuelan Short Stories*. Caracas: Monte Ávila, 1992.

7

Performing Arts

FOLK MUSIC

NUMEROUS FORMS of folk music exist across Venezuela. The oldest of them were not created exclusively to be listened to, but were linked directly to particular social activities. Some pieces formed part of religious or festive occasions; others were composed to be danced to during popular celebrations; and work songs were often sung as people carried out routine, daily tasks. In spite of the changes in patterns of life that have occurred, a significant proportion of this music is regularly performed today, for it remains an important component of communal life throughout the country.

European dances, such as the minuet, the polka, and the mazurka, were firmly implanted in Venezuela during the colonial period, and local composers later produced their own distinct versions of such forms. Many fine Venezuelan waltzes and polkas have resulted, for example. Some dance rhythms of Spanish origin, like the *malagueña* and the *jota* played in Anzoátegui state, have changed so much that they are now almost unrecognizable as the original European form. A similar process of development occurred with the songs that were carried to the Americas by the Spanish, such as the Christmas carols (which, as mentioned in chapter 3, evolved into a distinctive form known as the *aguinaldo* in Venezuela).

Throughout the colonial period, each region of the country produced its own new varieties of music and song resulting from the fusion of the Spanish musical tradition with those of the indigenous communities and of the African slaves. In villages in the interior of some states, music of indigenous origin now frequently incorporates the stringed instruments introduced from Europe, and on the coast, not far from Caracas, the predominantly black communities are famed for their Afro-Venezuelan music based on strong drum rhythms. However, it is perhaps the llano that has the country's best-known folk music, with a rich array of work songs, ballads, and highly inventive improvised verses, often sung in the form of a duel between two singers. Most famous of all is the *joropo*, a vibrant dance rhythm with many regional variants, typically played by groups consisting of harp, four-stringed guitar, and maracas, and at times accompanied by vocals. For the majority of Venezuelans, it is the country's most traditional and distinctive musical form.

During the twentieth century, many types of popular music from overseas had a considerable impact in Venezuela, but national folk music maintained a strong following. It was largely due to the many professional musicians who tapped those traditional forms, re-created them, and, through concerts and recordings, popularized them among a wide audience. Foremost of those artists has been the singer and songwriter Simón Díaz (b. 1928), who was born in the llano and has dedicated his life to propagating its music. He has written numerous songs in the folk idiom, many of which have enjoyed huge success, such as "Caballo viejo" (Old Horse), which, in the metaphorical language popular in the countryside, tells of a man who falls in love with a girl everyone considers to be too young for him. It has been recorded by many singers and groups worldwide. Díaz is particularly well known for his *tonadas*, slow, gentle ballads that were traditionally sung by ranch hands as they carried out the milking, partly in the belief that soothing the cattle in that way improved the yield. Noting that the *tonada* was disappearing as the work on the ranches was mechanized, Díaz sought to rescue and revive it. Regarded as a major ambassador of Venezuelan popular culture, he has won numerous awards and has become one of the country's most revered personalities.

Much of the distinctive sound of llano folk music is provided by the harp, and its best-known exponent, Juan Vicente Torreabla (b. 1917), has won international recognition for his renditions of traditional melodies and for his own compositions. He was one of a number of musicians whose radio performances in the 1950s helped to reawaken interest in traditional music. Other recording artists, like Reinaldo Armas, Reina Lucero, and Luis Silva, have developed more commercial variants of llano music, especially *joropo*. With songs about life, work, and love in the countryside, they regularly pack concert halls in the big cities.

Simón Díaz, popular singer and promoter of Venezuelan folk music. Photo by Nelson Garrido. Courtesy of the Fundación Bigott.

A number of groups have achieved considerable popularity through their successful reinterpretation of folkloric forms. The best-known are Serenata Guayanesa (Guayana Serenade) and Un Solo Pueblo (One People), both of which have won many national prizes for their services to Venezuelan music since their formation in the 1970s. The study and collection of forgotten songs and tunes has been central to their work. Serenata Guayanesa, a four-man group, has developed a vast and varied repertoire of folk songs and dance rhythms from different regions that have been recorded in over forty albums. Un Solo Pueblo is best known for re-creation of the music of the black communities of the coast, combining strong, energetic rhythms with lyrics about everyday life of those villages.

Venezuela's so-called New Song Movement, which emerged at the end of the 1960s, drew some of its inspiration from traditional folk music. Its members were interested in and attracted to traditional forms and themes, but what distinguished them as singers and songwriters from mainstream folk musicians were the political concerns that oriented their work. They were first and foremost protest singers, influenced by the left-wing student politics of the 1960s. Their use of song as a vehicle to raise awareness about the need for radical social change linked them to protest singers across Latin America during the same period, such as Argentina's Mercedes Sosa and Chile's Victor Jara. The best-known representatives of the New Song in Venezuela were Soledad Bravo (b. 1943), Ali Primera (1942–1985), and Gloria Martín (b. 1945). Although the political songs that made them famous nationally were very much the products of a particular era, all three have had a lasting impact on Venezuelan popular music. Soledad Bravo is perhaps the best-known internationally. She branched out from her songs of political commitment to record ballads, salsa, and other popular forms. Ali Primera became one of Venezuela's major songwriters; his simple compositions condemning exploitation and repression, and celebrating resistance, struck a chord among a wide public. Like Ali Primera, Gloria Martín combined her music with political activity in the 1970s, regularly performing at rallies and events in support of human rights and social justice.

OTHER POPULAR MUSIC

The diffusion of overseas popular music in Venezuela accelerated dramatically in the 1930s, as a result of the spread of radio throughout the country. The Argentine tango, Cuban music, and the big band sound from the United States (produced by the likes of Glenn Miller) acquired an avid following. So did merengue from the Dominican Republic, which was popularized by the most successful dance orchestra of the 1940s, Billo's Caracas Boys. Billo was the nickname of its leader, Luis María Frometa, who arrived from the Dominican Republic at the end of the 1930s. Many rival orchestras were formed, playing a variety of dance music. Venezuelan musicians soon adopted the imported forms, such as the rumba, the conga, and the *son*, which came from Cuba. They went on to produce their own distinct versions too, and the process of assimilation and re-creation was a dynamic force in Venezuelan popular music throughout the twentieth century.

There was, however, no shortage of composers and songwriters who sought inspiration from the national musical tradition, developing popular Venezuelan themes and forms into catchy, commercial melodies and songs. One notable example was Chelique Sarabia, well known for his love songs based on traditional rural ballads, above all "Ansiedad" (Longing), a song he wrote while still in his teens. Expressing the singer's longing for the lover from whom he is separated, it was a huge success in the 1950s and won him several awards. Hugo Blanco was another whose songs with traditional roots proved extremely popular during the same period. He is best known for "Moliendo café" (Grinding Coffee), which he wrote in 1957. In it a black worker sings about his frustrated love while he works at night, grinding coffee. Over two hundred cover versions of it have been recorded by many famous singers. The most popular singing voice of the 1950s, and for the next few decades, was that of the tenor Alfredo Sadel, who included both popular love songs and opera in his extensive repertoire.

British and American pop and rock music had an enormous impact on Venezuelan youth in the 1960s, and the first Venezuelan rock groups soon appeared. At the same time, many singers of the romantic ballad emerged, with José Luis Rodríguez, nicknamed "El Puma," the best known of them. His recordings and performances in shows around the world made him one of Venezuela's best-known show business personalities. Salsa became one of the most popular types of dance music in the late 1960s. Overseas artists like Cuba's Celia Cruz made it popular initially but once again Venezuela quickly produced its own interpreters of the genre, such as the group Dimensión Latina (Latin Dimension). Its charismatic lead singer, Oscar D'Leon, eventually embarked on a solo career, and enjoyed such success that he became one of the most popular salsa singers in Latin America.

The popular music industry boomed in Venezuela in the 1970s, helped by the increased consumer spending prompted by high oil prices. Caracas established itself as a world center for Latin music, its concert halls, nightclubs, and excellent recording studios attracting artists from all over Latin America. This buoyant atmosphere helped national musicians as well. The *gaita*, mentioned in chapter 3, was one type of Venezuelan music that flourished in those years, both in the traditional format, with its familiar rhythm and vocal style performed by groups such as Los Cardenales del Éxito (The Big Hit Cardinal-birds), and in a more modern style particularly associated with Guaco, a *gaita* group that introduced new instruments and rhythmic arrangements. Constant experimentation with new mixtures has characterized much of Venezuelan popular music. A prime example is jazz, which, developing in widely differing directions, clearly reveals the vast array of musical influences adopted in the country.

Perhaps the most striking aspect of Venezuelan popular music in the 1990s was the unprecedented importance of young consumers in the market. A number of rock bands, blending various styles and singing about issues of concern to youth, established a huge following. Two of the most successful were Zapato 3 (Shoe 3), who were influenced by British rock but steadily cultivated their own distinctive sound and lyrics, and Desorden Público (Public Disorder), who created their own style of ska (a fusion of Caribbean rhythms and jazz). Teenage groups enjoyed equal success, especially Salserín (Little Salsa Singers), whose young members produced a salsa tailored to the tastes of their age group. The popular music industry was thriving in Venezuela at the end of the 1990s, and the country seemed set to continue as a melting pot, with the constant fusion of the national and the cosmopolitan producing more new musical currents and innovations.

CLASSICAL MUSIC

For the first three centuries of its history, classical music in Venezuela was centered in the Catholic Church. The earliest information available on the subject refers to the songs and chants that formed part of religious worship in the 1520s, and it was the Church that created the first specialist musicians by establishing permanent posts for organists and chapelmasters. Music and singing were taught as integral elements of Catholic ritual, and it was such training that, for generations, produced most of Venezuela's best musicians and composers.

The growing commercial prosperity of the colony in the early eighteenth century enhanced music both in the churches and among the wealthy elite, for whom orchestral music and balls became a central part of social life. The 1760s saw Venezuela's first influential music movement. The Chacao School, named after the district in Caracas where its members met, was founded by a priest, Pedro Palacios y Sojo (1739–1799), who gathered a large group of young composers and instrumentalists to develop their skills. The most important school of its kind in Latin American at the time, it produced an impressive list of outstanding musicians, including the composers Juan Manuel Olivares (1760–1792), Juan José Landaeta (1780–1814), and the prolific José Angel Lamas (1775–1815). These and the other composers of the school produced a large body of religious music: choral pieces, psalms, and hymns. In the course of the nineteenth century, as musical activity gradually recovered from the disruption caused by the Wars of Independence, the first Venezuelan operas were composed and performed, and the waltz established itself as the most popular musical form. Musicians who had played in military bands during the war found a new role in the peace that followed, playing in the many town bands that were formed to entertain the public with concerts and to instill a sense of national pride and unity through patriotic music.

No new movement or school emerged to give further momentum to Venezuelan classical music in the nineteenth century, and it was the work of outstanding individuals, influenced principally by Romanticism, that dominated musical life. Foremost among them was the pianist and composer Teresa Carreño (1853–1917). She established her reputation in concerts overseas, becoming Venezuela's most internationally acclaimed musician of the century. Best known as a brilliant performer, she also wrote piano pieces, most notably waltzes. In the 1970s, the Venezuelan state paid homage to her by naming after her the impressive new concert hall and theater complex built in Caracas, and by transferring her remains to the Pantheon. Other major musicians of the period were José Angel Montero (1839–1881), the most prolific composer of the century, and Felipe Larrazábal (1816–1873), best known for his composition *Segundo trío* (Second Trio), an outstanding work of chamber music.

By the 1890s, however, composition was in a state of stagnation, out of touch with innovations elsewhere and repeating well-worn formats. It was not until the 1920s that a process of renovation was initiated by a new generation of composers and musicians. Much of this activity centered on the inspirational figure of Vicente Emilio Sojo (1887–1974), an original composer and an outstanding teacher. He helped to found the first major choral society in Venezuela, the Orfeón Lamas, as well as the Venezuela Symphony Orchestra, eventually taking charge of both of them. However, it was as director of the Academy of Music and Interpretation in the 1930s that he made his greatest contribution. His reorganization of the academy's music teaching included the creation of a school of composition, named, because of its location, the Holy Chapel School. It produced two generations of talented young composers who were encouraged to use traditional Venezuelan musical forms as the basis for their work. Some of Venezuela's most original classical music resulted.

Among the major composers to emerge from the school were Antonio Estévez (1916–1988), the creator of skillful orchestral and choral compositions, and Antonio Lauro (1917–1986), who wrote pieces for the guitar that are now frequently played by classical guitarists worldwide. Other influential musicians worked alongside Sojo to improve the quality and quantity of musical training and creativity, generally combining several different areas of activity. Juan Bautista Plaza (1895–1965), for example, was chapelmaster of the cathedral in Caracas for twenty-five years, a music teacher, and a dedicated researcher of Venezuelan colonial music. He was arguably the most accomplished musician of his generation. Of his many compositions, his moving Requiem of 1933, dedicated to his mother, stands out. José Antonio Calcaño (1900–1978) wrote on music history, taught music at university, formed new music groups, and composed ballet and choral works.

Choral music developed particularly strongly in Venezuela throughout the twentieth century, and no other area of classical music maintained such a consistently high level of activity and of quality. The success of the Orfeón Lamas, performing original works that fused traditional European songs such as madrigals with elements from Venezuelan folk music, stimulated the creation of many other choral societies. Several have won an international reputation, such as that of the Central University of Venezuela, the Orfeón Universitario, which was founded in 1943 and was still making hugely successful overseas tours at the end of the 1990s. Not only have these numerous choirs interpreted the work of major composers such as Bach, Handel, and Stravinsky, but they have also generated the production of an impressive body of choral compositions in Venezuela. In 1974, a national choral movement, called Cantemos (Let's Sing), was founded to provide continued support for choirs and their music.

Orchestral music developed more slowly, but finally experienced major expansion in the 1980s, with the proliferation of professional, amateur, and youth orchestras. Caracas supported four professional orchestras simultaneously during those years (*Gran enciclopedia*, 1998, 349). Most striking, and most important for the future of Venezuelan music, was the huge number of youth orchestras formed as the result of an initiative launched in the mid-1970s. Around the same time, new music schools, both public and private, and research centers dedicated to the conservation of the country's musical heritage were created. This institutional strength helped to offset, at least to some extent, the effects of the economic crisis of the 1990s, when a lack of resources reduced activity and led to the cancellation of many programs.

For many critics, Venezuelan classical music suffered from isolation and insularity for many centuries, making it slow to assimilate innovations and currents emerging in other parts of the world. In the second half of the twentieth century, however, the country's musicians and composers benefited considerably from the increasing opportunities that arose for cultural exchange with their counterparts abroad. Study overseas became more common, and events like the Caracas Music Festival, which was first held in 1954, increased access to the latest musical tendencies from around the world. The culmination of this process can be seen in the work of a number of highly inventive vanguard composers of the 1980s and 1990s, such as Ricardo Teruel and Alexis Rago, whose modernist, experimental compositions are the most cosmopolitan expressions within Venezuelan classical music. The attempts made in the 1990s to include such new forms in the concert repertoire demonstrate the vitality and variety that classical music had acquired in Venezuela during its centuries of development.

DANCE

Arguably, dance is the cultural activity in which the greatest number of Venezuelans participate. It extends well beyond the formal space provided by clubs, dance halls, and discotheques, for it is an integral part of most festivals, many musical events, and virtually every private party. It is the most natural way of celebrating in Venezuela, and everyone, regardless of age, is expected to join in. Imported dance forms such as salsa and merengue became increasingly popular in the last decades of the twentieth century, but Venezuela has a strong tradition of folk dance, with most regions contributing their own distinct varieties. Through the decades—indeed, the centuries—dance, as a form of popular cultural expression, has lost none of its vitality or dynamism while professional dance, both classical and contemporary, has slowly but surely established itself as a major art form within the country.

Folk Dance

Venezuela's best-known dance, widely regarded as one of the principal expressions of national culture, is the *joropo*. Lively and energetic, it is danced by couples and appears to be linked to the Spanish fandango, which was danced in Venezuela during colonial times. Couples move freely, not restricted to a fixed choreography, though obviously there are specific movements and steps, the man leading and the woman following. At times they dance holding each other, but then separate, to twirl and turn, and execute certain steps, most notably the *zapateado*, the rapid stamps that are one of the main characteristics of the dance. The *joropo* is distinguished by its rhythm, but there are regional variations in the music, steps, and musical instruments used. Like virtually all forms of folk dance, the *joropo* is strongest in the interior of the country, where it is regularly danced at parties and festivals, and in traditional bars and restaurants.

The different ethnic components that have formed Venezuelan society are all represented in the country's rich array of popular dances. Venezuelan varieties of such European imports as the waltz and the polka have evolved, and the *baile de tambor* (drum dance), a vibrant and frenetic dance of African

The *joropo*, Venezuela's national dance. Photo by Nelson Garrido. Courtesy of the Fundación Bigott.

origin, is popular in the festivals and celebrations of many of the predominantly black communities on the coast. In other regions, the country's indigenous groups still perform numerous traditional dances, either as an integral part of their religious rituals or as part of the social life of their community. There are, for example, sacred indigenous dances to effect a cure for illness, and others that prepare the participants for the successful accomplishment of a specific task, such as hunting or building a house.

A large part of Venezuela's popular dance tradition is rooted in ancient religious ritual, whether indigenous, Christian, or a fusion of them. As discussed in chapter 3, dancing has a central role in virtually all the country's religious festivals. The dancing devils of Corpus Christi are the most striking example, but there are also formation dances, such as *las turas*, which is performed in late September in villages on the border between the states of Lara and Falcón. Although part of the region's celebrations for the Virgin of Las Mercedes, it originated from an indigenous ritual dance paying homage to nature in thanks for the harvest. Danced in a circle, its movements represent the different tasks required for agricultural work. Another example is the dance of the Vassals of La Candelaria, which takes place in Mérida state in February and is dedicated to the Virgin of La Candelaria. It, too, celebrates the gifts of nature. The brightly costumed dancers, lined up in rows, enact such tasks as clearing the land, burning the scrub, and sowing the seed.

In the course of time, secular dances were incorporated into many religious celebrations, often becoming indispensable elements. In certain towns in Trujillo state, for example, the bottle dance is performed during the festival for San Benito. Each participant is required to dance around a full bottle of brandy, their feet passing as close as possible without knocking it over. At the end, when all have demonstrated their dexterity, the bottle's contents are consumed. In similar fashion, *la perra* (the dog) animates the festivities dedicated to St. John in some towns close to Caracas. Couples dance in turn, to the beat of the drums, the woman attempting to knock over the man with trips or blows of her hips. The onlookers gather around them in a circle, giving encouragement and mocking any man brought to the ground by his partner. Dances of popular entertainment are among the most striking folkloric manifestations of the northeastern states of Venezuela, where in many towns they are incorporated into carnival or Christmas celebrations. Perhaps the best known is a type of maypole dance, called the *baile del sebucán*, in which men and women dance while holding the ends of long ribbons attached to a central pole, some dancing to the right and some to the left, weaving between one another and interlacing the ribbons in the process. Also performed in the same states during festive periods are a number of dance-dramas, in which the participants enact a simple plot. In *el carite*, dancers in a mock fishing boat act the role of fishermen struggling to catch a fish, represented by another individual; *el pájaro Guarandol* narrates how a bird is pursued and wounded by hunters, then cured by a folk healer and able to fly freely again. Dance, theater, music, and song are fused in these performances, in which additional narrative is provided by a chorus of singers backed by musicians.

Though none of these dances have achieved the worldwide popularity of the Argentine tango or the Dominican merengue, the wealth of Venezuela's popular dance tradition has nonetheless received international recognition.

Much of that is due to the work of one of the country's best-known professional dancers, Yolanda Moreno, who, since beginning her career in the 1950s, has dedicated her life to adapting popular Venezuelan dances for stage performance. Her major successes have been achieved as director and principal dancer of Danzas Venezuela (Dances of Venezuela), a company created in 1965. Skillfully integrating dance, music, song, costume, and lighting, its colorful and high-quality productions have attracted huge audiences in many countries. They have, however, courted controversy. Some critics have argued that Moreno's work is a distortion of popular culture that, severing it from its social context, converts it into an extravagant spectacle for the commercial theater. In response, she describes her performances as "nationalist dance" that is inspired by popular tradition but does not seek simply to imitate it. The process of adaptation creates a different form, adding steps and movements as necessary, positioning the dancers to make maximum use of stage space and using lighting to full effect. In Moreno's interpretation of the *joropo*, for example, the men dance a series of steps at the back of the stage while the women move in file to the front, turning and swirling their wide and colorful skirts. Considerable attention is paid to the overall visual impact. Despite the arguments over her approach, Yolanda Moreno established herself as a high-profile and much acclaimed ambassador of Venezuelan dance, and Danzas Venezuela, which won prestigious prizes at international dance festivals, became one of the country's most successful companies.

Classical and Contemporary Dance

Dance as an art form was late to emerge in Venezuela. Though visiting dancers from overseas stimulated interest—the most famous example being the Russian ballerina Anna Pavlova, whose performances in 1917 were heralded as the most important cultural event in Venezuela for years—lack of institutional support and financial difficulties hindered development. Much of the pioneering work was done by foreign instructors who had experience with European dance groups, such as Galy de Mamay, one of the first ballet teachers to give formal classes in Caracas, and Steffy Stahl, who, having arrived from Europe in 1938, gave private classes and taught dance movement in schools. Not until the 1940s was formal and systematic dance instruction firmly established, thereby creating the conditions for the emergence of Venezuela's first major dancers and dance companies. The ballet courses taught in the Andrés Bello High School during those years, for example, helped to produce such outstanding artists as Nena Coronil and Vicente Nebrada, who played important roles in national dance over the decades that followed. In the late 1940s, Nena Coronil founded the National Ballet School, employing top-class professional teachers from abroad, and Venezuela's first ballet company, the Ballet Nena Coronil. Development was not restricted to Caracas, for schools were also created in Barquisimeto and Valencia around the same time.

Those initiatives bore fruit, and the 1950s saw the beginning of professional dance performance. Well organized, stable groups were launched, Teatro de la Danza (Dance Theater), founded in 1950, being one of the earliest. It was still difficult for a company to sustain itself financially, for state grants were extremely limited and private sponsorship was virtually nonexistent, but increasing public support and greater professional know-how gave them more security than their predecessors. A particularly significant landmark was the foundation, in 1957, of the National Ballet of Venezuela, under the directorship of Irma Contreras, which lasted until 1972. It was the first professional company to formally represent Venezuela aboard when it appeared at the First Ballet Festival of Havana in 1960, and in 1965 it became the first classical dance company to be subsidized by the state. It was also the company that launched the career of the country's best-known ballerina, Zhandra Rodríguez.

Dance was dynamic in the 1960s and 1970s, and initiatives became more audacious and experimental. Notable examples from the 1970s were the creation of the National Dance Company, which attempted to bring together classical ballet and contemporary dancers in its performances, and, most important of all, the foundation of the International Ballet of Caracas, which between 1975 and 1981 established a new level of professionalism, earning an international reputation and serving as an important example for subsequent groups. A firm base had been laid nationally, and the 1980s were boom years for Venezuelan dance. A plethora of new groups appeared; tendencies and ideas from abroad were assimilated into new projects; and the state played a role by creating the National School of Dance and, for training at a more advanced level, the Higher Institute of Dance. Venezuelan dancers won awards in prestigious competitions overseas, and festivals for young choreographers, organized by the Higher Institute, encouraged new talent. These years of expansion and new opportunity gave Venezuela worldwide importance as a center for dance.

Nevertheless, the development of classical and modern forms has been unequal, with that of contemporary dance being significantly more dynamic than that of classical ballet. Unrestricted by traditional concepts and techniques, the greater possibilities for free expression and experiment offered by the former have attracted more young dancers and choreographers. The foundations were laid by the Mexican dancer Grishka Holguín, who arrived in Venezuela in the late 1940s. He gave the first performances of modern dance in the country, and with the Venezuelan dancer Conchita Crededio he founded its first modern dance group, the Venezuelan School of Contemporary Dance. Only gradually could contemporary dance establish itself, however, for in those early years it had to contend with public incomprehension, on the one hand, and hostility from the devotees of traditional ballet, on the other. In time, however, the work of talented young artists of contemporary dance began to attract new audiences and gain recognition. Performances were fed by continual experimentation, and imaginative teaching regularly produced new dancers. José Ledezma, who established his contemporary dance workshop in 1974, was one of the most influential figures of that period, making a vital contribution as both an original choreographer and a highly regarded teacher.

Of the many women who have been at the forefront of the development of modern dance, none has been more prominent than Sonia Sanoja, who emerged in the 1960s. Tireless work on her body movement and facial expression resulted in a highly individualistic style, and she was hailed as one of Venezuela's most original modern dancers. In their work Graciela Henríquez, who moved from classical to contemporary dance, and Hercilia López, leader of an influential group called Contradanza (Contra Dance), explored, albeit in different ways, problems confronting women. The number of companies that flourished in the 1980s and 1990s, in and beyond Caracas, is a clear indication of the success that modern dance had achieved by that time. Arguably Danzahoy (Dance Today) became the best known of them, with carefully staged performances making full use of costume and lighting, focusing on issues of Latin American reality and culture. There were numerous young dancers experimenting in the 1980s, seeking to open up new directions in dance. Carlos Orta, creator and director of the group Coreoarte (Choreoart) used elements of popular urban culture; Luis Viana established himself as an outstanding choreographer and, as a solo dancer, the inventive creator of memorable characters; and Abelardo Gameche has passed through various stages of experiment since studying under Ledezma, and has formed his own company.

Though classical ballet did not expand at the same pace, it has maintained a strong presence. Two figures with major international reputations tower above all others: the choreographer Vicente Nebrada and the ballerina Zhandra Rodríguez. Nebrada began his career in the late 1940s and gained experience in several different countries, then rose to prominence in Venezuela in 1975, when he created the International Ballet of Caracas, which, under his artistic directorship, brought the country's ballet unprecedented recognition around the world. A choreographer of extraordinary versatility, he has enjoyed unrivaled success with works rooted in Latin American cultural identity, such as *Nuestros valses* (Our Waltzes), and with interpretations of works from the traditional repertoire, such as *Romeo and Juliet* and *Swan Lake*. He choreographed his first pieces in 1953, and was still receiving enthusiastic reviews in 1999 for his version of *The Nutcracker Suite*, a ballet regularly performed in Caracas at Christmastime in front of huge audiences. Zhandra Rodríguez established her reputation as a dancer with the American Ballet Company in the United States, and in 1974 the magazine *Esquire* declared her to be one of the world's best ballerinas (Monasterios, 1986, 66). Returning to Venezuela, she benefited considerably from her association with Nebrada, as prima ballerina with the International Ballet of Caracas. Their joint creations are considered by many to be the high point to date of Venezuelan classical dance. When that company dissolved in 1981, she founded a new one, the Caracas New World Ballet, achieving further success as its director.

Professional dance has made impressive progress in its short history. That is amply demonstrated by the expansion in dance education and training; the increasing number of dancers and choreographers making a living from their art; and the high level attained in choreography (Paolillo, 1994, 147). From being essentially students of the forms and techniques established overseas, dance professionals in Venezuela have become innovators in their own right.

THEATER

Records of the early history of theater in Venezuela are sketchy. Evidence indicates that before the arrival of the Europeans, indigenous communities included forms of theatrical performance in their sacred rituals. After the Conquest, theater played an increasingly important role in the life of the colony, serving as a vehicle to propagate Catholic doctrine and to consolidate the authority of the Spanish Crown. No texts of plays performed in Venezuela before the nineteenth century have survived, but reports from the colonial period suggest that the vast majority of works were imported directly from Spain. The first theater built was constructed in Caracas in 1784, on the orders of the governor of Venezuela, and it served as an important focus for drama until it was destroyed by an earthquake in 1812. Though no record of its performances survives, it is believed to have presented a wide variety of plays by major Spanish dramatists, and the fact that it had capacity for over 1,500 spectators demonstrates the popularity the theater had attained in Caracas.

National playwrights began to have some impact in the early nineteenth century, though French and Spanish plays, written by the likes of Alexandra Dumas, Victor Hugo, Mariano José de Larra, and José Zorrilla y Moral were still those most in demand. *Venezuela consolada* (Venezuela Consoled), written by Andrés Bello and performed in 1804, is the earliest known Venezuelan play. Neoclassical in style, it celebrates the introduction of the smallpox vaccine into Venezuela. Theatrical activity increased steadily as the century progressed, with a growing band of impresarios playing an increasing role in its expansion and gradual professionalization. Nearly fifty theaters of various types were opened in Caracas between 1835 and 1898 (Castillo, 1980, 32). For much of that time, light forms of entertainment dominated their repertoires, such as the *sainete* (comedy sketch) and the *zarzuela* (light operetta), both of which originated in Spain but were quickly adopted by Venezuelan writers. Many of the plays written during the century were strongly influenced by Romanticism, typified by the work of Eduardo Blanco (1839–1912), such as his romantic melodrama of 1879 entitled *Lionfort*, recounting the tragedy of love that can never be realized. Arguably the dramatist who enjoyed the most consistent success during the nineteenth century was the prolific Heraclio Martín de la Guardia (1829–1907), who produced highly popular family dramas, romantic at first but marked by realism and naturalism toward the end of his career.

Political pressures, and the tastes of the bourgeoisie, who made up such a large percentage of the theatergoing public, allowed little space for social criticism in nineteenth-century drama. Many *costumbrista* plays, focusing on regional customs and problems, and full of local color, were produced in Venezuela; they employed satire but were generally superficial in terms of social analysis. Nevertheless, *costumbrista* drama represented the first attempt by Venezuelan playwrights to confront the social reality of the nation and to seek inspiration there, rather than exclusively in European models. Nicanor Bolet Peraza was one of the major exponents, writing humorous plays highlighting patterns of social and political behavior typical of the period. He was also one of the dramatists who developed a curious genre called "theater for reading only"—works composed of dialogues written in verse but not intended to be staged. They were popular until the 1940s, when such well-known writers as Andrés Eloy Blanco and Miguel Otero Silva published examples, usually humorous, in literary journals and newspapers.

In fact, some of the most notable attempts to modernize Venezuelan drama in the early twentieth century, and to expand it beyond mere entertainment, were made by writers who achieved fame through other forms of literature. Many years before his novels, Rómulo Gallegos (1884–1969) wrote plays that explored conflicts within Venezuelan society and their effects on the psychology of the characters, and Arturo Uslar Pietri (b. 1906), in two plays in the late 1920s, dispensed with traditional plot and introduced the vanguard techniques of such movements as futurism and surrealism. But these attempts at innovation were the exceptions, and they had only limited effect at the time. The Gómez dictatorship of 1908–1935 imposed severe restrictions on drama, as it did on all the arts. The theater was the favorite form of entertainment of the wealthy, and it was still light forms—musicals, comedy reviews, and colorful romances—that they demanded. Furthermore, a large part of the professional theater space available was provided by foreign companies, especially Spanish, often relegating national theater to secondary status. The *sainete* and the comedy of manners were the most popular genres, though they were ephemeral works and relatively few texts have survived. It is reported that when the *sainete* was at its height, one of its most successful creators, Rafael Guinand (1881–1957), a famous actor as well as a dramatist, was producing a new one each week, with parody and satire the major components (Barrios et al., 1997, 67).

It was not until the 1940s, when the death of Gómez had created new conditions for cultural activity, that radical renovation gave rise to a modern, dynamic theater in Venezuela. The state played a significant part, promoting drama education and subsidizing theater groups, most notably the Teatro Obrero (Workers' Theater), which, created in 1938 and changing its name several times over the years, provided theater for factories, trade union organizations, and working-class communities for several decades. It represented the first attempt in Venezuela at a popular theater. Its director, Luis Peraza (1908–1974), did more than anyone else to develop Venezuelan drama during the 1940s. A prolific playwright, he also created the University Theater in the Central University in Caracas, and founded, with other artists and intellectuals, an independent organization called the Society of Friends of the Theater. Between 1942 and 1946 it supported new playwrights, offered prizes for plays, and staged new works. The modernization of drama, delayed by the sterility of the Gómez years, was particularly helped by the arrival of talented foreigners bringing the latest ideas, techniques, and training. The Argentine actress Juana Sujo, the exiled Spanish director Alberto de Paz y Mateos, and the Mexican Jesús Gómez Obregón all became influential teachers and organizers of theater under whose guidance many young actors and directors emerged.

For many critics, the most important figure in the creation and consolidation of the modern Venezuelan theater was César Rengifo (1915–1980), also a talented journalist and painter. His career in the theater, for which he wrote over forty plays, extended across five decades. Profoundly committed to radical political change, Rengifo wrote plays that focus on the continual struggle by the Venezuelan people against oppression and injustice in all its manifestations. That basic concern was established in his first known work, *Por qué canta el pueblo* (Why the People Sing), dating from 1938, which deals with the fight against Gómez's tyranny. Numerous aspects of national reality are covered in his work. There is an extensive group of plays exploring Venezuela's history, others critically examining the effects of the oil industry, and another body of works that focus on alienation and marginalization in the expanding cities. Inspired by Marxist thought, Rengifo conceived of the theater as an instrument for stimulating social transformation and as an activity of popular involvement. His theater group, Máscaras (Masks), formed in 1951, toured working-class districts, prisons, and workers' centers, presenting plays with political content. The ideological orientation of his work meant that during his lifetime his plays were hardly ever performed by professional groups in mainstream theaters, but rather by amateur and student groups in community buildings and during drama festivals. He won many prizes for his work, but only toward the end of his life was he accorded the recognition he merited. More than anyone else, Rengifo established a theater of critical social analysis in Venezuela, in opposition to the traditional, commercial theater.

The Pérez Jiménez dictatorship imposed restrictions on cultural production in the 1950s, and the group Máscaras, for example, had to devise a form of metaphorical theater to express its social concerns. Nonetheless, it was by no means a lost decade for Venezuelan drama. Experiments continued, such as the search for a new poetic language and atmosphere for the theater, represented particularly by two women dramatists. Ida Gramcko (1924–1994) wrote plays that explored the mythical and magical elements of Venezuelan culture, such as *María Lionza*, staged in 1957; and Elizabeth Schön (b. 1921) produced a highly original work in 1956, titled *Intervalo*, which used surrealist elements to investigate problems of human communication. Schön was one of a number of dramatists who, having launched their careers in the 1950s, became major figures in the Venezuelan theater during the following decades. Others were Román Chalbaud (b. 1931), José Antonio Rial (b. 1911), and José Ignacio Cabrujas (b. 1937). Drama was thus able to recover its vibrancy rapidly once democracy was restored in 1958. The following year was extraordinarily productive for the theater, with groups revitalizing their activities both in Caracas and in the provinces, new plays being staged, and the First Festival of Venezuelan Theater being held.

Political repression, social nonconformity, and sexual liberation were recurring themes in the drama of the 1960s. It was also a decade of wide-ranging experiment. Major theories and currents, such as the political theater of Bertolt Brecht, Eugène Ionesco's theater of the absurd, and Antonin Artaud's theater of cruelty, oriented the work of some groups. Others explored novel ways of integrating music, lighting effects, film projection, and audience participation. The new possibilities for interpretation and presentation gave the director greater importance than ever before. Arguably the most successful vanguard play of the period was the 1966 musical *Vimazoluleka*, by Levy Rossell and his group Bohemio. Performed by a cast of fifty young actors, it used songs, dance, and slogans to express the youth protest that marked the period. Some of the experimentation of the 1960s had a lasting impact; other elements were superficial and soon forgotten. Overall, however, the new creativity applied to production and performance made it an important phase in the development of the Venezuelan theater.

Román Chalbaud, José Ignacio Cabrujas, and Isaac Chocrón (b. 1930) were the most successful and influential playwrights of the decade. They became known as the "Holy Trinity" of the Venezuelan theater, reflecting the importance they had attained. Chalbaud was perhaps the most acclaimed of all in the 1960s. He is best known for his plays focusing on the most marginalized sectors of society, such as *Los ángeles terribles* (The Terrible Angels), of 1967, which, using Brechtian techniques to encourage the audience to reflect critically on the situations presented to them, explores the effects of alienation on the psychology of the characters. The contradictions of contemporary Venezuelan society became Chalbaud's principal concern. Many of his works sought to disturb or even shock the public by confronting it with a sordid and violent social world that was in sharp discord with official presentations of a stable, democratic society whose steady modernization was supported by a prosperous, oil-based economy. Chalbaud also proved to be a talented theater director, and later his conversion of some of his plays, such as *La quema de Judas* (The Burning of Judas), into highly successful films established him as one of the country's leading filmmakers.

Versatility has been one of the main attributes of Isaac Chocrón's work. Always eager to experiment with new theories, he has constantly incorporated different techniques and new forms of expression to produce plays of great variety. His early works, centering on the isolation and frustration suffered by individuals in modern society, were broadly realist in approach. He has also written some highly experimental plays, such as *Tric-trac*, in 1967, which, though referring to problems confronting Venezuela, dispenses with plot and any attempt at character development. His most accomplished works, however, have been penetrating analyses of the human anguish that results from social taboos and prejudices, frustrated relationships, and the relentless passage of time. In the 1970s it was Chocrón, along with Cabrujas, who wrote the plays that, because of the richness and complexity of their themes and character portrayal, had greatest impact in Venezuela. Cabrujas began his career with plays on historical subjects, their approach strongly influenced by Brecht. The examination of Venezuela's past was used to shed light on contemporary issues, and it was Cabrujas's desire to deepen his exploration of national reality that provided the inspiration for his major works in the 1970s. The first of those was *Profundo* (Profound), staged in 1971, a powerful play focusing on the frustration arising from lost illusions. Caustic humor has been a recurring feature of his writing, which, in addition to his many plays, has included film and television scripts.

The 1970s and early 1980s were extremely productive years for the Venezuelan theater. Building upon the advances of the previous decades, and backed by state funding, the theater was more solid and vigorous than ever before. At the same time, the ideological orientation of drama production became more diversified as the utopianism underlying many of the plays of the 1960s gave way to a multiplicity of new tendencies. Collaboration among Chalbaud, Chocrón, and Cabrujas made a vital contribution, for in 1967 they joined forces to create the Nuevo Grupo (New Group), a company that would be a dynamic focal point for national drama over the next twenty years. It was launched with the presentation of Chocrón's *Tric-trac* and went on to stage works by over thirty Venezuelan playwrights, many of them among the finest plays produced in the country during that period. Diverse currents and forms were represented, and a wide range of plays from other countries was included. The group became renowned for the high quality of its productions, and it was instrumental in establishing the careers of many new directors, actors, and dramatists.

While the Nuevo Grupo flourished, Rajatabla, another highly successful company, began its activities. Founded in Caracas in 1971, it sought a new style of expression oriented toward the critical exploration of social issues. Its first production was *Tu país está feliz* (Your Country Is Happy), a musical of political protest written by Antonio Miranda, which was so popular that its planned run of three days stretched into three years. It attracted huge audiences of young people, many of whom had had little previous contact with the theater, and it made Rajatabla renowned nationally. Until his death in 1993, Carlos Giménez, an outstanding director, was the driving force behind the group, receiving international acclaim for some of his productions. Like the Nuevo Grupo, Rajatabla benefited from state support, and it developed an increasingly international repertoire in the 1980s, with adaptations of works by Brecht, Shakespeare, Leo Tolstoy and Gabriel García Márquez. It remained active throughout the 1990s, with tours and televised productions popularizing its work.

Caracas became one of Latin America's most important centers for drama in the 1970s, winning international recognition for the strength of its theatrical production and for the work of groups based in the city, such as Nuevo Grupo and Rajatabla. Activity intensified in the provinces as well, often centered in the universities or in drama festivals. In Maracaibo and Valencia, for example, the talent of Rodolfo Santana (b. 1944), the major new playwright to emerge from this period of expansion, first became recognized. Rejecting the social realism preferred by many earlier playwrights, he continually introduced new forms of dramatic expression into his work. His early plays revealed an interest in the metaphysical and in science fiction, but he turned his attention toward political and social issues in the 1970s and 1980s, as in his internationally acclaimed *Los criminals* (The Criminals), of 1972, focusing on the anguish and violence bred by social inequality. He is the most prolific playwright in the history of the Venezuelan theater, and the consistent quality of his plays, acknowledged through the numerous prizes awarded to them, has been remarkable. No other Venezuelan dramatist had a higher profile than Santana in the closing decades of the twentieth century, though the boom years produced many others who made valuable contributions. Notable among them were Mariela Romero, who became Venezuela's best-known female playwright through explorations of women's experience in the big city, and Edilio Peña, whose best plays examine human relationships under strain.

The most innovative theater of the 1980s was produced by vanguard groups such as Theja, the Dramatic Society of Maracaibo, and Grupo Actoral 80 (Drama Group 80), all of which attempted to break new ground with audacious experiments. In 1983, for example, the Dramatic Society of Maracaibo staged a work titled *Traje de etiqueta* (Formal Dress), in which the spectators became participants in the events presented, thereby dissolving the traditional division between audience and actors. Such works were in the minority, however. Venezuelan drama as a whole found it difficult to sustain the impressive dynamism of the previous decade. Many plays repeated the formulas that had proved successful in the 1970s. The works that enjoyed most critical acclaim tended to be those by established writers, like Isaac

Chocrón's *Clipper*, staged in 1987, which sought inventive ways of exploring the values and customs central to middle-class family life. In the late 1980s, the state attempted to encourage new talent by giving generous support to drama training programs, though, not for the first or last time, there were complaints that political favoritism in the way the funds were distributed disadvantaged many valuable drama groups and projects.

Like most of the other arts, the theater suffered the effects of the country's economic crisis in the 1990s. The subsidies that were so vital to most drama groups were reduced, audiences were smaller, and the number of theaters regularly presenting plays declined. Those conditions help to explain the preference in the 1990s for simple plays with low production costs, such as Mónica Montañés's *El aplauso va por dentro* (The Applause Goes Within), a big box office success in 1996, consisting of a monologue in which a woman confides details of her daily life to the audience. The existence of new talent was demonstrated by the work of young dramatists such as Gustavo Ott, whose 1998 play, *Comegato* (Eat Cat), found a novel form through which to provide a penetrating analysis of the state of Venezuelan society and culture. Such examples gave cause for optimism about the future of the country's theater in the midst of the difficulties and uncertainties it faced at the end of the twentieth century.

REFERENCES

Azparren Jiménez, Leonardo. *El teatro venezolano y otros teatros.* Caracas: Monte Ávila, 1977.

Barrios, A. L., C. Mannarinor, and E. Izaguirre. *Dramaturgia venezolana del siglo XX.* Caracas: Centro Venezolano del ITT/UNESCO, 1997.

Castillo, Susana. *El desarraigo en el teatro venezolano.* Caracas: Editorial Ateneo de Caracas, 1980.

Ficher, Miguel, Martha Furman Schleiter, and John M. Furman, eds. *Latin American Classical Composers: A Biographical Dictionary.* Lanham, MD: Scarecrow Press, 1996.

Gran enciclopedia de Venezuela. Vol. 8, 339–349. Caracas: Editorial Globe, 1998.

Monasterios, Ruben. *Cuerpo en el espacio: El baile teatral venezolano en nuestros días.* Caracas: Gramoven, 1986.

Moreno Uribe, Edgard Antonio. *Teatro 96: Apuntes para su historia en Venezuela.* Caracas: Kairos, 1996.

Paolillo, Carlos. "50 años de coreografía en Venezuela. Mil rostros y una danza." *Itinerario por la danza escénica de América Latina,* 121–147. Ed. Paulina Ossona et al. Caracas: CONAC, 1994.

Peñín, José. "La música." In *La cultura de Venezuela, historia mínima,* 141–172. Ed.

Elías Piño Iturrieta et al. Caracas: Fundación de los Trabajadores de Lagoven, 1996.

Ramón y Rivera, Luis F. *La música popular en Venezuela*. Caracas: Armitano, 1976.

Womutt, Andreina. *Movimiemto perpetuo*. Caracas: Findarte, 1991.

8

Art and Architecture

THE VISUAL ARTS were one of Venezuela's strongest areas of artistic activity in the twentieth century. The European avant-garde provided the initial inspiration for a process of renovation, with the best Venezuelan artists using the forms they discovered overseas as a starting point for creating painting and sculpture of great originality and vitality. Institutions to support those arts grew more numerous as the century progressed, with some impressive museums and private galleries being founded. At the same time, new possibilities for modern architecture were created by the rapid urbanization discussed in chapter 3; some startling, often controversial, buildings were erected. It was these achievements in the second half of the twentieth century that finally drew world attention to Venezuelan art and architecture, though previous eras had produced work of cultural value and importance.

The most impressive form of ancient artistic expression found in Venezuela is petroglyphs (designs carved into rock), of which numerous examples exist in Amazonas state. Most consist of huge figures in linear form, and probably served a magical-religious function. Other art produced by pre–Hispanic communities was neither elaborate nor monumental in scale, but archaeologists have discovered a range of significant artifacts. The oldest pottery dates from about 1000 B.C. Sophisticated in technique and designs, it has certain similarities with the Chavín culture which flourished in Peru at that period. From later centuries there are examples of funeral urns, animal and human figurines in pottery, and body adornments of shells and stones.

Religious imagery dominated the art of the colonial era. Sculpture was plentiful, if not of outstanding quality, with altarpieces and carvings of saints the most common items. The need for religious iconography led to the emergence of skilled painters who specialized in that genre, and three notable centers of production became established: in El Tocuyo in Lara state, in Mérida in the Andes, and in Caracas. Toward the end of the eighteenth century, a small but prosperous bourgeoisie, the result of expanding commerce, began to sponsor art which until then had been dominated by the Church. Portrait painting became increasingly common. After 1800, religious art started to decline as the political and ideological conflicts that led to the Wars of Independence generated new concerns.

PAINTING

As the new republic was consolidated in Venezuela, painting was used to record the struggle against colonialism and to pay homage to the sacrifice made by the nation's heroes. Juan Lovera (1776–1841) was the first major painter in this line, well known for his evocation of historical scenes, such as the formal declaration of independence made on July 5, 1811. Subsequent generations of artists carried on the task of producing epic paintings to reinforce republican ideals and satisfy patriotic sentiment. Martín Tovar y Tovar (1827–1902) was the most celebrated exponent. He was commissioned by the Venezuelan state to produce an extensive series of historical scenes and portraits of revolutionary heroes. His depiction of the crucial battle of Carabobo, which decorates the ceiling of the Elliptical Salon in the Congress Building, is his most famous painting. Arturo Michelena (1863–1898) was another important representative of the genre. He demonstrated considerable versatility in his brief career, though he is best remembered for his paintings of Simón Bolívar and Franciso de Miranda.

The most original painter of the nineteenth century was Cristóbal Rojas (1857–1890), another whose output was limited by premature death. His earlier work included religious pieces and patriotic paintings in the style of Tovar y Tovar, but he came to reject such traditional subject matter to focus on other themes, most notably social topics, as seen in his painting of a beggar, *El mendigo*, dating from 1884. A sense of anguish and forboding haunts many of his works. In the late nineteenth century, themes became increasingly diverse as painters relied less on commissions and concentrated on subjects of personal interest, including still lifes, landscapes, and urban scenes, usually hoping to sell the work to well-off inhabitants of the cities.

Nonetheless, officially sanctioned patriotic art still dominated in the opening decades of the twentieth century. It was epitomized by the work of Tito Salas (1888–1974), whose enormous paintings depicting key moments in the life of Bolívar adorn the Congress Building and the Pantheon. Those works, in bold, simple style for maximum emotional force, made Salas a national celebrity. The limitations of such art were clear, however. Produced in accordance with imposed criteria, it was conservative in its conception and conventional in its execution. Pressure for renovation mounted. The first important movement for change occurred in 1912, when a group of students at the prestigious Academy of Fine Art in Caracas rebelled against what they saw as its conservative and rigid approach by breaking away and establishing their own group, known as the Fine Arts Circle. Inspired by French impressionism and its experiments with tone, light, and color, the Circle aimed to free the painter from the conventions of academic art in order to attain free, personal expression.

Many of the young artists involved in the Circle became important figures in Venezuelan painting. Manuel Cabré (1890–1983) specialized in landscapes and, on huge canvases, painted numerous pictures of the Ávila mountain range north of Caracas. Rafael Monasterios (1884–1961) is best known for his paintings of the towns and countryside of his native Lara, and Federico Brandt (1879–1932) produced still lifes, portraits, and intimate studies of daily life. These were all highly skilled painters who won national recognition, but one member of the group was a unique talent who became one of Latin America's most original twentieth-century artists: Armando Reverón.

Armando Reverón

After graduating from the Academy and spending several years studying in Europe, Reverón (1889–1954) joined the Fine Arts Circle in 1915. In 1921, he decided to move away from Caracas, his birthplace, and settle in Macuto, where he spent the rest of his life in a home he ironically called El Castillete (The Little Castle), consisting of two wooden huts he built, surrounded by a brick wall. With his wife, Juanita, as his only companion, he lived a life devoid of comforts, a virtual recluse totally dedicated to his painting. Paying little heed to previous forms, he developed a highly individual style. Juanita, and rag dolls he made, served as models for some of his paintings, but his best-known works are his coastal landscapes. He died in a Caracas sanitarium after many years of mental illness. In the decades since, his extraordinary life, and the vibrancy and originality of his painting, have made him a figure of legend.

In one of the most authoritative studies of Reverón's work, Alfredo Boulton (1979) identifies three main phases in the painter's career. In 1919–1924, his blue period, he already showed a clear concern for tone and, in

Armando Reverón at work in the 1930s. Photo courtesy of the Museo de Arte Contemporáneo de Caracas Sofia Imber.

some paintings, the influence of impressionism. His later experiments with ways of capturing the luminosity of the Caribbean coast led him into phases dominated by white (1924–1934) and by sepia (1935–1954). He painted numerous portraits and nudes, but his fascination with the effects of sunlight on the sea, land, and tropical vegetation produced his most famous works, with pale palm trees and white or light brown skies. The searing heat and glare of the sun are vividly conveyed. Color and tone came to preoccupy him obsessively, and the figures and landscapes in many of his sepia paintings blur and merge into the background, barely distinguishable in some cases.

Reverón received little recognition for his work during his career, but in the last year of his life, as his health was failing, he was awarded the National Prize for Painting. Several major exhibitions were organized after his death, in Venezuela and overseas, and El Castillete was eventually reconstructed and made into a museum. Today, publications on Reverón's work abound, and no other Venezuelan artist captures the imagination of the public to the same degree.

New Directions in the 1940s and 1950s

The 1940s was a crucial decade for Venezuelan painting. While established artists at the height of their powers continued to paint memorable landscapes—Reverón, Monasterios, and Marcos Castillo (1897–1966), whose varied work was marked by constant experiments with color—other painters sought a new approach, responding to the political circumstances of the time. The return of democracy to Venezuela after a prolonged period of dictatorship affected painting just as it did all forms of artistic expression. In the new atmosphere of open debate and free expression, a number of social realist painters began to explore national reality and culture. A major influence was the mural painting produced in the wake of the Mexican Revolution. Many Venezuelan artists were attracted to its visual power and its effectiveness in conveying social comment. Héctor Poleo (1918–1989) was among them. His *Los tres comisarios* (The Three Commissioners), one of the country's most famous paintings, refers to Venezuela's history of political turbulence. It depicts three men, wrapped in ponchos, who are huddled in conversation, suggesting a conspiracy. César Rengifo (1915–1980), already discussed as a playwright, conveyed social protest in his studies of the poor and the marginalized.

But the 1940s were also years of innovation as young painters became attracted to such European movements as cubism, Fauvism and surrealism. The varied experiments that resulted represented the beginnings of modern art in Venezuela. Again rebellion by students played an important role. The main art college in the country was the School of Plastic Arts, which had replaced the Academy of Fine Art in 1936, but many of the young artists who studied there found it too restrictive. Discontent came to a head in 1945, when a strike by students demanding reforms led to the expulsion of a large number of them. The exodus increased as others decided to seek alternatives. Some went abroad to study, particularly to Paris, where they formed a vanguard group called The Dissidents; others formed their own group in Venezuela, called the Free Art Workshop, as a way of encouraging free experiment in opposition to institutionalized art. These students, in Paris or Caracas, pursued their own particular interests. Their work was diverse, but they shared the desire to create abstract or nonfigurative art.

Inspiration was sought from many different sources, not all of them the main international centers of modern art. Oswaldo Vigas and Humberto Jaime Sánchez, for example, used designs from pre–Hispanic pottery as the basis for developing their abstract painting. By far the greatest influence, however, was provided by European artists, such as the Russian Wassily

Kandinsky, one of the founders of pure abstract painting, and the Dutchman Piet Mondrian, whose compositions centered on geometrical shapes. Geometrical abstractionism dominated Venezuela in the 1950s, attracting many young artists. Its main theoretician and most prominent advocate was Alejandro Otero, who had been one of The Dissidents in Paris. Back in Venezuela, he produced paintings he described as "color-rhythms," a type of optical art consisting of vividly colored geometrical shapes on a white background striped with black. He later turned his attention to sculpture, and it was in that medium that he achieved worldwide recognition. The large mural became a popular form for producing geometrical abstract art, and examples by such painters as Mateo Manaure, Pascual Navarro, and Carlos González Bogen adorned the campus of the Central University of Venezuela in Caracas when it was redesigned in the 1950s. In 1952, Manaure and González Bogen established Venezuela's first gallery dedicated to abstract art. One particularly important development of this interest in geometrical forms and optical effects was the experiments in kinetic art—art involving movement or creating the illusion of movement—that Jesús Soto and Carlos Cruz Diez carried out with their murals. Kineticism, which had a huge impact in Venezuela, will be discussed later.

There were, of course, painters who turned to other forms of expression, and an intense debate took place in the course of the 1950s over the respective merits of abstract art and figurative art. For the likes of Otero, abstractionism permitted Venezuelan artists to transcend national frontiers and create work with a universal dimension. Others, however, argued that original expression was best achieved through commitment to national life, culture, and problems, and criticized what they saw as the common tendency to uncritically adopt artistic innovations from around the globe. Rejecting abstractionism, a number of painters produced neofigurative art, the themes of which became increasingly diversified in the 1960s as those concerned took on board the ideological and political conflicts of the period. Prominent among the representatives of this approach were Luis Guevara Moreno, who, after producing many abstract works, returned to urban and rural scenes and historical topics, subjecting them to new treatment, and Alirio Rodríguez, perhaps best known for his paintings of dramatic, monstrous human figures. This work was far removed from earlier social realist painting. More imaginative, and free in form, it incorporated some elements and techniques of abstract art, noticeable in the use of color and tone. Social criticism is evident in the work of some of neofigurative painters, notably Régulo Pérez and Pedro León Zapata, who both use caricature as a vehicle for political satire.

Jacobo Borges

Venezuela's outstanding neofigurative painter, and undoubtedly one of the best in Latin America, Borges (b. 1931) has contributed to several areas of artistic activity. His work as a filmmaker was referred to in chapter 5, and he has also been prominent as a set and costume designer for theater productions. He demonstrated his talent as a painter while a teenager, with work he produced in the Free Art Workshop. His early paintings revealed an interest in Venezuela's folkloric traditions and natural environment, but social protest came to dominate, resulting in work that—combative, highly symbolic, and frequently satirical—explored the country's institutions and class relations. Typical is his 1973 painting *Encuentro con un círculo rojo o rueda de locos* (Meeting with a Red Circle or Circle of Madmen), in which figures of power, some in military uniform, are seated in a semicircle. It has echoes of official photographs of members of the oligarchy or leading figures of state, but the inclusion of a prostitute and a blood-red carpet undermines their supposed respectability and legitimacy. In other paintings by Borges, figures dramatically dissolve into an explosion of color. The vibrant use of color is one of the main features of his later work, which by the 1980s had brought him worldwide recognition.

The Later Twentieth Century

Increased diversification characterized Venezuelan painting during this period. In the early 1960s, art of political satire and protest was notable, promoted by a number of groups active in Caracas, such as the Goldfish Circle, in which Jacobo Borges participated, but other forms soon came to prevail. Surrealism was rediscovered, perhaps best represented by Alberto Brandt, who created a dreamlike world of extraordinary characters and fantastic landscapes. At the same time, new styles of abstract and figurative painting were developed. Geometrical abstract art, often incorporated into modern building projects, retained its popularity for several decades, but many painters preferred a freer, more personal form of abstractionism. Humberto Jaime Sánchez and Luisa Richter were two of its most important practitioners, with compositions emphasizing mood and tone. Of the figurative artists, one of the most original to emerge was Edgar Sánchez. He produced a new view of the human form, powerful but compassionate, through large-scale, detailed close-ups of parts of the face, such as magnified lips or the skin of the cheek. Caracas has long dominated artistic production in Venezuela, but signif-

icant efforts were made in the last decades of the twentieth century to promote regional art, largely through the creation of museums, competitions,
and awards. Maracaibo established itself as the second most important center
for painting with the emergence of a significant number of artists who have
concentrated on the imaginative re-creation of their region's social life, cultural history, and environment. In fact, many parts of the country have
retained their distinctive artistic traditions, which find regular expression in
the work of local artists. A notable example is the tradition of naive painting
in the Andes region, represented by the work of Josefa Sulbarán, whose vivid
rural scenes depict the area's mountainous terrain and village life. This popular art has frequently been a source of inspiration for the many professional
painters who have sought innovation through merging national and international cultural forms.

SCULPTURE AND MIXED MEDIA

Sculpture was slow to emerge as a major art form in Venezuela. Throughout the nineteenth century, and well into the twentieth, painting took precedence, and sculpture was consigned to secondary status. Conservative and
conventional, it was largely limited to the production of busts and statues of
Bolívar and other national heroes, commissions for which increased as the
nineteenth century progressed. Among the few sculptors of note, Eloy Palacios (1847–1919) stands out. The best-known of the neoclassical works
that he produced is a statue of an Indian woman, known as *La india del
Paraíso* (The Indian Woman of Paradise), which, atop a high column in a
busy district of Caracas, symbolizes the liberty obtained in the battle of Carabobo against the Spanish forces in 1821.

Two major factors permitted sculpture to modernize and develop beyond
these confines in the second half of the twentieth century. The first was the
experience obtained by the many Venezuelan artists who studied in Europe,
some having won grants or awards, and others paying their own way. Their
contact with vanguard art movements in France and Italy encouraged them
to explore the full potential of sculpture. The second factor was the arrival
in Venezuela of foreign artists, who not only introduced new styles of sculpture but also played an important role as teachers. Major examples were
Ernesto Maragall, from Spain, and the Dutchman Cornelis Zitman, both of
whom have important work on display in Caracas. In contrast to the rapid
and dramatic changes that occurred in painting, modern sculpture evolved
gradually. Artists experimented with new, stylized versions of the human

figure, which had long been the dominant subject of sculpture, but hardly any examples of abstract sculpture existed in Venezuela before 1950.

In the latter decades of the century, urban development provided important new outlets for modern sculpture, which was increasingly used to embellish the new buildings, plazas, and other public spaces. Such attempts to integrate art and architecture constituted an important new phase for the visual arts in Venezuela. It is most noticeable in Caracas, where a huge variety of sculptures, installations, and murals is found in parks, streets, and squares. Whereas clearly defined parameters restricted sculpture in earlier decades, sculptors now freely experimented with form, technique, and materials, using iron, aluminum, glass, and plastics. This freedom of expression led some artists to produce hybrid works of art: assemblages or installations that mixed sculpture, painting, and collage, and fused diverse materials. This mixed-media art, innovative and polemical, expanded rapidly in the last decades of the century.

Francisco Narváez

Narváez (1905–1984) was the pioneer of modern sculpture in Venezuela. Having studied at the Academy of Fine Art in Caracas and the Julian Academy in Paris, he produced his first works in the late 1920s. Those first sculptures, broadly neoclassical, are large, idealized figures, some of which represent Venezuela's various ethnic groups: indigenous, mestizo, and black. The most famous example of this phase of his work is the monumental fountain known as *Las toninas*, in the Plaza O'Leary in Caracas, which he completed in 1943. Graceful female figures recline above relief sculptures of waves and dolphins. His most original work, however, was produced from the 1950s on. Inspired by such artists as Jean Arp and Henry Moore, he gradually moved away from realism in his treatment of his human subjects, creating semiabstract forms that alluded to the human figure. By the 1970s, pure abstractionism dominated his work, and he became well known for his simple, austere geometrical sculptures. In the last phase of his career, he experimented with different types of stone and wood, and also worked in bronze. His increasing interest in the properties of each material became central to his sculptures, many of which had one part of the wood or stone smoothed and polished, and another left in its rough, natural state. Employing all available techniques to produce work of widely varying form, Narváez exerted a fundamental influence on the development of Venezuelan sculpture.

Alejandro Otero

No one did more than Otero (1921–1990) to promote abstract art in Venezuela. He experimented with various forms, but the remarkable sculptures he produced, which became increasingly sophisticated and ambitious in scale, are undoubtedly his major achievement. He was one of the country's first artists to explore kinetic art, and movement and light were the central concerns in his most impressive work. In the late 1960s he began to produce the huge aluminum and steel sculptures for which he became renowned. A famous example is the massive and elaborate construction titled *Abra solar*, made of numerous metal poles and plates. Completed in 1982, it occupies a central place in Plaza Venezuela, in Caracas. The effects created by the changing reflections of the sun and the shadows cast are a major element of such sculptures, another example of which is *Delta solar*, in the National Air and Space Museum in Washington, D.C. Otero became particularly interested in using natural energy—wind and water—to create motion within the work of art, seen in the 1986 sculpture *Ala solar*, built near the Guri hydroelectric power station in Bolívar state. It consists of a fifty-meter steel tower topped with a wheel that reflects different colors as it rotates in the breeze. Shortly after Otero's death, a museum dedicated to the evolution of Venezuelan modern art, established in Caracas, was named for him in recognition of his contribution.

The Kinetic Art of Jesús Soto and Carlos Cruz Diez

The work of Soto (b. 1923) has been more widely diffused than that of any other Venezuelan artist; examples of his kinetic sculptures and murals are found in museums around the world, as well as in public spaces in many Venezuelan cities. During his art studies in Europe, he became interested in the possibilities of optical illusions and effects, and used them as the creative principle for his painting. Soto soon established himself as the leading figure in Venezuelan kineticism as it gained recognition and popularity. His work developed through a continual search for ways of converting sculpture from a solid and static form into a fluid one dominated by movement. One of the results that has attracted most attention has been the sculptures he describes as *penetrables*, consisting of a frame from which hang hundreds of nylon wires through which the public is invited to walk, as if through a forest of hanging vegetation. A development of this is his famous 1989 construction, *Esfera Caracas*, located alongside a major freeway in the city, in which an orange, sunlike globe is marked on the threads, shimmering as they move.

Cruz Diez (b. 1923) developed kineticism in a different direction, motivated by explorations in the use of color. Combining colors in different patterns, his murals, mosaics, and sculptures are transformed into different geometrical formations as the spectator views them from different positions or as the light changes. He, too, has created art for public spaces and buildings, producing work of unprecedented scale, such as the mosaic that covers the floor and walls of the entrance hall of the Caracas international airport, and a mural that runs for one and a half kilometers alongside the River Guaire in the same city. Venezuelan kinetic art flourished for several decades, sponsored by the state and by private business interests. By the 1980s, other artists had begun to challenge its privileged position and to promote alternative forms of expression, though different manifestations of kineticism continued to be produced, emphasizing its role as one of Venezuela's most dynamic art movements.

Eclecticism in the Late Twentieth Century

All the major international artistic currents that emerged in the final decades of the twentieth century were assimilated by artists in Venezuela. There was a common tendency among them, however, to combine elements from the various movements, creating highly individualistic mixed-media works that defied classification. The influence of pop art, for example, is noticeable in the work of a number of artists in the 1970s and 1980s, such as Marisol Escobar, who moved to the United States to live and work. She created humorous characters, carving the figures from blocks of wood or stone, painting on faces and features, and adding details made from metal, plastic, or other materials. Satire is prominent in this work, and is also evident in that by Carlos Zerpa, whose assemblages of cheap consumer products, such as tacky costume jewelry, advertising material, and bottles, conveys a sardonic view of Venezuela's modern consumer culture.

Provoking controversy is a key objective of many of these artists, none more so than Meyer Vaisman, who uses parody and comedy to pass critical comment on social behavior and the concern with self-identity. One of his most startling creations was a series of stuffed turkeys, each dressed in clothes alluding to social status, ethnicity, and fashion. Chosen by the National Council for Culture (CONAC) to represent Venezuela at the 1995 Venice Biennale, he proposed as his project the full-scale reconstruction of a Caracas shanty, putting typically middle-class furniture and furnishings inside it in order to highlight the social contrasts in modern Venezuela. CONAC requested that he submit a more dignified exhibit; he refused, and withdrew from the Biennale. The incident demonstrated the underlying tension between state-sponsored art and art of critical social comment. In fact, Vaisman was only one of a number of artists whose work invited reflection on the state of Venezuelan society and culture at the end of century. Rolando Peña created installations consisting of stacks of oil drums painted gold, that, multiplied by mirrors on the floor, evoked the myth of "Saudi Venezuela" (a reference to the oil-rich country of Saudi Arabia) that took hold as a result of the economic boom of the 1970s. Another example is the protest street art of Juan Loyola, who identified symbols of urban deterioration, such as abandoned cars, and painted them in the colors of the national flag as a way of emphasizing the social decay he perceived around him.

While avant-garde artists challenged the traditional ways in which art is produced and displayed, and focused on ideas rather than on aesthetic criteria, other sculptors continued to work within a more traditional framework, developing the forms that had long been established in the country. Geometrical abstract sculpture was continued by Carlos Medina, working in bronze, marble, and wood, and new representations of the human figure were produced by Abigail Varela, with her groups of silhouettes made of iron. Increasing heterogeneity of style and technique was a feature common to many of the arts in Venezuela as the twentieth century drew to a close, and nowhere was it more in evidence than in the country's sculpture.

ARCHITECTURE

Venezuela's pre–Hispanic and colonial architecture was elementary. Its indigenous groups did not construct any elaborate religious or ceremonial buildings like those found in other parts of the Americas, and since their housing was made almost entirely from local materials that perished quickly—tree trunks, branches, and fibers—hardly any remains have been found by archaeologists. The lack of fine churches or palaces from the colonial era testifies to the low priority Venezuela was given by the Spanish Crown. Colonial buildings were simple, austere, and functional. The most significant constructions of the sixteenth and seventeenth centuries were the military fortresses along the coast, built as part of Spain's defense system, though buildings did increase in number and in sophistication in the course of the eighteenth century, as Venezuela's cacao and tobacco exports became increasingly lucrative. In 1728 the Real Compañía Guipuzcoana, a monopoly trading company, was set up to control trade and combat illegal commerce by Spain's European competitors. The increased mercantile activity created by the company prompted the construction of new administrative, industrial, and commercial buildings in the main ports, La Guaira and Puerto Cabello, and the families that prospered from the commerce had ornate houses built in the cities.

The first really significant period of Venezuelan architecture was that of the liberal governments of President Guzmán Blanco, in the 1870s and 1880s. Political turbulence had hindered building during most of the nineteenth century, but Guzmán Blanco ushered in an era of order, stability, and modernization. His regime was strongly centralized in Caracas, and it was there that the vast majority of building projects were carried out, with new administrative buildings, hospitals, schools, roadways, and squares. The most imposing architecture was designed to symbolize the enlightened progress that the Guzmán Blanco regime saw itself as representing, and many of Caracas's best-known landmarks date to this period. The Congress Building in the city center was constructed in the 1870s, along with the most famous square in Caracas, the Plaza Bolívar, where the statue of The Liberator was erected in 1874. Generating a sense of patriotic pride, with Bolívar its principal vehicle, was a prime objective of many construction projects, and 1876 saw the completion of the Panteón Nacional, the mausoleum for Venezuela's national heroes, which was built on the ruins of an old church. The recreation and cultural life of the elite was served in buildings such as the Teatro Guzmán Blanco, finished in 1881 (later renamed the Caracas Municipal Theater). Neoclassical and neo-Gothic styles dominated this period of architecture, and Juan Hurtado Manrique (1837–1896) was the major architect. The use of building projects to celebrate national modernization was continued by the governments that held power in the early decades of the twentieth century. A disciple of Hurtado Manrique, Alejandro Chataing (1873–1928), was responsible for many of the monumental and ornate public buildings that resulted. His work was varied and eclectic, borrowing from a range of European architectural styles, including the neobaroque, neo-Romantic, and *morisco* (Moorish) forms.

The late 1920s marked the beginnings of modern architecture in Venezuela. The dictator Gómez suppressed most areas of cultural activity, but he did dedicate resources to building projects, especially as oil revenues increased. The architects who emerged to undertake the work included foreigners like the Catalan Manuel Mujica, and young Venezuelans who had trained abroad. Over the decades that followed, they introduced new building techniques and approaches to architectural design, such as the organic architecture of the American Frank Lloyd Wright, seeking to harmonize buildings with their natural surroundings, and the functionalist approach of the Frenchman Le Corbusier. Obviously, the neoclassical and neocolonial architecture did not disappear overnight. Examples continued to be produced not only in Caracas but also in Maracaibo, Valencia, and the place that Gómez made the seat of his government, Maracay. Gradually however, modern design, with its smooth shapes, simple style, and rejection of elaborate ornamentation, became increasingly visible, first in the private sector, in the houses and apartments built in exclusive urban districts for the prosperous social sectors, and then in public buildings, such as schools, colleges, and hospitals.

There were many pioneers who contributed to that first phase of modern architecture. Three of the most important were Carlos Guinand Sandoz, Gustavo Wallis, and Cipriano Domínguez. Guinand trained as an architect in Germany, and quickly established a professional reputation on his return to Venezuela by designing a series of exclusive private houses in Caracas. His later public buildings, like that for the Ministry of Development, which was completed in the capital in 1934, illustrate as well as any other work of the period the fusion of the elegant with the functional. Guinand was one of the first Venezuelans to make landscaping a major concern of the architect. Wallis trained as an engineer, then studied architecture in the United States before returning to Venezuela in 1928 to apply the construction techniques he had learned. The Teatro Principal in Caracas, for example, is believed to be the first building in the country to have a metal frame, and to be multifunctional, with a cinema and shops on the ground floor, and offices above. Wallis undertook a number of other major projects in the center of the capital, their smooth geometrical form sometimes adorned with art deco ornamentation. Domínguez was strongly influenced by the theories of Le Corbusier, which he put into practice in his best-known work, the Simón Bolívar Center in Caracas. A complex of government offices and shops built between the late 1940s and early 1950s, the two slim thirty-floor towers that dominate it were an early example of the high-rise buildings that soon dramatically changed the skylines of most Venezuelan cities.

One name stands apart from all the others, however: that of Carlos Raúl Villanueva (1900–1975). Nobody has played a more significant role in contemporary Venezuelan culture. Between the 1930s and 1970s, he designed many of the country's finest examples of modern architecture, winning numerous national and international prizes and awards and earning recognition as one of Latin America's most talented architects of the twentieth century. He used traditional forms in his early work, seen in his neobaroque design for the Hotel Jardín in Maracay, and the *morisco* style he employed for the bullring in the same city. Neoclassical columns give a distinctive appearance

Sculpture, murals, and modern architecture on the campus of the Central University of Venezuela, Caracas. Architectural design by Carlos Villaneuva. Photo courtesy of Mark Dinneen.

to the Museum of National Art, his best-known work in Caracas from that period. At the end of the 1930s, in the same city, he produced his first clearly modern work. His design for the Gran Colombia School, which makes use of green spaces incorporated into the plan of the building through colonnades. Adapting his buildings to the tropical conditions of the country was one of Villanueva's prime concerns, as seen in his careful consideration of light and ventilation.

His most famous work is undoubtedly the campus of the Central University of Venezuela, in Caracas. The most ambitious architectural project undertaken in Venezuela, it occupied Villanueva from 1944 until 1959. Covered passages through garden areas link the buildings, but it is the integration of works of art into the design that is its most striking feature. The campus abounds in murals and sculptures by well-known Venezuelan and overseas artists. Of the many buildings that Villanueva designed for the complex, which include an Olympic stadium and an Olympic swimming pool, it is the university's Great Hall—the Aula Magna—that is his most celebrated

Exhibition of the designs of Carlos Villanueva, at the Museum of Contemporary Art, Caracas. Photo courtesy of the Museo de Arte Contemporáneo de Caracas Sofía Imber.

piece of work. What makes the project such an outstanding achievement is its overall conception, the blending of environmental, aesthetic, and functional considerations.

Nowhere was Villanueva's contribution more significant than in housing, which in the 1940s and 1950s became a major problem in the large cities as their populations steadily increased. The state attempted to address the issue through the largest project of subsidized housing in Latin America, using a government agency, the Banco Obrero, created in 1928, to organize the work. Villanueva was the main architect, producing excellent examples of high-density, high-quality housing. Between 1941 and 1943, the elegant El Silencio development, a mixture of neoclassical and modern forms consisting of 845 apartments with 400 shops below, was built in the heart of Caracas. He subsequently designed several other housing projects, the best-known being the huge 23 de Enero development, also in the capital, that was composed of high-rise blocks. Vast and varied, Villanueva's work continually incorporated new ideas and methods, seen in the use made of prestressed concrete in the construction of the Museum of Fine Art in Caracas; dating from the early 1970s, it was one of the last designs he completed.

Much of Villanueva's best work was carried out in the 1950s, a decade in which building boomed in Venezuela. Another dictatorship, that of Pérez Jiménez, invested heavily in huge public works, and there were important initiatives from the private sector as well. Along with the massive housing projects, there was a significant increase in construction of hotels, recreation facilities, infrastructure, and commercial buildings. Many of the latter showed the influence of North American models, with the appearance of the skyscraper, though there were continued efforts by some architects to create modern designs suited to local climate and patterns of life. Fruto Vivas was noted for designs and choice of materials that carefully considered the geographical surroundings of the site, and its natural light and climatic conditions. He designed a number of impressive private residences and the striking Club Táchira, a private club with a sculptural, curved roof, completed in Caracas in 1956.

In 1960 construction began on Ciudad Guayana, the first attempt to create a new city in Venezuela in accordance with modern planning criteria. Most of the commercial and office buildings were banal and unimaginative, but that built as the headquarters of the Venezuelan Guayana Corporation—the EDELCA Building—designed by Jesús Tenreiro in the mid-1960s, is one of the finest modern administrative buildings in the country. Technically very advanced, with a metal frame covered with brick, it is constructed in the form of a pyramid. It established Tenreiro's reputation as one of Venezuela's most imaginative architects. Another major figure was Tomás Sanabria, whose office blocks in Caracas—the building for the Banco Central de Venezuela and that of INCE (technical college), both finished in 1967—incorporated elements into the facade that offered protection from the sun and, by creating patterns of light and shadow, made them visually striking. In spite of achievements such as these, town planners and architects faced considerable criticism in the 1960s. In the rush to modernize urban areas, old districts in Maracaibo and Caracas were bulldozed with little thought about what might be worth preserving and at times, insufficient consideration about the new buildings constructed. Creating freeways and avenues was a major objective, for the car had become so important that it was a determining factor in the redesign of urban areas. At the same time, the pressure for housing in the big cities had grown so great that the state turned increasingly to standardized, prefabricated blocks, cheap to design and to construct, that did little to enhance the urban environment and often began to deteriorate very quickly.

The oil boom between 1973 and 1983 led to frenetic construction activity by both the state and the private sector. Opulence and a high level of technology characterized many of the buildings. Again, the principal examples were constructed in Caracas. Close to the center, the Spanish–Venezuelan company Siso, Shaw and Associates built the massive Parque Central development, consisting of blocks for housing and commerce, and two mirror-windowed skyscrapers of over sixty floors. Luxury office blocks for banks and other major companies, and large shopping centers incorporating restaurants, cafés, and cinemas, were the most noticeable products of private capital. Huge geometrical glass structures were perhaps the maximum expression of the wealth and technology of the period, exemplified by the aptly named Cubo Negro (Black Cube), designed by Carlos Gómez and completed in 1977, and the Parque de Cristal (Crystal Park), by Jimmy Alcock, dating from the 1980s. They have become famous landmarks in Caracas. Alcock, who began his career in the mid-1960s, became one of the country's best-known and most versatile architects in the closing decades of the century. He was also responsible for the Poliedro in Caracas, a major concert and events arena for five thousand spectators, notable for its eye-catching domed roof, like an enormous shell.

Buildings built in Caracas were subsequently used as models in other cities, such as Puerto Ordaz and Maracaibo, where economic growth increased demand for high-quality office space. The huge sums invested in construction permitted projects of massive scale to be undertaken, often incorporating audacious designs epitomized by the Teresa Carreño theater complex in Caracas. The work of Jesús Sandoval and Tomás Lugo, it was finished in 1983.

Different geometrical forms compose its overall structure, which houses carefully designed concert and theater halls, practice rooms, and open spaces. The 1980s also saw the construction of the first stations for the Caracas subway system, which produced some innovative designs. Attractive but practical, cool and spacious, and often incorporating works of art, the stations offer respite from the noise and frenzied activity of the city streets. No particular current or school dominated those years of intense construction. Buildings were varied, their conception usually linked to the latest styles and techniques used overseas.

The closing decades of the twentieth century saw considerable debate in Venezuela about the appropriateness and quality of the buildings being constructed. Critics argued that architecture had become too imitative of foreign forms, and was failing to harmonize with the environmental characteristics and cultural traditions of the country. In a newspaper article in 1998, Oscar Tenreiro, himself an architect, argued that though architecture as a profession had expanded quickly in Venezuela—from little more than three hundred architects in 1960 to almost fifteen thousand by 1998—the standard of architecture had fallen due to adverse economic and political factors (Tenreiro, 1998). Certainly, major problems were created by the economic crisis that began in the mid-1980s. It led to a severe contraction of the construction industry, and a consequent reduction in the opportunities available to architects. Commentators looking for more positive signs pointed to talented new architects at work, such as Celina Bentata and Carlos Brillembourg, and to recent buildings that were innovative, distinctive, and of high quality. There were some more impressive office blocks built, and the Caracas mosque by Oscar Bracho, completed in 1992, was an outstanding achievement of the period. Nonetheless, it was clear that as pressures on the urban environment continued to increase, due to many social and economic factors, the challenges that lay ahead for Venezuelan architects would be more formidable than ever.

PHOTOGRAPHY

In the mid-nineteenth century photography began to have an impact in Venezuela, following the arrival of the daguerreotype in 1841. For many decades it was principally used for portraits, partly because of the limitations of the equipment and partly because it represented good business to its practitioners. From the 1850s, photographic studios were established in the large cities, offering a portrait service to the public. A new phase of development began in the 1880s, when technical advances improved quality, and the press started to use photographs in its publications. During its existence from 1892 to 1915, the Caracas-based journal *El Cojo Ilustrado* (The Enlightened Cripple) did much to promote photography. It invited photographers, professional or amateur, to submit examples of their work, many of which were reproduced in the journal, forming a valuable record of life across the country. Among the photographs were some by Henrique Avril, the most significant photographer of the period. He traveled throughout Venezuela, taking pictures of local scenes, customs, and traditions.

Press photography developed steadily in the first half of the twentieth century, especially after the death of the dictator Gómez in 1935. Freed from the censorship imposed by his regime, photographers began to record the social and political life of the nation, with all its contradictions and conflicts. As the press modernized in the post–Gómez era, photography was given much greater importance. The work of Juan Avilán became particularly well known because whole pages of the paper *Ahora* (Today) were given over to his photographs. The most important press photographer of the period, however, was El Gordo Pérez (Francisco Edmundo Pérez), who, working for such papers as *El Heraldo* (The Herald), *El Universal* (The Universal), and *El Nacional* (The National) established new levels of quality in photographic journalism. During the 1960s, photography extended its role as a vehicle for social exploration and documentation with images of life in the shantytowns, the poverty-stricken rural villages, and the prisons—previously seen by only a few—appearing in publications. The expansion of the newspaper, magazine, and advertising industries, and the high status they gave to photography, increased the number of professional photographers over the following decades. The work of some of them became well known. Such was the case with Luigi Scotto, whose striking and creative photographs appeared regularly on the front page of *Diario de Caracas* (*Caracas Daily*) beginning in the late 1970s.

Photography as a medium of personal, artistic expression began to emerge in the 1920s in Venezuela. The first major name to appear was Alfredo Boulton (1908–1995), who was well known as an art historian and critic. He became the first Venezuelan photographer to receive international recognition. His pioneering photography—landscapes, nudes, surrealist studies, and the iconography relating to Venezuela's national heroes—had an important influence on subsequent generations of Venezuelan photographers. Like others before him, he took numerous pictures of both the urban and the natural environment, but he was more concerned with aesthetic criteria than with the desire to document. Boulton's work was widely diffused, appearing in many books and exhibitions beginning in the mid-1930s. By that time, photographic artists had formed their own club in Caracas, and major institutions such as the Museo de Bellas Artes (Museum of Fine Arts), the Caracas Ateneo (Atheneum), and the Venezuelan–American Center had started to present exhibitions of photography.

Opportunities continued to open up over the decades that followed, as increased demand for creative photography came from magazines such as *Shell* and *El Farol* (The Lantern), private foundations publishing books on national culture, and, from the 1970s particularly, the publicity and fashion industries. One of the most talented photographers of those years was Fina Gómez (c. 1917–1997), who was influenced by the avant-garde approaches she discovered in France and the United States. Among her best-known photographs are those showing the fantastic, humanlike forms of twisted tree trunks, roots, and debris from the sea. The 1970s was dominated, however, by documentary photography, with a large body of work produced on folkloric themes, such as dance and festivals, indigenous groups, and urban life and architecture. Recognizing the importance of this work, collections and archives were founded, the most important being that of the Biblioteca Nacional (National Library) in Caracas.

During the 1980s, Venezuelan photography reached a high level of sophistication. New forms of expression were sought. Much of what was produced aimed to provoke thought rather than to provide a visual record of a given subject or to create an aesthetically pleasing piece of work. Luis Brito (b. 1940), who won the National Prize for Photography in 1996, offers a good example. The human subject is the center of interest for much of his work, such as a 1976 collection showing the activities undertaken during Holy Week. It is, however, the compassionate study of human behavior, emotion, and everyday experience that makes his photography particularly powerful and moving. In the 1980s he produced an extensive series of fragmented, close-up images of human hands, faces, and feet that convey a sense of solitude and vulnerability. Many photographers became increasingly experimental during those years, producing work that was symbolic, allegorical, or even abstract. Collage techniques were employed, different uses of color were attempted, and alterations, such as staining, were made during the processessing of the negative to create striking visual effects. The photography of Enrique Hernández D'Jesús (b. 1947), also a writer, integrates image and text, creating a very personal expression that mixes the surreal, the erotic, and the fetishistic. Vasco Szinetar (b. 1948) is best known for his unorthodox portraits of well-known personalities, such as writers and politicians. He deliberately seeks to subvert the conventions of traditional portrait photog-

El ángel exterminador (The Angel Exterminator), a satirical photograph by Nelson Garrido. Courtesy of Nelson Garrido.

raphy, presenting an alternative, more intimate view of his subjects by placing them in an incongruous setting or photographing their reflection in a mirror with himself alongside them.

Two of the most original photographers to emerge in the 1980s were Nelson Garrido (b. 1952) and Francisco Beaufrand (b. 1960). Garrido's output has been extensive. For journals and books he has produced a large body of colorful and vivid photographs of daily life and folkloric traditions in different regions of Venezuela. In marked contrast is his startling and provocative avant-garde photography, which challenges the viewer to see things that are familiar, even cherished, from a new perspective, free from the myths and stereotypes in which they are usually shrouded. Macabre humor and satire are evident in many of his photographs. Some seek to shock, such as a series he produced in the 1990s that reconstructs familiar religious iconography in a bizarre, surreal form. Other photographs have a disturbing effect, showing, for example, dead or decomposing animals. Images of death abound in his work. Like Garrido's work, that of Beaufrand breaks with any attempt to document, and turns instead to the allegorical and the theatrical, though the direction he takes is very different. It is exemplified by a series of photographs of individual models, carefully posed and partially draped in cloth, with flowers sometimes used as props. These enigmatic images are sensuous and exotic, creating a dreamlike, nostalgic atmosphere. Numerous connotations are suggested through the symbolism and carefully arranged composition.

Alongside this experimentation, the use of photography for documentary purposes continued. The examples from the 1990s, however, often borrow from other genres, and are more concerned with atmosphere and texture than earlier documentary work. Luis Lares, for example, produced poignant images of the industrial environment of the town of Matanzas, in the east of the country, and an exhibition by Pablo Krisch, titled "Hidden Venezuela," explored the myths and popular beliefs integral to everyday life through scenes taken in different regions.

In 1994, the National Council for Culture (CONAC) announced that it would give photography a higher priority as an art form, creating a specialized journal and funding a national center for photography and video. Photography had long been heavily centered in Caracas, but CONAC drew up plans to extend higher education in the subject throughout the country via a network of regional centers. National photography prizes were launched. New possibilities were promised by this expansion at the institutional level, and others were emerging as a result of technical advances, in particular the use of digital technology.

REFERENCES

Bethell, Leslie, ed. *A Cultural History of Latin America*. Cambridge: Cambridge University Press, 1998.

Boulton, Alfredo. *Reverón*. Caracas: Ediciones Macanao, 1979.

Boulton, María Teresa. *Anotaciones sobre la fotografía venezolana contemporánea*. Caracas: Monte Ávila, 1990.

Calzadilla, Juan, and Pedro Briceño. *Escultura, escultores: Un libro sobre la escultura en Venezuela*. Caracas: Maraven, 1977.

Gran enciclopedia de Venezuela. Vol. 8, 28–81, 167–297. Caracas: Editorial Globe, 1998.

Guédez, Víctor. *La poética de lo humano en cinco fotógrafos venezolanos*. Caracas: CONAC, 1997.

Liscano, Juan. *Testimonios sobre artes plásticas*. Caracas: CONAC, 1981.

Moholy-Nagy, Sibyl. *Carlos Raúl Villanueva and the Architecture of Venezuela*. New York: Praeger, 1964.

Noriega, Simón. *El realismo social en la pintura venezolana, 1940–50*. Mérida: Universidade de los Andes, 1989.

Paez, Rafael, et al. *Pintores venezolanos*. Caracas: EDIME, 1974.

Palacios, Inocente. *La creación artística en Venezuela: Reflexiones sobre su evolución histórica.* Caracas: Congreso de la República, 1988.

Rodríguez, Bélgica. *Breve historia de la escultura contemporánea en Venezuela.* Caracas: FUNDARTE, 1979.

Tenreiro, Oscar. "Más arquitectos y menos calidad." *Diario de Caracas.* July 29, 1998, 8.

Glossary

aguinaldo: traditional Christmas song.

arepa: roll of fried or baked corn flour.

arepera: snack bar specializing in *arepas*.

baile de tambor: popular dance accompanied by energetic drum rhythms.

baile del sebucán: maypole dance.

barrio: working-class housing district.

bolas criollas: open-air lawn bowling.

cachapa: sweet pancake of corn flour.

carite, el: a type of fish; also the name given to a traditional dance enacting the work of fishermen.

cazabe: crisp bread made of yucca.

chicha: drink made of corn or rice.

chigüire: capybara, the world's largest rodent, eaten during Lent.

chimbángueles: battery of drums used at certain saints' festivals.

Cinemateca Nacional: organization created in 1966 to promote new films and research on the Venezuelan cinema.

CNAC: state agency formed in 1994 to stimulate film production.

cofradía: brotherhood.

comida criolla: typical Venezuelan cuisine.

compadrazgo: system of kinship ties established through the naming of godparents.

CONAC: National Council for Culture, founded in 1975.

CONIVE: National Indigenous Council of Venezuela.

costumbrismo: artistic expression focusing on daily life and local customs.

criollismo: tendency in the arts which emphasizes national identity and values.

criollo: typically Venezuelan.

culebrón: literally "long snake"; a popular term for a long-running television soap opera.

curandero: folk healer.

dulce de lechosa: sweet conserve of pawpaw.

farándula: news and gossip about show business and the media.

FOCINE: agency formed to coordinate distribution of state funds for film production.

gaita: traditional song from Zulia state, popular at Christmastime.

hallaca: traditional Christmas dish consisting of corn dough, chicken, beef, pork, raisins, tomatoes, and olives, wrapped in plantain leaves.

INCIBA: National Institute for Culture and Fine Art; existed from 1964 to 1975, when it was replaced by *CONAC.*

joropo: traditional dance and musical form associated particularly with the plains.

jota: traditional dance of Spanish origin.

llorona, la: according to popular belief, the ghost of a woman who weeps incessantly.

mal de ojo: evil eye; curse.

malagueña: traditional dance of Spanish origin.

modernismo: Spanish–American literary movement seeking to renovate the language and themes of literature, and to prioritize its aesthetic qualities.

novenario: Reciting of the rosary for nine consecutive evenings after someone's death, to ensure the eternal rest of the deceased.

pabellón: Venezuela's national dish, consisting of shredded beef, black beans, rice, and slices of fried plantain.

pájaro Guarandol, el: traditional dance enacting the hunting of a bird.

pan de jamón: bread containing ham and olives.

papelón: drink of water, raw sugar, and lemon juice.

paradura del niño: popular ceremony celebrating Christ's birth.

parranda: popular festivity in which a group of musicians goes from house to house, playing and singing.

pastores, los: traditional popular Christmas ritual mixing dance and theater.

perra, la: popular dance by couples, in which the woman attempts to knock over the man.

Polo Patriótico: political coalition formed under leadership of Hugo Chávez in the 1990s.

quinta: large detached residence.

rancho: owner-built shack, shanty.

Real Compañía Guipuzcoana: Monopoly trading company established by the Spanish Crown in 1728 to consolidate control over Venezuelan trade.

sainete: comedy sketch; farce.

santería: popular religion of Cuban origin.

Sayona, la: according to popular belief, the wife of the devil.

tamunangue: series of traditional dances particularly associated with Lara state.

telenovela: television soap opera.

tonada: traditional ballad originally sung by rural workers as they milked the cattle.

turas, las: traditional formation dance, danced in a circle.

umbanda: popular religion of Brazilian origin.

urbanización: relatively prosperous area of planned housing.

yerbatería: herbalist shop.

zapateado: rapid steps that form part of certain folk dances.

zarzuela: musical comedy; operetta.

Selected Bibliography

Alexander, Robert J. *Rómulo Betancourt and the Transformation of Venezuela*. New Brunswick: Transaction Books, 1982.

Berryman, Phillip. *Religion in the Megacity: Catholic and Protestant Portraits from Latin America*. New York: Orbis Books, 1996.

Bethell, Leslie, ed. *The Cambridge History of Latin America*, vol. 8. Cambridge: Cambridge University Press, 1991.

———, ed. *A Cultural History of Latin America*. Cambridge: Cambridge University Press, 1998.

Coronil, Fernando, *The Magical State, Nature, Money and Modernity in Venezuela*. Chicago: University of Chicago Press, 1997.

Ewell, Judith. *Venezuela, a Century of Change*. London: Hurst, 1984.

———.*Venezuela and the United States: From Monroe's Hemisphere to Petroleum's Empire*. Athens: University of Georgia Press, 1996.

Ferguson, James. *Venezuela in Focus: Guide to the People, Politics and Culture*. London: Latin American Bureau, 1994.

Fox, Geoffrey E. *The Land and People of Venezuela*. New York: HarperCollins, 1991.

Goodman, Louis W., J. Mendelson Forman, Moisés Naím, Joseph Tulchin, and Gary Bland, eds. *Lessons of the Venezuelan Experience*. Washington D.C.: Woodrow Wilson Center Press, 1995.

Goodnough, David. *Simón Bolívar: South American Liberator*. Springfield: Enslow Publishers, 1998.

Hellinger, Daniel. *Venezuela: Tarnished Democracy*. Boulder: Westview Press, 1991.

Hillman, Richard S. *Democracy for the Privileged: Crisis and Transition in Venezuela*. London: Lynne Rienner, 1994.

Kamen-Kaye, Dorothy Allers. *Venezuelan Folkways: Twentieth-Century Survivals of*

Folk Beliefs, Customs and Traditions of Caracas. Detroit: B. Etheridge Books, 1976.

King, John. *Magical Reels.* London: Verso, 1990.

Klein, Elizabeth. *A Traveler's Guide for Venezuela.* Caracas: Armitano Editores, 1994.

Levine, Daniel. *Popular Voices in Latin American Catholicism.* Princeton, N.J.: Princeton, 1992.

————. *Religion and Politics in Latin America.* Princeton, N.J.: Princeton, 1981.

Lewis, Marvin. *Ethnicity and Identity in Contemporary Afro-Venezuelan Literature.* Columbia: University of Missouri Press, 1992.

Lieuwen, Edwin. *Venezuela.* Westport: Greenwood Press, 1985.

Márquez, Patricia C. *The Street is My Home: Youth and Violence in Caracas.* Stanford: Stanford University Press, 1999.

McCoy, Jennifer, Andrés Serbin, William C. Smith, and Andrés Stambouli. *Venezuelan Democracy Under Stress.* New Brunswick: Transaction Publishers, 1995.

Moholy-Nagy, Sibyl. *Carlos Raúl Villanueva and the Architecture of Venezuela.* New York: Praeger, 1964.

Morrison, Marion. *Venezuela.* Philadelphia: Chelsea House, 1999.

Rudolph, Donna Keyse. *Historical Dictionary of Venezuela.* Lanham: Scarecrow, 1996.

Salazar-Carrillo, Jorge. *Oil and Development in Venezuela during the Twentieth Century.* London: Praeger, 1994.

Sinclair, John. *Latin American Television: A Global View.* Oxford: Oxford University Press, 1999.

Sullivan, Edward J. *Latin American Art in the Twentieth Century.* London: Phaidon Press, 1996.

Tenenbaum, Barbara. *Encyclopedia of Latin American History and Culture* (5 volumes). New York: Scribner's, 1996.

Waddell, David A. G. *Venezuela.* Oxford: Clio, 1990.

Wells, Alan. *Picture-Tube Imperialism? The Impact of U.S. Television on Latin American Television.* Maryknoll: Orbis, 1972.

Wright, Winthrop R. *Café con leche: Race, Class and National Image in Venezuela.* Austin: University of Texas Press, 1990.

Index

About the Author

MARK DINNEEN is an Assistant Professor in Latin American Literature and Cultural History at the University of Southampton, United Kingdom. He has written frequently on Latin American topics.